Texts in developmental psychology

Series Editor:
Peter Smith
Goldsmiths College, University of London

ALSO IN THE *TEXTS IN DEVELOPMENTAL PSYCHOLOGY* SERIES:

THE CHILD AT SCHOOL
Peter Blatchford and Anthony Pellegrini

ATTACHMENT AND DEVELOPMENT
Susan Goldberg

FRIENDS AND ENEMIES
Barry H. Schneider

Child Development: Thinking About Theories

Phillip T. Slee
School of Education, Flinders University, Adelaide

Rosalyn H. Shute
School of Psychology, Flinders University, Adelaide

First published in Great Britain in 2003 by
Arnold, a member of the Hodder Headline Group,
338 Euston Road, London NW1 3BH

http://www.arnoldpublishers.com

Distributed in the United States of America by
Oxford University Press Inc.
198 Madison Avenue, New York, NY10016

The advice and information in this book are believed to be true and
accurate at the date of going to press, but neither the authors nor the publisher
can accept any legal responsibility or liability for any errors or omissions.

British Library Cataloguing in Publication Data
A catalogue record for this book is available from the British Library

Library of Congress Cataloging-in-Publication Data
A catalog record for this book is available from the Library of Congress

ISBN 0 340 808179 (hb)
ISBN 0 340 808187 (pb)

1 2 3 4 5 6 7 8 9 10

Typeset in 10 and 13pt Plantin by Dorchester Typesetting Group Ltd
Printed and bound in Great Britain by MPG Books Ltd, Bodmin, Cornwall

What do you think about this book? Or any other Hodder Arnold title?
Please send your comments to feedback.hodderarnold@hodder.co.uk

Contents

List of figures and tables

Figures

Tables

Preface

This book is part of a series that addresses a range of theoretical and applied issues in developmental psychology. Our purpose is to provide a broad overview of theories of child development, although practice is certainly not neglected. As well as being academic psychologists, we have strong professional interests: Phillip has a background in teaching, educates student teachers and has produced internationally utilized materials to address school bullying; Rosalyn is an experienced coordinator of professional postgraduate psychology programmes and provides clinical psychology services to young people and their families. Most of our publications address applied issues. At first sight, then, it is perhaps a little curious that a book on theories of child and adolescent development should be written by two people whose primary interests are applied. However, we take a holistic approach to our work, and see theory as underpinning all aspects of it, including research, teaching and professional practice. We therefore considered it important to include a chapter on the implications of theory for practice, especially given the primary readership of the book (higher-level undergraduates, honours students and postgraduates), who are at the stage of considering the connections between their undergraduate education and future career plans.

We also considered it important to have some empirical basis for decisions about how to structure the book. As well as drawing upon the developmental literature, guidance from the series editor and book proposal referees, and our own experience with writing texts, we held a focus group of honours psychology students at our university to ask them what they would like to see in a book such as this. One of their main issues was that they wanted to gain an overall picture of various theories and how they fitted together, in contrast to the fragmented image they felt they had gained as undergraduates. We have therefore attempted to make some explicit historical and theoretical links between different schools of thought. They also felt that the university culture of critique left them with only a sense of 'what was wrong' with various theoretical approaches, and they also wanted to know 'what was right' with them. They asked to see examples of the implications of theory for practice, which accorded well with our own conception of the book, and reported being put off by too much abstract writing without examples and too many pages of unbroken text. Within the constraints of the series style, we have aimed to address all these issues, in an attempt to avoid the type of text described by Jones (1991):

> ... dry, distanced monologues bereft of the warm breathing human being who wrote them ... obscure and difficult ... simply commodities in the academic marketplace ... 'valuable' perhaps for the students forced to wade through their pages and reproduce their arguments in return for grades.

Other texts are available that provide a detailed exposition of many of the classical theories of child development. In the present volume, we have focused in the main upon more recent critiques and trends, including issues of epistemology – the theory of knowledge. However, we have also sought to provide a sense of historical development of various schools of thought, and have included information about some theorists whose work is less well known today.

As we set about discussing the content of this text and the placement of the various chapters we realized that it had a developmental feel to it (no pun intended!). While the early chapters cover mainstream theories, later chapters consider the contributions of postmodern thinking to theorizing about child and adolescent development. We felt that postmodern critiques were important to include, as they are generally found in journal articles and specialist books but not in child development textbooks, which adopt a standard scientific perspective. In setting out the text in this way we were then confronted with the tensions that characterize current modern and postmodern debate concerning the nature and role of developmental theory. This, in turn, raised for us the significant question of whether one is able to articulate a middle ground for developmental theory. Is there a position that takes the best that modernism has to offer while also accommodating postmodern views of human development, and the theory and practice surrounding it, as inhabiting a historical time and culture? We are hopeful that, as the story of this text unfolds, readers will be challenged and encouraged to consider such issues in addition to the more familiar ones about nature/nurture and continuity/discontinuity in development.

We begin the book with an overview of some of the historical, cultural and philosophical influences on theorizing about children's development. This is followed by a chapter on biological explanations for development. Chapters follow based on organismic, psychoanalytic and mechanistic theories, followed by dialecticism and contextualism. The postmodern influence becomes apparent as we move into a consideration of sociocultural and feminist theories. Having considered these diverse schools of thought, we examine the prospect of a more integrated approach to developmental theorizing, and complete the book with a discussion of implications for practice.

We have provided ideas for further study in an appendix (Appendix 2) rather than integrated into the relevant chapters, to enable those wishing simply to read the book to do so (this is in line with the wishes of our focus group students). However, we felt it important to provide some exercises and ideas for further study for those students or lecturers seeking them, hence their inclusion in Appendix 2. (This also includes references to some relevant websites.)

We thank the referees who commented on the original book proposal, and who asked for some additional areas to be covered. We have been able to incorporate most, but not all, of their ideas, given the space constraints placed upon us. We have tried, however, to select examples (including some from our own work) to illustrate some important themes and trends in the developmental path of theorizing in the field, and to create the sense of connection between different theories that our students requested.

We also hope the fact that we are writing from the Antipodes has helped to give a broader perspective than that found in many texts and, where appropriate, we have provided examples from Australia and other Pacific nations.

Our thanks go to Peter Smith for his invitation to write this text and for his very helpful comments on the first draft. We also thank Wilhelmina Drummond for permission to use her illustration of the Maori model of human development (Figure 9.1). We also thank Robyn Fogarty and Elen Shute for their secretarial assistance. Finally, and especially, we thank our families for their forebearance during the completion of this project. Phillip thanks Elizabeth for her support, and their sons (Matthew, Nicholas and Christopher), who helped him maintain some balance to his life with trips to the movies to see *Star Wars* and *Spiderman*. Rosalyn apologizes to Jason for weekends spent at the word processor rather than tiling the bathroom!

Phillip Slee and Rosalyn Shute
Adelaide
July 2002

1 Ways of knowing about development

Introduction

Some of our readers may be habitual 'Preface-skippers,' and if that applies to you we do refer you back to the Preface so that the rationale for this book and our general approach to it are clear. As one would expect from an introductory chapter, our purpose here is to set the context within which the following chapters are embedded. After giving some consideration to the nature of developmental psychology, the main body of the chapter is devoted to a consideration of some ways of knowing about children: knowing them from various philosophical and theoretical perspectives, knowing them in a cultural sense and knowing them as beings placed in historical contexts. Throughout this book, we will be using the word 'child' in a generic sense to include all stages of development from conception through infancy, childhood and adolescence.

Developmental psychology

Psychology is a discipline which has wholeheartedly embraced a positivist philosophy and the scientific method. The field of study in psychology that is concerned with how the individual grows and changes from conception until death is known as developmental psychology. Human development is complex – indeed, one writer has gone so far as to describe it as 'the most complex phenomenon in the universe' (Charlesworth, 1992: 14). Even when we limit ourselves (as in this book) to a consideration of child development, we find that many different ways have been proposed of theorizing about this multifaceted phenomenon.

The study of child development, like psychology in general, is a young science and the systematic study of children is a relatively recent undertaking. Cairns (1998: 26) has noted that 'developmental psychology has its own distinctive history, which is associated with, but independent of, the history of experimental or general psychology'. In reading the literature one becomes aware of how acutely theorists such as Charles Darwin, Sigmund Freud, Margaret Mead, Jean Piaget and Eleanor Maccoby commented upon child development. Today, courses in child, adolescent and family development embrace a range of professions including teaching, psychology, social work, child care and nursing, to name but a few.

We have laid out some historical 'milestones' in developmental psychology in Appendix 1. However, just as individual development can be portrayed as happening in either a stage-like or continuous manner, so there have been ongoing debates and cross-fertilizations underlying the major turning points in developmental theorizing (Pellegrini and Blatchford, 2000). Currently, psychologists are being challenged to consider whether theoretical diversity or integration is the way of the future. We are also being encouraged to think beyond mainstream empirical ways of researching and understanding child development, and to embrace a more critical outlook regarding the theories and assumptions that underpin the field. Debate in the literature appears to us to be polarizing thinking in terms of a modern versus postmodern dichotomy. We are not at all sure that this is a helpful trend and we are concerned not only to identify where this happens but to encourage some informed debate on the issue.

Several broad questions are addressed in this text.

- How do children change as they develop?
- What factors influence the developmental changes?
- What individual differences exist in growth and development?

In each of the chapters we encourage readers to return to these questions as a way of reviewing the nature of the theories presented, and to use the discussion questions, activities and websites listed in Appendix 2 to facilitate this contemplation.

Why study child development?

The reasons for studying children are as broad and complex as the field itself. It is reasonable to argue that a dominant theme in the field, as verified by an examination of the contents page of significant journals, is that of raising children. This concern, exemplified at many stages throughout this book, arose from the writings of early philosophers such as John Locke and Jean-Jacques Rousseau, and religious writers such as John Wesley.

It is also recognized that through the study of children we may come to understand adult behaviour better. As John Milton commented in *Paradise Lost*: 'The childhood shows the man as morning shows the day'. Gabriel Compayre, a French educationalist who observed and wrote about child development over a hundred years ago, also believed that information concerning the child's early years would serve to illuminate later development: 'If childhood is the cradle of humanity, the study of childhood is the cradle and necessary introduction to all future psychology' (Compayre, 1896: 3).

From a somewhat different perspective, Charles Darwin believed that the child was the link between animal and human species. The birth of his son William Erasmus (nicknamed 'Doddy') on 27 December 1839 prompted Darwin to begin a diary description of the development of his son – 'a baby biography'. By observing the development of the infant, Darwin believed some understanding could be reached of the species itself. For example, in *The Expression of the Emotions in Man and Animals* (first published in 1872), Darwin argued that emotional expression was basically a physiological matter and that expressive gestures were largely universal and innate:

> Everyone who has had much to do with young children must have seen how naturally they take to biting when in a passion. It seems instinctive in them as in young crocodiles, who snap their little jaws as soon as they emerge from the egg.
>
> (Darwin, 1965: 241–2)

More recently, Medinnus (1976) identified four main reasons for studying children:

1. an intellectual curiosity concerning natural phenomena;
2. the need to gain information to guide children's behaviour;
3. to increase our ability to predict behaviour;
4. the need to understand our own (adult) behaviour.

A point that we will strongly argue in this text is that the study of development does not occur in a historical, cultural or philosophical vacuum. It is a salutary point to consider that the very words 'child' and 'childhood' have changed their meaning within the context of recent western history and have different meanings in different cultures. Thus, the historical element in developmental theories is highlighted when, with the benefit of hindsight, we note that Charles Darwin's observations were designed to explore the links between animal and human species. The infant was essentially depicted as a biological organism influenced and shaped to a greater or lesser degree by the environment. A surge of interest in the study of children along with the study of so-called 'primitives' arose as the perceived key to a better understanding of the development of 'normal' behaviour. The concept of 'recapitulation' – understood as the idea that 'ontogeny recapitulates phylogeny' or that the individual in her/his lifetime demonstrates the patterns and stages exhibited in the development of the species – underpins the writing of many of the early theorists, such as G. Stanley Hall (see Chapter 3). The identification of children's stages of development and the obsession with minutely recording normal growth and development characterized much early research, such as that of Gesell (see Chapter 4).

A postmodern outlook would suggest that the conduct of this science went hand in hand with the development of an empirical methodology that clearly separated the observer from the observed in the best interests of the scientific endeavour. The child was objectified, in the spotlight of this critical gaze. This exercise involved a gendered division of labour, with men viewed as having the necessary credentials to conduct objective, verifiable observations: 'Women were excluded from the investigative enterprise because they were declared constitutionally incapable of regarding their children with the requisite objectivity' (Burman, 1994: 12). So, in a postmodern context, our attention is drawn to the various factors impacting on and shaping the study of child development, which in turn is related to the way in which we conduct science. Some of these issues facing contemporary psychology are examined in more detail in the chapters considering cross-cultural and indigenous psychology and feminism.

Factors shaping views of development

Writers have identified a number of factors that have shaped western views of children and families over the centuries (Aries, 1962; Clarke-Stewart, 1998; Elkind, 1987; Schorsch, 1979; Young 1990). Two factors consistently identified are history and culture. As Aries (1962) has reminded us, little, if anything at all, escapes history and culture, not even the central elements of life itself for women, men and children. A third factor that will also be discussed in this chapter is the philosophy of science. We begin our discussion by examining the child in a historical context.

History

As noted by Kennedy (2000), 'Looking back to the foundations of the western philosophical tradition, the child does not fare particularly well in adult male construction (we do not hear from the females)' (2000: 518). In beginning a study of childhood, it is important to appreciate the view expressed by the social historian Philippe Aries that childhood, as it is understood today in western society, is a relatively recent phenomenon. Following Aries' (1962) pioneering writings on the history of childhood, a number of writers have supported his views. For example, Schorsch (1979: 11) observed that, 'thinkers of the 16th century, and of the preceding centuries as well, agreed that the child is nothing more than a lower animal – "the infant mewling and puking in the nurse's arms" as Shakespeare put it baldly but succinctly'. Of course, Aries' thesis is not without its shortcomings, and there also exists the idea that, at various times throughout European history, the infant has been revered as an embodiment of New Testament depictions of 'sinlessness'. For examples of this ideal, consider the ways in which infants and young children were represented by Renaissance painters.

Elkind (1987) captured some of the complexity of the changing views of childhood from antiquity to the present time. In Ancient Greece the stress was upon educating children into the laws and cultural mores of the time. Children in Babylon went to school at the age of six, while in Roman times the children attended school around the age of seven to acquire reading and writing skills. However, children in medieval Europe fared far less well. During this time the prevailing image was of the child as a chattel or piece of property of the parent and state. All in all, during the medieval period the child did not account for much in the eyes of society, as a sixteenth-century rhyme (cited in Schorsch, 1979: 23) indicates:

> Of all the months the first behold,
> January two-faced and cold
> Because its eyes two ways are cast
> To face the future and the past.
> Thus the child six summers old
> Is not worth much when all is told.

In western societies, history shows that for centuries children have been looked upon as property and, more particularly, as the property of their fathers. Paternalism and patriarchy have been significant elements in parent–child relationships for quite some time. Some basis for understanding the contemporary status of children in western societies is found in the writings of the Greek philosopher Aristotle. In Bertrand Russell's description of Aristotelian ethics, he noted that, while Aristotle considered human beings as 'ethically equal', 'the justice of a master or a father is a different thing from that of a citizen, for a son or slave is property, and there can be no injustice to one's own property' (Russell, 1974: 186). Law elaborated in Europe between AD 1300 and AD 1800 prescribed the relationship between parent and child in terms of trust. The parents' rights came from the state, and the state reserved the right to intervene and protect the child's rights and interests. However, while the court would protect children's interests, it could not present their grievances and had no guarantee of independent representation (Fraser, 1976).

Apart from the law, some interesting insight is gained into the status of children in western society from the writings of seventeenth- and eighteenth-century philosophers such as Thomas Hobbes, John Locke and John Stuart Mill. Hobbes, writing in the seventeenth century, argued that children were cared for solely because they were capable of serving their father and should be assigned a position of complete dependence. 'Like the imbecile, the crazed and the beasts over ... children ... there is no law' (Hobbes, 1931: 257). The implication of Hobbes' argument is that children have no natural rights and no rights by social contract, because they lack the ability to make formal contracts with other members of society and cannot understand the consequences of such contracts.

Later in the same century, John Locke, arguing from a different perspective, considered children to be under the jurisdiction of their parents until they were capable of fending for themselves. Until such time, children were thought to lack understanding and therefore could not assert their will (Russell, 1974). Unlike Hobbes, Locke believed that both adults and children possessed certain natural rights, which needed protection. Parental benevolence was believed to be sufficient to ensure that children's rights were protected. Locke's outlook rejected the proprietary aspect of parenthood, replacing it with the concept of children as God's property. Locke's description of children as lacking in understanding reflected the view that children need to develop adult capacities for reasoning and understanding. Until such time, parents were under a God-given obligation to care for children. By implication, where parents failed to fulfil their obligation to children, the state would be empowered to do so.

The late eighteenth and nineteenth centuries in Europe were witness to the dramatic social and economic changes wrought by the Industrial Revolution. In large part children fared very poorly in the face of these changes. Schorsch (1979) noted that children as young as four years of age worked in the cotton mills of England:

> A child over seven worked from sunrise to sunset six days a week with two and a half days off a year; children between six and sixteen earned slightly more than half a woman's wages and only a fourth of a man's.
>
> (Schorsch, 1979: 143)

The nineteenth-century French novelist Emile Zola, in his book *Germinal* (first published in 1885), depicts 12-year-old children working alongside their fathers, and older brothers and sisters, in the mineshafts of France.

Eventually child labour laws were enacted, the first being in Britain in 1833, to protect children from the excesses and exploitation of the Industrial Revolution. The nature of childhood and the way it was viewed by western society were beginning to change. New emphasis was given to education and recognizing the special needs of young children. Childhood was gradually recognized as a distinct stage in human development. Readers might pause to consider how western views about children and their relationship to adults is reflected in such behaviours as corporal punishment (see Box 1.1).

Most recently the field of developmental psychology has contributed to the recognition of divisions in the concept of childhood itself. Beyond infancy, at least four stages of child development are commonly recognized in western societies today: early childhood, middle childhood, late childhood and adolescence. Overall, setting child development in a historical context would suggest that the status of children, attitudes toward children, and the value society attaches to children are best understood in historical context. For example, Collard, writing about Australian Aboriginal culture, has emphasized the role of history in providing people with a sense

---

Box 1.1. Children and punishment

There was an old woman, who lived
in a shoe
She had so many children she didn't
Know what to do.
She gave them some broth without
Any bread
Then she whipped them all soundly and
Sent them to bed.

In Australia, as in other western countries such as the United States of America, the notion of the iniquitous child as reflected in the use of corporal punishment still continues to elicit controversy as reflected in media reports and the research literature. Sweden became the first country in the world to ban corporal punishment of children, and a number of European countries have followed this example including Denmark, Norway, Finland, Austria, Cyprus, Italy, Croatia and Latvia. Proponents of corporal punishment such as Dobson (1970) have argued that excessive permissiveness in child-rearing and at school has contributed to social problems such as drug-taking and delinquency. Alternatively, writers such as Paintal (1999) have argued that corporal punishment is a dehumanizing, ineffective practice that models aggression. In a position paper on the issue of banning corporal punishment, Paintal noted that in the United States of America corporal punishment in schools is still legal in about half the states, a situation that has not changed a great deal since Viadero (1988) reported on the matter. In Australia all states have banned the use of corporal punishment in public (i.e. state-run) schools.

---

of belonging: 'in considering the present it is important to look at the past, particularly an Aboriginal account of history, which has either been conveniently ignored or omitted from the official history of Australia' (Collard, 2000: 22). We will revisit this theme in Chapter 9.

Culture

A second important factor shaping the way we understand children and adolescents is that of culture. Kessen (1979) has gone so far as to speak of children and child psychology as 'cultural inventions', highlighting that we cannot easily separate the influence of culture from any discussion of the nature of children and families. The ideas of the American anthropologist, Margaret Mead, help us to appreciate the role played by culture in shaping our views of children and the family. We will take up the contribution of

Margaret Mead to child development in Chapter 8. In her book *Culture and Commitment* (1970), she calls upon knowledge she gleaned from studying children in Manus, Bali and New Guinea following their lives into adulthood.

The issue of culture in child-rearing is exemplified by considering the case of Australian Aborigines. In traditional Aboriginal communities, the values stressed included sharing, mutual cooperation, kinship obligations and personal relationships (Jenkins, 1988). Aboriginal children were largely brought up by their mother and her sisters: 'In the case of boys, education was later taken over by the father, learning by emulating adults rather than by formal instruction' (Lippman, 1970: 21). Each society had rich oral, spiritual traditions, which conveyed knowledge about their lands and seasons and, upon initiation at puberty, the amount of learning and community responsibility greatly increased for the Aboriginal child (Collard, 2000).

The mix of the population should be taken into consideration when examining the effect of culture on child development. For example, between 1947 and 1985, nearly three million migrants settled in Australia and 56 per cent of these were of non-British origin (Storer, 1985). However, while we might have accurate statistics on the number of migrants who have settled in Australia, we have far less knowledge about how being raised in Australia affects children and adolescents from migrant families. A recent study by Leung (2001) comparing the adaptation of Chinese migrant adolescents in Australia and Canada pointed to the significance of social support in ensuring adaptation, as did a study by Kovacev and Shute (1999) of resettled adolescent refugees from the former Republic of Yugoslavia. In an examination of income and employment data, Storer (1985) reported that male migrant workers from Mediterranean countries earned less than Australian-born or English-speaking migrants and had higher unemployment rates. These factors have an obvious impact on the family in terms of 'social capital' and 'human capital'.

In the process of migration, the extended family is often broken up and some members remain in the home country. The migrating members may experience 'culture shock' when they encounter 'new attitudes, values, customs, ideas and relationships' in their adopted country (Aspin, 1979: 297). The scene is then set for some conflict between parents and children in terms of values, attitudes and morality (Storer, 1985). For example, southern European girls are more restricted and supervised in their activities than their Australian-born counterparts (Storer, 1985). Storer also notes that adolescents (10 years and older) of migrant families settling in Australia are likely to experience 'extreme cultural confusion' exacerbated by a lack of proficiency in either their own or the English language. These adolescents are more at risk of falling victim to delinquency and illegal drug use, and often become confused about their identity as a result of the conflict that can arise from the family's struggle to maintain its ethnic identity in the face of Australian mainstream culture (Storer, 1985).

In summary, in contemporary developmental thinking, it is clear that the role of culture in shaping the way children grow and develop is increasingly being recognized. Bruner and Haste (1987) note that, 'It can never be the case that there is a "self" independent of one's cultural-historical existence' (1987: 91). Thus, in order to appreciate the study of children fully one should step outside the traditional bounds of views offered by the social sciences, education and science. Echoing Bruner's sentiment, Kennedy (2000) has argued that childhood is best viewed as a cultural and historical construction in order to appreciate '… the ways in which characterizations of children function symbolically as carriers of deep assumptions about the construction of human subjectivity, about the ultimate meaning of the human life cycle, and about human forms of knowledge' (2000: 514).

Philosophy of science

While developmental psychology has never hesitated to draw upon disciplines such as biology, anthropology and sociology, recent developments in the philosophy of knowledge have largely been ignored (Teo, 1997). This rather curious omission has occurred despite the fact that influential writers and researchers in the field, such as Piaget, had epistemology as the basis for their work. Teo suggests that the primary reason for the failure to integrate the latest philosophical thinking in developmental psychology has to do with the rise and dominance of empiricism, particularly as reflected in mainstream North American psychology.

The philosophy of science has significant ramifications for the theoretical and conceptual foundations of developmental psychology, shaping the very way we view the subject: 'In the broadest sense of the term a world view helps people interpret, understand and bring some order to their lives' (Slee, 1987: 8). More particularly, a paradigm or worldview helps to shape how we use terms like 'knowledge', 'information' and 'science'. That is, it helps to specify the types of theory used in research, and identifies problems worthy of study and the methodology to be employed in investigating a problem (Lerner, 1986).

In reading the developmental psychology literature one becomes aware of how strongly 'common sense' initially prompts and informs the interpretation of behaviour, such as Darwin's observations regarding the emergence of emotions in children (cited earlier), or Piaget's careful noting of the behaviour of his children in relation to their use of their senses and motor activity to acquire knowledge about the world (see Chapter 4). These scientists attempted to bring some order and coherence to their observations in a systematic way, such as by gathering further examples or experimenting in an attempt to reproduce the initial findings. As Overton (1998: 155) notes, 'This issue – the route from common sense to science –

constitutes the methodology of science'.

Presently, the dominant western model of 'reality' draws heavily upon the belief in a particular view of the scientific method as the only valid approach to the acquisition and understanding of a systematic body of knowledge. The basis for the prevailing scientific method is drawn from the worldview of empiricism. Empiricism as a philosophy of science has exerted a powerful influence on scientific practice. In a very direct way, it has shaped the way we have conducted the science of child study. Thus, in modelling itself upon the natural sciences such as physics and chemistry, the empirical method of child study has placed a great deal of importance in studying children on a search for causes of behaviour with an emphasis on reducing the complexity of behaviour to its basic components. In 1977 Bronfenbrenner noted that a survey of child development research indicated that some 76 per cent was of an experimental laboratory nature, contrasting with only 8 per cent that used naturalistic observation designs.

While the empirical method eschews interpretation, at the beginning of the twentieth century psychology struggled with the method of 'Verstehen', or understanding, as a methodology. Ultimately, the method drowned in the sea of empiricism, which became the dominant scientific discourse in developmental psychology. Presently, the role of interpretation is undergoing a re-examination in relation to its role in understanding human development. The pressure for this comes from the contributions that postmodern and feminist thinking are making to the field along with a reappraisal of the role of philosophy.

What is a theory?

As defined by *The Macquarie Dictionary*, a fact is 'what has really happened or is the case; truth; reality; something known to have happened'. Research into child development is uncovering facts at a rate that sometimes outstrips our ability to integrate them into a coherent framework. Facts are very important to any science. They have been called the building blocks of science. However, just as a pile of bricks does not make a house, a collection of facts does not make a science: 'A theory may be considered as a way of binding together a multitude of facts so that one may comprehend them all at once' (Kelly, 1963: 18). But to backtrack a little ...

The word 'theory' has its origins in the Greek 'theoria' – contemplation, spectacle, mental conception. Harvey (in Williams, 1976) relates theory to 'fantasy', suggesting that theory is quite inferior to practice. However, any understanding of the concept of 'theory' should look to embed it in historical context (Morawski, 2001). In relation to psychology, theory has held a rather troubled and uneasy place. From a logical-positivist perspective 'a judiciously crafted theory, sparse and logically pristine, could be submitted to hypothetico-deductive method; that is, it could yield tidy hypotheses for laboratory testing' (Morawski, 2001: 434–5). As Morawski further notes, theory unrestrained has frequently resulted in 'profligate claims about human nature'. Moreover, theory has existed uneasily alongside practice. Theory was distinguished from 'practice' by Bacon (1626), and the word 'praxis' links theory and practice such that ' "praxis" is practice informed by theory' (Williams, 1976: 268). In the last chapter of this book, we will consider further the link between theory and practice.

Evaluating theories

In reading the literature it is evident that a number of attempts have been made to evaluate developmental theories (e.g. Gewirtz and Pelaez-Nogueras, 1992; Green, 1989; Kelly, 1963; Lerner, 1983; Thelen and Smith, 1994). These authors have suggested various criteria for evaluating theories, but we can identify little in the way of consensus on this. However, one feature of development about which there is universal understanding is that development implies 'change' (Overton, 1998). Rather simplistically this notion has focused psychologists' attention on 'changes in observed behavior across age' (Overton, 1998: 109). Overton has elaborated on the nature of change, identifying four types.

1. Transformational change is really morphological change that involves the emergence of novelty. An example is that of the single-celled zygote differentiating and emerging into ever more complex forms.
2. Variational change describes the individual differences that occur in development – e.g. the age by which a child walks in relation to the norm.
3. Expressive-constitutive change focuses on the essential features of what changes – e.g. Piaget focused on the 'schemes' that change.
4. Instrumental-communicative change focuses on what it is that changes – e.g. Skinner focused on the operants that change.

In evaluating theories for their usefulness, readers might therefore apply a number of criteria concerning change, based on the key points raised earlier in this chapter.

- How well do the theories explain how children change as they develop? What empirical support is provided for their explanations?
- How do the theories account for the various factors, such as culture, that influence developmental change?
- How well do the theories account for individual differences that exist in children's growth and development?
- Finally, the parsimony or simplicity of explanation is an important attribute of a good theory.

(Gewirtz and Pelaez-Nogueras, 1992)

At this point, we would also like to introduce the philosophy of science articulated by Lakatos (Ketelaar and Ellis, 2000), as this provides a broad framework for making decisions about whether to accept or reject a theory. The Popperian view that science proceeds by falsification of hypotheses remains well accepted in psychological research, and psychology students are well versed in this approach. However, Lakatos proposed that falsification should not be used to reject a theory, only to reject specific statements derived from the theory. Lakatos distinguished between metatheories and middle-level theories. A metatheory is based upon certain core assumptions. This core is surrounded by a 'protective belt' of middle-level theories and auxiliary hypotheses that give rise to specific, testable statements. In this way, competing statements derived from the same basic metatheory may be tested. Rather than experimental results leading to all-or-none acceptance or rejection of the basic metatheory, they contribute to evaluation of the performance of the protective belt – to a decision about whether the metatheory in general is progressive or degenerative. In Chapter 11, we will apply this idea in discussing the status of evolutionary theory.

How do children change as they develop?

We now consider the nature of change in the light of the following frequently debated questions in development. These key concepts are identifiable in various theories and provide a useful heuristic for understanding development. They include:

- heredity versus environment
- continuity versus discontinuity of development
- similarity versus uniqueness
- stability versus instability of behaviour
- activity versus passivity of behaviour
- thinking versus feeling.

Heredity and environment

The role that heredity and environment play in shaping the person is a major issue not only in psychology, but also in education, sociology, politics and related disciplines. Everyday observations reveal similarities and dissimilarities between people. Thus, we may observe that people differ in such diverse ways as physical appearance (for example, tall or short), mental capacity (for example, creativity) or emotional make-up (calm versus excitable). An important question raised by observations such as these concerns the extent to which one is born with particular characteristics. Are the characteristics innate or were they shaped by environmental forces after (or even before) birth? The debate engendered by this question is often referred to as the nature/nurture debate (see Chapter 2). At various times in history, one or another view has held sway. The nature/nurture debate has raged inconclusively in social science literature because the issues involved have not been clearly identified nor have the basic terms been defined. Now it is generally accepted that heredity and environment must interact in order to produce behaviour. The issue, then, is not so much one of how much each contributes to an individual's development but rather how they combine.

Continuity versus discontinuity

The second important issue is whether an individual's development is gradual (continuous) or occurs in sudden leaps (discontinuous). The continuous viewpoint emphasizes slow methodical changes over time. The analogy here would be that of a gum tree growing from a small seedling. That is, growth from the small seedling to sapling and finally mature gum tree is steady and continuous with no apparent 'sudden' transformations or changes into another form. Some psychological theories and praxis such as behaviourism and behaviour therapy draw heavily on the notion of continuity to explain human growth (see Chapter 6).

An alternative viewpoint emphasizes the discontinuity of development. The analogy here would be a caterpillar changing into a butterfly. Psychological theories such as those proposed by Jean Piaget (cognitive-developmental theory) and Sigmund Freud (psychoanalytic theory) emphasize a stage-like or discontinuous view of human development (see Chapters 4 and 5).

Wohlwill (1973: 236) has argued that 'The usefulness of the stage concept remains an open question today and its potential promise unfulfilled'. The concept of stages in the psychological literature has proved difficult to define, despite the observations made by parents, teachers, social workers and others who spend time with children that not all functions are present at birth and that some do appear in most children at a particular time in their development.

Moreover, the use of the concept of stages differs from psychological theory to psychological theory. Thus, in Erik Erikson's psychosocial theory of human development the concept of stages is broad, descriptive and evocative in nature, and does not 'refer clearly to anything definite or measurable in behavior' (Meadows, 1986: 19). Meadows observes that the use of the term 'stage' in relation to other psychological theories is more specific. In Jean Piaget's cognitive-developmental theory, during the child's 'sensori-motor stage', for example, it is generally possible to clearly identify observable aspects of a child's thinking. For example, a favourite toy hidden from a six-month-old child under a handkerchief will not elicit a search reaction on the part of the child, who acts as though 'out of sight is out of mind'. More particularly, some stages are associated with identifiable, clearly defined behaviours, such as the crawling stage in a 10- to 12-month-old infant. So it appears that the use of the word 'stage' varies along a continuum from less to more specific in terms of associated behaviours.

In order to enhance the descriptive and explanatory power of stage theories it is desirable to achieve the following.

1. Establish clearly the relationship between structure and behaviour at any one stage (Kagan *et al.*, 1978).
2. Account for or explain the factors contributing to the child's movement from one stage to the next (Meadows, 1986), such as through biological maturation or environmental input.
3. Clearly relate the structure of one stage to the succeeding stage (Kagan *et al.*, 1978).
4. Specify the behaviours subject to age changes that make up the stages (Meadows, 1986).

Similarity versus uniqueness

The next issue is the matter of similarity versus difference. One view put forward is that people are essentially similar despite superficial differences. That is, the search is for general principles that can be applied to everyone. For example, Carl Jung provided important insight into the complex interaction between similarity and uniqueness in human personality. The Australian writer Peter O'Connor (1985) noted that in his theory of psychological types Jung identified differences in the way people prefer to use their minds – specifically in the way they perceive (that is, are aware of things) and make judgements (that is, reach conclusions about what has been perceived). In Jung's theory, the ways in which we perceive the world relate either to sensing (using sight, touch, taste, hearing and smell) or intuition, which involves indirect perception. The ways of judging are thinking, or logical reasoning, and feeling, or appreciating things. Underlying the complexity of human behaviour, therefore, there are essentially similar processes common to all people. An alternative view is that each human being is unique and that psychology should be concerned with appreciating the special qualities that distinguish one person from another.

Stability versus instability

Another principle of human development deals with the extent to which we regard human behaviour as stable or unstable. One outlook in psychology emphasizes the fixed and unchanging nature of an individual's personality. For example, psychoanalytic theory as expounded by Sigmund Freud suggests that an individual's personality has largely been shaped and moulded during the early years of childhood (Wollheim, 1974). An alternative outlook is that an individual's characteristics (or personality) are constantly changing. The psychological theory of Erikson (1963) is in accord with this outlook. Erikson proposed that an individual continues to develop throughout their lifespan. At various times in her or his life, the individual is faced with certain normative crises that must be addressed and dealt with, thereby allowing the person to proceed to the next stage. For example, from the ages of 13 to 19 years the individual is primarily concerned with establishing an identity or sense of self, particularly in relation to sexuality and occupation.

Activity versus passivity

A further principle of developmental psychology concerns the extent to which children are initiators as opposed to passive reactive organisms. The former view presents the individual as an agent. An agent is someone who takes responsibility for her or his behaviour, is understood to be capable of acting for certain purposes or goals, attaches some freedom of choice to his or her actions and may cite reasons for behaviour – reasons that are often guided by values (Battye and Slee, 1985). Arguments were mounted as the twentieth century progressed that such a view of child development was gaining sway in the psychological literature (Bruner, 1986; Gauld and Shotter, 1977; Harré and Secord, 1972).

Alternatively, individual development can be considered to be shaped by powerful forces that are largely beyond the individual's control. In this view, the individual is seen as essentially a passive/reactive organism. Writers such as Gauld and Shotter (1977) argued that this view of human behaviour has been promulgated by such lines of thought in psychology as that represented by learning theory.

Thinking versus feeling

The final key concept in developmental psychology is the thinking/feeling dichotomy. Writers such as Piaget emphasized the study of children's thinking while theorists such as Freud and Erikson focused on the emotional or affective development of the individual. The complex interplay between thinking and feeling in governing behaviour was revealed in a famous experiment by Schacter and Singer (1962). They gave adrenaline injections to individuals who were told that it was a vitamin compound. These people were then each asked to wait with another individual who was supposed to have received the same 'vitamin' injection but who was, in fact, in collaboration with the experimenters and had not received the injection. Shortly, the subject began to experience the physical effects of adrenaline (for example, rapid breathing and hand tremors). The collaborator then began to act in either an angry or aggressive fashion or a playful, euphoric fashion. The subjects who waited with the 'angry' collaborator were observed to become angry while those who waited with the 'euphoric' collaborator became euphoric. Subjects injected with a placebo of saline solution showed no emotional reaction regardless of how the collaborator behaved, and similarly subjects who had been forewarned that the 'vitamin' injection had side-effects such as rapid breathing or hand tremors showed no emotional reaction regardless of the collaborator's behaviour. It was concluded that emotion consists of more than physiological arousal. A state of physiological arousal for which the individual has no immediate explanation will encourage the person to search his or her environment for an explanation or label, and the choice of label will determine the emotional response (Schacter and Singer, 1962: 379–99).

A commentary on these controversies about developmental change

The various controversies, such as those presented here, suffer from a number of limitations (Overton, 1998). In the first instance their 'either/or' nature suggests that one or the other represents the 'right' or 'real' nature of development. This in turn suggests that empirical inquiry will soon uncover the correct answer. 'The simple empirical observation that generations of empirical observations have failed to resolve any of these issues demonstrates the inadequacy of this assumption' (Overton, 1998: 113). Instead, the focus may best be shifted away from 'which one' questions, to the nature of functioning of each end of the continuum, and the exploration of the relationship between the ends of the continuum (Overton, 1998).

Nevertheless, the classical developmental theories do have their advantages. Rose and Fischer (1998: 123) think that a strength of theories 'such as those of Freud (1973), Piaget (1985), and Werner (1948), has been their sense of the richness and complexity of human beings, in contrast to the oversimplifications that are often evident in more narrowly empirical research'. (This issue of complexity is apparent in the real world, and the link between theory and practice is further considered in Chapter 12.) A contrasting, postmodern, perspective decries the value of theory: 'Theory is taken to be a conceit of modernist knowledge seekers who imagine (and can only imagine) an epistemology of truth – of foundational, transhistorical knowledge. Theory in such a postmodern view resembles its earlier depiction as fantasy' (Marawski, 2000: 436).

Images of children

As outlined in the preceding pages, the factors of history, culture and the philosophy of science play significant roles in shaping how we view children and adolescents. It is possible to draw out a number of 'images' of children influenced by one or more of these factors, including the experiential child, the iniquitous child and the virtuous child. These three views are identified in Figure 1.1.

A mainstream view of children identifiable in the psychological literature might be labelled the experiential child. Inherent in this view is the notion that at birth the infant is like a blank slate, or *tabula rasa*, a concept that has developed from the worldview of empiricism, the primary force behind this view being the English philosopher John Locke (1632–1704). Empiricism did much to replace scholasticism – a worldview of a God-ruled static cosmos. Empiricism advocates that all knowledge is derived from experience. As Locke noted:

> Let us suppose the mind to be, as we say white paper, void of all characters, without any ideas; how comes it to be furnished? Whence comes it by that vast store, which the busy and boundless fancy of man has painted on it with an almost endless variety? Whence has all the materials of reason and knowledge? To this I answer in one word; from experience: in that all our knowledge is founded, and from that it ultimately derives itself.
>
> (Cited in Russell, 1974: 589)

The Scottish philosopher David Hume (1711–76) further developed Locke's view. He focused specifically on sensation, advocating that research drawing directly upon experience through the senses was the means by which we acquire knowledge of the world.

Empiricism became the building block of science in the nineteenth century. Science triumphed over philosophy as the means for gaining knowledge about the world. As viewed by the French philosopher Auguste Comte (1798–1857), science referred to the natural sciences such as biology, chemistry and physics. However, the implication for the social sciences was that human behaviour could be investigated and studied by applying the methods and principles of the natural sciences. The philosophy of Comte is better known as positivism. Comte had identified three ages of thought: the early theological; a metaphysical age that during his time was, in his view, just finishing; and an era of positive science. During the twentieth century, positivism was further refined in relation to the philosophical writings of the Vienna Circle composed of such influential figures as Schlick, Godel and A.J. Ayer. Logical positivism focused on reduction, and induction, which complemented causal explanation.

Empiricism, as reflected in positivism, has firmly established itself in developmental psychology as the predominant means of gaining knowledge about the world (Battye and Slee, 1985). Underpinning this worldview are four propositions regarding the nature of science that have had

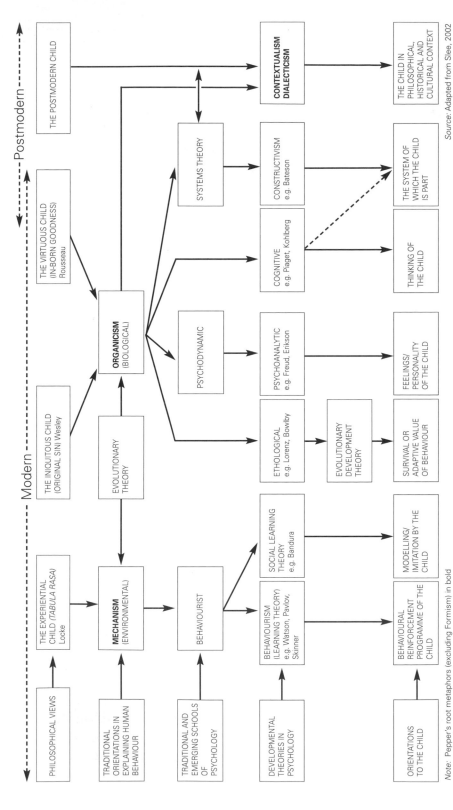

Note: Pepper's root metaphors (excluding Formism) in bold

Figure 1.1 'Images' of children as influenced by history, culture and the philosophy of science

Source: Adapted from Slee, 2002

significant implications for the development of psychology as a science. These four propositions, developed by Evans (1979), may be labelled under two headings: scientism; and the unity of science thesis.

Scientism maintains the following.

1. Science gives us the whole truth about the nature of reality.
2. Science gives us the ultimate truth about the realities it deals with.

The unity of science thesis holds the following.

3. There is one method that all the genuine sciences employ.
4. This one method consists of giving deterministic causal explanations that are empirically testable.

As already noted, in its most basic form positivism is concerned with establishing causes and with predicting events or behaviours. Science is to be conducted in a neutral, value-free manner. Overton (1998) has noted two features of logical positivism. First, there is the reduction of all scientific theories and propositions to words whose meaning could be directly observed, requiring a 'neutral observation language – completely objective, and free from subjective or mind-dependent interpretation' (Overton, 1998: 158). Second, 'to be scientifically meaningful, any universal propositions (e.g. hypotheses, theories, laws) had to be demonstrably nothing more than summary statements of the pristine observations themselves'.

This outlook presented humans as passive or inert organisms whose behaviour is directed or shaped by external forces. That is, at birth the infant is a *tabula rasa* and all that the child becomes is determined by the environment. A modern exponent of this view was B.F. Skinner whose theory of operant conditioning is described in Chapter 6.

A second view of children, as iniquitous, accepts the proposition regarding the inherent sinfulness of the human race (see Figure 1.1). Because the child is thought to be born into original sin, the task of the parents becomes that of breaking the will of the child. This may be accomplished by teaching the children to submit to the will of parents and God (see Box 1.1). In the Puritan tradition of seventeenth- and eighteenth-century England and the United States, the inherent sinfulness of the child was an accepted outlook of educators and the establishment in general. The English churchman, John Wesley (1703), wrote forcefully:

> Break their wills betimes, begin this work before they can run alone, before they can speak plain, perhaps before they can speak at all. Whatever pains it costs, break the will, if you would not damn the child. Let a child from a year old be taught to fear the rod and to cry softly; from that age make him do as he is bid, if you whip him ten times running to effect it. If you spare the rod you spoil the child; if you do not conquer you ruin him.
>
> (Cited in Southey, 1925: 304)

Wesley's views were incorporated into regulations for running a girls' boarding school. Faint-hearted parents intending to enrol their children at his school were warned off. The girls' daily life included a 4 am rise, an hour of religious instruction followed by public worship, breakfast and then the school day, which ended at 5 pm. All children were supervised, with no time allowed for play (Cleverley and Phillips, 1976). A contemporary exploration of the iniquitous view of the child is found in William Golding's portrayal of children's nature in his book *Lord of the Flies*. In this book a group of children is stranded on a desert island; free of the restraint of traditional culture and adult supervision, the iniquitous nature of the children comes to the fore.

An alternative outlook concerning the nature of children to that presented by either the experiential or iniquitous view is the idea of the virtuous child (see Figure 1.1). An exponent of this ideal was the seventeenth-century French philosopher Jean-Jacques Rousseau (1712–78). He disputed the prevailing view that the task of parents and educators was to shape and mould an obedient child from an inherently sinful one. Rousseau took issue with Locke's ideas about children, proposing instead the concept of an innocent child whose development was powerfully directed by nature. He thereby affirmed the inherent goodness of children. Rousseau also rejected Locke's notion of the rational child; he argued that the capacity for reasoning does not develop until around 12 years of age. In his book *Emile* (1762), Rousseau applied his ideas to education: 'God made all things good; man meddles with them and they become evil' (Rousseau, 1914, Book 1: 5). He believed that in educating the innocent and amoral child, it made no sense to punish the child for wrongdoing: 'Before the age of reason we do good or ill without knowing it, and there is no morality in our action' (Rousseau, 1914: 34). If a child committed some wrong action, such as breaking a household object, Rousseau blamed the parents for leaving it within the child's reach.

Rousseau's views are reflected in the more recent thinking of the educator A.S. Neil (1968). Adopting Rousseau's notion of inherent goodness, Neil also rejected the idea of original sin or evil, and advocated non-interference in the education of children. He believed in some innate driving force that would lead children to make the best decisions if left to their own devices. Neil became famous for incorporating his philosophy into the education of children.

David Elkind presented an arguable case (1987) that there exists a fourth contemporary outlook, which he labelled the 'competent infant'. This view presents 'infants and young children as having much more capacity to learn academic skills than children, regardless of background, actually have' (1987: 8). Elkind argued that this view had been adopted by such educators as Bruner, with his now famous statement in 1962 that it is possible to teach any child any subject matter at any age in an intellectually responsible manner. Elkind believed that Bruner may not have appreciated how sincerely parents and educators would take up this statement as a rallying call. A new optimism was generated regarding the capabilities and competences of the infant that, in Elkind's view, overstepped the mark.

Elkind also argued that a second factor contributing to the image of the competent infant concerns Bloom's (1964) idea that one should teach as much as possible to young children because their minds are growing so rapidly. A third influential factor developed by Hunt (1961) is that intelligence is malleable and not fixed. Finally, Elkind (1987) argues that the historian Aries, in pointing out that the concept of childhood is largely a social invention, contributed to the idea that we have been ignoring children's true potential. According to Elkind, in overemphasizing the competence of children we have distorted the true nature of young children and how they really grow and learn.

To highlight how perceptions of children impact on society, we can consider the emerging debate in the literature and the moral panic generated in the media regarding the extent to which children are seen as 'out of control' and 'at risk' (see Box 1.2).

Box 1.2 Children and moral panic

To highlight how views about children impact on society, consider the emerging debate in the literature regarding the extent to which children are seen as 'out of control', 'in crisis' and 'at risk'. Fears are held for the safety of children (e.g. in relation to victimization) and regarding the 'risk' that children present to others (e.g. in relation to school bullying and homicide). Wyness (2000) and Scraton (1997) have both raised questions about whether such a 'crisis' is actually taking place. One outcome of the perceived 'crisis' in childhood relates to the manner in which children have become the subject of both overt and covert regulation (James and James, 2000). This can be reflected in the way that adults are now attempting to control and restrict children's use of public space. For example, in our home city of Adelaide, South Australia, in the last year there was considerable public debate about the provision and location of a skateboarding park for young people. One point of view held that it should be located in the centre of Adelaide where, presumably, behaviour could be regulated, controlled and scrutinized. In contrast, it was argued that locating it in the city centre would attract 'undesirables'. It was finally built and located away from the city centre in a disused part of a railyard. Valentine (1996: 205) has noted that 'postmodernism's concern with the geographies of "others" has revived interest in children's marginalization as a social group'.

Metaphors and theoretical orientations

In considering different theoretical orientations to child development (e.g. Smith *et al.*, 1998), some writers have drawn upon the work of Pepper (1942) on metaphor. Rich discussions of metaphor are to be found in such diverse fields as anthropology, philosophy, sociology, linguistics and psychology (and in Chapter 10 we discuss the use of metaphor in feminist theories). While metaphors can be non-linguistic (e.g. ritual or gestural), it is the linguistic metaphors that have gained most attention. The literature on metaphor has a long history in western civilization (see, for example, Aristotle's *Rhetoric and Poetics*). More contemporary writing on the topic is found in works by Richards (1936), Black (1962), and Lakoff and Johnson (1980). As described by Rosenblatt (1994: 12), 'A metaphor is a figure of speech in which a word or phrase that ordinarily applies to one kind of object or idea is applied to another, thus suggesting a likeness or analogy between them'. Rosenblatt gives the example of an individual exclaiming, 'My love is a red, red rose', which transfers all the meaning we attach to a red rose (such as passion, colour and delicacy) to the loved one, thereby clearly communicating why the person is loved. Lakoff and Johnson (1980) have argued that metaphor is a common everyday facet of language, which guides our everyday thinking regarding a wide variety of topics.

As identified in Figure 1.1, two traditional orientations to behaviour that flow from the experiential, iniquitous and virtuous views of children are the mechanistic and organismic orientations. Pepper (1942) identified these as two of four 'root metaphors' influencing various schools of thought in developmental psychology. Following Pepper, Dixon and Lerner (1992) identified mechanism and organicism as two metatheoretical traditions in developmental psychology.

Theories within the mechanistic tradition, such as behaviourism, use a machine analogy and emphasize that the environment is all-important in shaping what we become and how we develop. Notions of classical science or 'Newtonianism' in the seventeenth and eighteenth centuries highlighted an image of a 'world in which every event was determined by initial conditions that were, at least in principle, determinable with precision. It was a world in which chance played no part, in which all the pieces came together like cogs in a cosmic machine' (Toffler, 1984: xiii).

The organismic tradition encompasses a wide range of theories, such as that of Jean Piaget. It draws upon the notion of the iniquitous or virtuous child, or the competent child, or a mixture of these. As later chapters indicate, the organismic view does not consider the infant to be a blank slate, or *tabula rasa*, at birth – for example, infants may differ in terms of temperament. Organicism draws heavily upon the image of the growing organism unique in its own right but whose development is significantly shaped by mutual influence and the patterning of its parts. Although humanistic theory can be considered to belong to this tradition, we do not cover it in this book as it did not focus upon child development. However, ethological, psychoanalytic, cognitive and constructivist theories are considered. In addition, dialectical theories (such as Vygotsky's) can be seen to belong to the organismic tradition, although they can also be seen as providing a bridge between mechanistic and organismic theories, with the organism and the environment in mutually influential interaction. Dixon and Lerner (1992) categorize dialectical theories separately from organicism.

Systems approaches to development could be considered in the organismic tradition although, like dialecticism, they too emphasize mutual interaction between the organism and the environment. In fact, the notion of systems should perhaps be considered as an additional metaphor to those suggested by Pepper. Emphasizing holism, systems theories focus on the organization of and relations among systems, and how these are transformed over time (Sinnot, 1989). The writings of Gregory Bateson (1972), deriving principally from cybernetic theory, significantly shaped the development of systems theories. So too did the writings of Watzlawick *et al.* (1974) in distinguishing between first- and second-order change: first-order change represents a western positivist ideal of change as orderly, predictable and progressive; second-order change can be sudden and spontaneous, resulting in the emergence of unpredictable new patterns and behaviours.

We mentioned that organicism and mechanism were two of four root metaphors described by Pepper (1942) reflecting different philosophical positions. The other metaphors are contextualism and formism.

Contextualism is concerned with placing the developing child within a historical time and culture, and Dixon and Lerner (1992) identified it as a separate metatheoretical tradition. Contextualists such as Dewey and Mead are considered in this book, their studies laying some of the groundwork for more recent sociocultural and indigenous approaches. For example, for Dewey the essential problem is 'to understand the relation between universal aspects of human nature and its different forms of expression in different social circumstances or arrangements' (Cahan, 1992: 207).

Pepper's metaphor of formism is concerned with classification. It draws upon the metaphor of the similarity of objects, and highlights their classification into discrete and hierarchical categories. Using this metaphor the world is seen to consist of 'things' or 'entities' that can be classified using some schema or system, as in psychiatric diagnostic systems. The notion of formism does not appear to link with any particular theoretical tradition, and thus does not appear in Figure 1.1. However, attempts to classify theoretical approaches are in themselves an expression of formism. In reality, while groupings of theories are convenient, they are not always clear-cut. We do not expect that all readers will endorse the classification scheme shown in Figure 1.1, but we offer it as a useful heuristic for conceptualizing theories in developmental psychology. We revisit the notion of metaphor in relation to categorization in the chapter on feminism (see Chapter 10).

The root metaphors described by Pepper essentially have no common measure and as such are not comparable in any respect (Seifert, 2000). It is perhaps sufficient to use them to help us understand the various lines of thought and the distinctions between them that have informed our theoretical understanding of child development.

Dixon and Lerner (1992) identified evolutionary theory, especially Darwinian theory, as playing a seminal role in the five metatheoretical traditions they identified (organicism, mechanism, contextualism, psychodynamic and dialectical). Discussions of evolutionary theory and Darwin's contribution appear at various points in this book.

A postmodern view of knowledge and children

Finally, we acknowledge the very different philosophical framework embodied in postmodernism, to which we have alluded at various points in this chapter. Influential postmodern philosophers include those in the German critical-theoretical tradition (Habermas and Holzkamp), the French postmodernists (Lyotard, Derrida and Foucault), and a broad range of feminist and ethnic theorists (Teo, 1997). Tierney (2001) has identified five attributes underpinning postmodern thinking. The first of these relates to the conceptualization of knowledge, which is not understood as something that is 'discovered' as though it is there somehow waiting to be unearthed or found. Rather, knowledge is understood as being constructed. Social constructionists argue that knowledge is produced by people working in groups, and is thus a social product with a political basis (Tierney, 1996: 359). In highlighting the politicized nature of knowledge, Tierney has commented that it is no accident that science has been a largely male enterprise that has ignored women's concerns or interpreted them in a patriarchal manner (Tierney, 2001).

The second attribute of postmodernism relates to the challenge that it directs at modernism's faith in science, and the efforts that it expends in analysing underlying assumptions and frameworks. The contrasting epistemological position of modernism with its positivist assumptions has been contrasted with postmodernism's 'critical questioning, and often outright rejection, of the ethnocentric rationalism championed by modernism' (Cooper and Burrell, 1988: 92, cited in Tierney, 2001). Central to this attribute is the idea of 'power', and that knowledge is not something neutral but part of the scientific endeavour.

The third attribute relates to the contrasting identities of the modernist and postmodernist scientist. Contrast the popular image of the nameless and faceless scientist labouring away in a laboratory with what Tierney calls the 'fractured nature of the postmodern identity' (2001: 362). Contributing to the idea of a 'fractured identity' is the interdisciplinary nature of a great deal of research today, which is searching for a greater comparative understanding of the world. We consider the notion of developmental psychology as a fractured discipline in Chapter 11.

A fourth attribute of postmodernist knowledge relates to the chaos, uncertainty and disorganization that a great deal of postmodern thinking encourages. This is in direct contrast to the causal, linear modernist thinking, searching for certainty and predictability. Tierney suggests that the political and cultural underpinnings of postmodern thinking are significantly broadening our understandings about the nature of knowledge.

Finally, Tierney has suggested that what we have witnessed in the latter part of the twentieth century is the death of the 'nation-state' wherein the university is no longer seen as the sole arbiter, producer and purveyor of knowledge. Instead, in the face of globalization, and the decline of the nation-state, the role of the universities in relation to the production of knowledge is now a matter for redefinition and debate. We will return to this point in the final chapter.

What would a 'postmodern child' look like? We would suggest that this child would be one understood in philosophical, historical and cultural context; one who is valued for him- or herself rather than simply as a means of understanding the adult condition; one whom the researcher strives to understand without exploitation, and whom the practitioner seeks to help in a full understanding of the social and historical contexts within which the child, practitioner and other relevant parties operate. The very fact that the structure of this chapter reflects some of these issues implies that we are indeed open to such reflection on our theory and practice. Critiques of traditional schools of thought in developmental psychology appear especially in our considerations of cultural and indigenous psychologies, feminism and implications of theory for practice.

Conclusions

In this chapter we have set the scene for the text that follows. While acknowledging the positivist tradition of development psychology, we have also deliberately embedded theoretical thinking in the context of history, culture and philosophy. In contextualizing theory in this manner we believe that it provides a richer account and understanding of influential theories in this postmodern era. As noted at the beginning of this chapter, though, we are hopeful, in presenting such material, of engendering debate regarding this very point.

2 From Darwin to DNA: biologically based theories of development

Introduction

In this chapter we consider theoretical frameworks that place a heavy emphasis upon the biological roots of development. Unsurprisingly, these have often emanated not from psychologists, but from workers in other fields such as biology and medicine. We first consider evolutionary theory in relation to behavioural development, beginning by questioning the often-repeated view that Charles Darwin heavily influenced various theoretical traditions in developmental psychology. We then consider more recent applications of evolutionary theory, including ethology, sociobiology and, most recently, evolutionary developmental psychology. We also consider behaviour genetics and neurological perspectives on development, both of which encompass the modern nature/nurture debate. We end by discussing the medical model as applied to children's behavioural and emotional problems.

How far was Darwin really the forefather of developmental psychology?

When a well-accepted historical 'fact' is challenged, this is worth mentioning, especially when it concerns a fundamental tenet of the field. Darwin's impact on the field of biology was, of course, profound. He has been described as 'having attained sainthood (if not divinity) among evolutionary biologists' (Gould and Lewontin, 1979: 589). As we observed in the previous chapter, it has been proposed that Darwinian evolutionary theory was the precursor of five major families of developmental theory (Dixon and Lerner, 1992), and developmental psychologists in the latter part of the twentieth century often claimed that Darwin had a dramatic and revolutionary effect on the child development field (Charlesworth, 1992). Similarly, in modern child development texts he may be credited as the 'forefather of scientific child study' (Berk, 2000: 12), and various developmental theorists mentioned in this book have acknowledged a debt to Darwin.

However, it can be argued that the influence of Darwinian theory specifically may not have been as direct or strong as commonly supposed (Charlesworth, 1992). It is difficult to identify the direct ancestors of developmental psychology, especially as this field began to emerge concurrently with Darwin's work. This raises the possibility that Darwin himself might have been significantly influenced by the new discipline or its precursors, although in the light of the available evidence Charlesworth dismissed this notion. Historians of psychology have identified the strong impact of Darwin on the field of psychology in general, especially in emphasizing the notion of continuity between human and animal minds, the importance of individual differences, the adaptation of organisms to the environment and a broadening of investigative methodologies. Although Charlesworth did not argue against these Darwinian influences on psychology as a whole, he contended that, when it comes to the specific area of developmental psychology, the evidence indicates that Darwin's influence is 'weak, indirect and somewhat distorted' (1992: 7), and that Darwin had no significant influence on either developmental psychology's empirical research or its theorizing. In particular, he concluded that the most distinctive feature of Darwin's theory – natural selection – has been missing from developmental psychology.

Charlesworth suggested three reasons for this actual lack of influence of Darwinian theory on the field of child development. One is a conceptual issue concerning the differentiation of phylogeny (changes over evolutionary time) and ontogeny (individual life histories). Whatever emphasis one might place upon genetic contributions to behaviour, the subject matter for developmentalists is individual organisms and not populations and lineages: 'It is not surprising, then, that evolutionary speculation about different ancestors fighting it out in different environments now long gone is viewed as having little utility in guiding research' (Charlesworth, 1992: 11). A second reason for the weak influence of Darwin follows from the previous one, and concerns methodology. Developmentalists are attracted to studying readily available, proximate factors rather than the ultimate factors that stretch back across evolutionary time. A third reason concerns moral values. Even though natural selection is not universally accepted by biologists as the primary evolutionary mechanism (Leakey and Lewin, 1996), the Darwinian perspective that 'less fit' organisms do not survive implies a harsh fate for infants and children born into a range of disadvantaged circumstances. Charlesworth suggested that this perspective is sharply at variance with the underlying motivation of many developmental psychologists to improve the lot of the world's children – an ideology he called 'meliorism'.

Notwithstanding these reasons for a lack of a profound Darwinian influence on developmental psychology, Charlesworth observed that at the time he was writing (the early 1990s) the implications of evolutionary theory for developmental psychology were just beginning to be recognized. As discussed later, by the turn of the millennium evolutionary developmental psychology was being hailed as an emerging field of interdisciplinary inquiry. Prior to this, however, came the fields of ethology and sociobiology, both of which were primarily concerned with the influence of biological heritage on human behaviour.

Ethology

During the middle of the twentieth century, the work of two Nobel Prize-winning zoologists, Lorenz and Tinbergen, became highly influential in understanding animal behaviour and, later, human development (e.g. Lorenz, 1981; Tinbergen, 1973). The ethologists studied innate behaviours (instincts) that fitted animals for survival, examining these both in the natural environment and the laboratory. A particularly important ethological concept was that of the critical period (later modified to sensitive period) – a time early in life when it was crucial for certain environmental conditions to be present in order to enable an instinct to be properly realized (Sluckin, 1970). For example, newly hatched chicks normally become attached to, or imprinted upon, their mother over the first day, but if instead of their mother they are exposed to a suitable alternative, such as a person, they become imprinted on that instead (readers will doubtless be familiar with famous photographs such as those of Lorenz being followed around by goslings). Imprinting is a clear example of gene–environment interactions at work. Such ethological concepts influenced researchers into early parent–child relationships, such as Bowlby (see Chapter 5) and Hinde. Ethology is a field that values research based on the observation and description of natural events, and it can be argued that developmental psychology's neglect of this approach in favour of theory-derived hypothesis-testing is detrimental (Hinde, 1992a). For example, Bowlby's highly influential research on attachment arose from observations that disturbed adolescents had disrupted early childhood relationships; this key area of research would not have happened if it had relied solely on existing theory to drive it. Blurton Jones (e.g. 1972), a former student of Tinbergen, was particularly influential in promoting the application of ethological methods to provide objective descriptions of children's behaviour. While acknowledging the pioneering nature of this work, Hinde (1982) suggested that Blurton Jones had gone too far in his rejection of alternative data-gathering methods, such as rating scales and parent interviews.

Although ethologists, like evolutionary biologists, were interested in innate behaviours subject to natural selection, they (like developmental psychologists) were nevertheless more interested in proximate behaviours than ultimate factors (Charlesworth, 1992).

Sociobiology

In the mid-1970s, a far more radical view about the role of biological heritage was proposed by certain biologists. They argued that human beings, and their behaviour, exist merely to provide the means for genes to survive and reproduce. This new discipline – sociobiology – was put forward by Wilson (1975). The notion that human behaviour is subservient to genes (which compete with other genes for survival) was encapsulated in the title of Dawkins' (1976) book *The Selfish Gene*. This perspective has profound implications for our understanding of human reproductive and child-rearing behaviours. In particular, sociobiologists argued that since males can produce numerous gametes (sperm) the best strategy for their genes to survive would be to impregnate as many females as possible, with a low subsequent investment in parenting these many offspring personally. By contrast, females, with their smaller potential for producing offspring, would best ensure their genes' survival by being very choosy about their children's father and by investing heavily in raising their small number of offspring to maturity. Hence greater male promiscuity and the role of females, rather than males, in parenting were seen as biological imperatives. Furthermore, aggression between males was seen as a natural consequence of male competition for females. It was even proposed by one writer that if a man discovered that his wife had had sexual relations with another man, then being jealous to the point of murder (whether of the woman or her lover) could be seen as biologically sensible (Freedman, 1979). Not surprisingly, feminists were outraged at such biological apologies for sexist and violent behaviour (see Chapter 10), and theorists (whether feminist or not) mounted various arguments against sociobiology. Notably, Lerner and von Eye (1992) critiqued three major tenets of sociobiology.

First, they took issue with the way in which sociobiologists use interspecies comparisons and the notion of homology – the idea that if behaviours of separate species can be described similarly this implies an evolutionary connection between them. For example, arguments for an evolutionary impetus for human male promiscuity and even rape have been based on fruit fly and monkey behaviours. Yet similarities in observed behaviours provide no proof at all of evolutionary connectedness, and they are more appropriately seen as analogies, not homologies. Neither do such similarities provide any evidence for how far the behaviours in question are constrained or produced by genetic means.

Second, Lerner and von Eye critiqued the notion of heritability as used by sociobiologists. Heritability estimates, which vary between 0 and 1, represent an estimate of the *variation in genetic inheritance between individuals*. However, sociobiologists and others sometimes use the term to imply that the higher the heritability estimate, the more the behaviour in question is determined by genes and not the environment. In fact, heritability estimates say nothing about how genes or the environment determine the behaviour of individuals. Lerner and von Eye provided the following clear example to illustrate how heritability estimates can be misinterpreted in this way. Imagine that a law permits men, but not women, to be elected to government office. A person's eligibility for office could then be absolutely predicted by their genes (possession of an XX or XY pair of chromosomes) – giving a perfect heritability estimate of 1. Clearly, this should not be taken as evidence that eligibility for office is genetic, yet this is exactly how heritability estimates of various behavioural traits are often interpreted. Conversely, traits that are universal, such as the capacity for language, have zero *heritability* but are clearly *inherited*, a point that is often overlooked even in texts about the nature/nurture debate (Wells, 2000).

A third principle of sociobiology that has been attacked is the assumption that what exists is necessarily an adaptation – that the physical features and behaviours that are observed in animals or humans represent ideal outcomes of evolution. Darwin himself observed that sutures (gaps) in the skulls of infants are a perfect adaptation to childbirth, giving flexibility to the skull as the child descends the birth canal; but how is their existence to be explained in baby birds, which simply have to escape from shells (Lerner and von Eye, 1992)? Thus, some features may develop for no particular purpose or become coopted for a purpose for which they did not originally evolve. This point was previously made by biologists Gould and Lewontin (1979), who used a now-famous architectural analogy. Cathedrals and churches may have rounded arches in their ceilings with triangular spaces between them which contain designs that fit the space perfectly; while no one would argue that the arches were placed there *in order to* provide the spaces for the designs, biologists frequently make similar arguments for the evolutionary origins of animal structures and behaviours. Similarly, it has beeen argued that *post hoc* explanations for the evolutionary pressures that may have determined various forms and functions may be no more scientifically valid than a Kipling Just So Story. (For the sake of my co-author PS, and any other readers who may not be familiar with Kipling's stories, I have included Box 2.1. A distinctly Lamarckian evolutionary theory is apparent – RS.)

Overall, Lerner and von Eye concluded that the problems with sociobiological explanations for human behaviour are so great that this theory is not relevant for understanding human development or sex differences. While powerfully argued, this view is perhaps an extreme one. While agreeing that a primary role for genes should be rejected, that homologies should not be confused with analogies, and that heritability estimates should not be misinterpreted, Hinde (1992b) – a researcher in the ethological tradition – suggested that these criticisms are too sweeping. For example, analogous behaviours might provide evidence that similar selection pressures have been at work, and Lerner and von Eye focused on aggression rather than cooperation, which has also been considered from a sociobiological perspective. The value of their critique may be to help balance the more extreme views espoused by some sociobiologists (Hinde, 1992b). Hinde (1992b) has also praised the ethological approach as bringing a broader perspective to bear on explanations of behavioural development than has been evidenced by most developmental psychologists. This perspective is that, in order to fully understand any biological structure or behaviour, questions need to be answered not only about its development and cause, but about its function and its evolution: while some sociobiologists have overemphasized function and evolution, developmental psychologists have largely neglected them. The potential for sociobiology to inform developmental psychology was identified by Smith (1987), who discussed several relevant sociobiological concepts, such as viewing the whole human lifespan as an evolved strategy for replicating genes. Such notions are increasingly being given attention under the rubric of 'evolutionary developmental psychology'.

Box 2.1 The elephant's child

Then the Elephant's Child put his head down close to the Crocodile's musky, tusky mouth, and the Crocodile caught him by his little nose, which up to that very week, day, hour, and minute, had been no bigger than a boot, though much more useful. ... Then the Elephant's Child sat back on his little haunches, and pulled, and pulled, and pulled, and his nose began to stretch ... and at last the Crocodile let go of the Elephant's Child's nose with a plop that you could hear all up and down the Limpopo ... he ... wrapped it all up in cool banana leaves, and hung it in the great grey-green, greasy Limpopo to cool.... The Elephant's Child sat there for three days waiting for his nose to shrink, but it never grew any shorter ... the Crocodile had pulled it out into a really truly trunk same as all elephants have today.

(Kipling, 1975: 45–6; first published 1902)

Evolutionary developmental psychology

Despite the backlash against evolutionary approaches to human behaviour sparked by sociobiological theory, evolutionary theory seems to be gaining new influence in psychology, being described as a 'new science of the mind' (Buss, 1999). More specifically, evolutionary *developmental* psychology has been described as an emerging interdisciplinary field, its goals being 'to identify the genetic and ecological mechanisms that shape the development of ... phenotypes and ensure their adaptation to local conditions' (Geary and Bjorklund, 2000: 57). The interplay between genetic and ecological conditions to determine the phenotype (physical and behavioural characteristics) is known as epigenetics (imprinting, as described by ethologists, is a good example of epigenetics). Like sociobiology, evidence is drawn from other animal (especially primate) species, from fossil records of ancestors of *Homo sapiens* and from a consideration of modern hunter-gatherer societies.

In a manner reminiscent of Havighurst's notion of developmental tasks (see Chapter 3), evolutionary developmental psychologists divide the life-span into a number of stages defined by differences in physical development, social dependence and social goals – for example, infancy, childhood, juvenility, adolescence and adulthood (Bogin, 1997, cited in Geary and Bjorklund, 2000). An important function of the extended pre-adult period of development in humans is said to be to provide the opportunity for practice of skills needed for survival and reproduction (for example, competition for mates), through play, social interactions and exploration of the environment. It has also been argued that social and cognitive immaturity may themselves serve adaptive functions that are concerned with the shorter-term survival of the young individual rather than being a preparation for adulthood. For example, children's short auditory memory span might aid comprehension of language by reducing the amount of information to be processed (Geary and Bjorklund, 2000).

In infancy and childhood, attachment to parents is seen as the central social relationship, functioning to keep the young organism alive by keeping it close to parents and increasing the level of parental investment in their offspring (see Chapter 5). Readers are also referred to Susan Goldberg's (2000) book (*Attachment and Development*) in this series for a rich discussion of this issue. The fact that there are individual differences in quality of attachment, as shown by the studies of Ainsworth (e.g. Ainsworth and Wittig, 1969) is taken as evidence that attachment is an epigenetic process, with the contribution of genes and environment yet to be studied.

As children grow older, the shift away from parents towards peers, especially same-sex peers, is seen as preparatory for adult reproductive activities. For example, boys' social relationships are concerned with status and dominance, which can be interpreted as being preparatory for competition for mates in pre-industrial societies, while girls' more intimate relationships with each other can be seen as fostering a supportive network for later parenting activities (Geary and Bjorklund, 2000). It is of interest that this traditional sex-typed interpretation (competing males but cooperating females) has required modification in the light of recent research (e.g. Crick and Bigbee, 1998) which has broadened the definition of aggression from physical and verbal types to social forms more typical of girls, such as spreading rumours about others and keeping them out of friendship groups. Thus Geary and Bjorklund acknowledge that girls also compete with one another, proposing that perhaps upsetting the social networks of competitors lays the groundwork for later competition for mates. In fact, our own research does show that competition between teenage girls over boyfriends is one (of several) triggers for social aggression (Owens *et al.*, 2000).

The evolutionary framework has been applied to cognition as well as to social development. It has been proposed that there are hierarchically organized modules of the mind that have evolved to process both social and non-social (ecological) aspects of the world (see Table 2.1) (Geary, 1998, cited in Geary and Bjorklund, 2000). This theory is an exemplar of Pepper's (1942) formism metaphor, in that it is based upon dividing the world into categories. Modules related to the social world are divided into those concerning different social groups and those that are individually based, such as theory of mind. Ecological modules are divided into the biological and the physical. While the basic neural structures underlying these modules are seen as inherent, they develop as children initiate activities and gain competence in 'folk psychology, folk biology and intuitive physics' (Geary and Bjorklund, 2000: 62). In other words, epigenetic processes are responsible for phenotype, although the mechanisms involved are poorly understood. The notion of the sensitive period is incorporated, with the additional suggestion that sensitive periods may be related to the position of modules/submodules in the hierarchy, with the sensitive period being shorter and earlier for lower-level than higher-level modules.

Table 2.1 Evolutionary developmental theory: evolved domains of mind

Domain of information:	social		biological	physical
Subdomain:	individual	group		
Function of information-processing modules:	online monitoring of dyadic interactions; maintaining interpersonal relationships	parsing social universe into kin, friends and competitors	categorizing and representing behaviour/ growth patterns of flora and fauna, e.g. food sources	guiding/ representing movement in three-dimensional space; using physical materials
Examples of information-processing modules:	language	ingroup	flora	movement
	theory of mind	outgroup	fauna	representation

Source: based on information in Geary and Bjorklund, 2000

A goal of evolutionary developmental psychology is to understand how biases and constraints on behaviour determined by evolutionary pressures are relevant for the modern world (Geary and Bjorklund, 2000). For example, while children the world over are biologically predisposed to learn language, reading is a cultural expression of language (Snowling, 2000) and thus inherently more difficult to learn. Similarly, Geary and Bjorklund suggest that while deadly male-on-male violence is an understandable result of evolutionary pressures to compete, this could be channelled more safely into alternative competitive activities, such as athletics (a view, incidentally, that would be strongly challenged by some sociologists concerned with gendered aspects of education, who would see this as encouraging harmful 'macho' attitudes (Gilbert and Gilbert, 1998).

While many theories of development focus on specific aspects, the above overview makes clear the breadth of coverage afforded by evolutionary developmental theory: 'an evolutionary perspective should provide a useful framework for conceptualizing and guiding future research across many of the developmental specialties (e.g. social, cognitive, and neuroscientific)' (Geary and Bjorklund, 2000: 63). This implies that evolutionary theory could play an important role in integrating otherwise diverse theories, a possibility raised previously by Hinde (1992a; 1992b) and discussed further in Chapter 11 of this book.

The evolutionary perspective on human development carries some dangers, however, some of which we have alluded to already. Hinde (1992b) warned against drawing simplistic and anthropomorphic parallels between animal and human behaviour. He provided the example of the removal of an infant from its mother in both humans and rhesus monkeys. While in both cases the greater the disruption to the mother–infant relationship, the more the infant's behaviour is disturbed, the dynamics differ in the two cases. Human children are more disturbed by spending the separation in a strange environment, while monkey infants are more disturbed by remaining in the familiar group environment (because of the effect of removal from the group on the mother's social relationships on her return). Thus, rather than simply drawing parallels, animal data should be used to suggest principles that can then be tested in the human case. More recently, and in a similar vein, Archer (2001) has argued that the value of evolutionary psychology lies in suggesting novel hypotheses that can be tested. However, Segal (2001) suggests that evolutionary-based tales of wicked step-parents (with their lack of genetic investment in their step-children), competitive men and nurturing women are simply clichés repackaged as new insights. Other opponents of the evolutionary approach maintain that, while our evolutionary history clearly empowers and limits our behaviour, this is at such a level of generality as to be unhelpful in considering most specific human behaviours (Rose and Rose, 2001). Readers interested in pursuing this debate in more detail are referred to Archer's (2001) article and the supportive and opposing papers that follow it, and to a paper by Ketelaar and Ellis (2000), which addresses the question of whether evolutionary explanations are unfalsifiable; we discuss this further in Chapter 11. Further information about evolutionary developmental psychology can be found in Bjorklund and Pellegrini (2002).

Behaviour genetics: a focus of today's nature/nurture debate

Evolutionary theory focuses upon characteristics of the human species in general. However, evolution (at least by natural selection) depends upon the existence of individual differences. Individual differences in behaviour and development are the subject matter of the field of behaviour genetics, which is an important focus of the familiar nature/nurture debate today. Genetic explanations for human phenomena are very much in the public eye as a result of the Human Genome Project, aimed at mapping the genes on human chromosomes and discovering the complete sequence of nucleotides on each gene. Plans for this project were initiated in 1986, and in June 2000 a working draft of the human genome sequence was announced (Dickson, 2000).

The notion that genes set limits on development has been in existence for some time, with the 'reaction range' being bounded by the upper and lower limits of possible developmental outcomes (Gottesman, 1974). Imprinting again provides an example, with chicks, for example, only becoming imprinted on objects if they possess certain characteristics in terms of size and movement, a role which under normal circumstances would be fulfilled by the mother. More recently, however, genes have come to be seen as playing a much more active role in development. Scarr (1992) has built a theory that draws upon the finding of behaviour genetics research that similarity in genetics correlates with similarity in behaviours. She acknowledges the role of the environment in promoting phenotypical behaviours, but points out that in reality the environment is very similar for many individuals, and that the genes, in effect, rely on the existence of that environment for their expression. She has promoted the notion of the 'average expectable environment' whereby, assuming a 'normal' environment, genes will express their potential. Variations of environment within the normal range are functionally equivalent. Provided the environment is indeed 'normal', environmental changes such as extra stimulation will have no effect. Only if the environment is outside the range of normality (for example, in abusive families) will such environmental change significantly alter behavioural outcomes.

Furthermore, the phenomenon of 'niche-picking' is introduced, whereby, rather than environments shaping passive organisms, organisms also shape their environments. Indeed, genotypes drive experiences. Acknowledging that this notion runs counter to mainstream developmental theory, Scarr has presented various kinds of evidence that individuals are active shapers of their own environment rather than passive recipients of it (which accords with organismic theories of development, as discussed in Chapters 3 and 4). Overall, Scarr has argued that '*genotype-environment correlations,* rather than gene-environment interactions, predominate in the construction of experiences' (1992: 8). Scarr sees the effect of genes becoming stronger as children grow older and become increasingly able to select environments that suit their genetic make-up.

Similar in many ways to Scarr's model is that of Plomin, who refers to his work as environmental genetics (e.g. Hetherington *et al.*, 1994). He has introduced the notion of the 'non-shared environment'. This concept can be exemplified by considering siblings. Behavioural differences between siblings are often very apparent despite their sharing 50 per cent of genetic material and being raised in the same family. Plomin maintains that being raised in the same family does not constitute being raised in an identical environment: the 50 per cent of genetic material that differs between siblings causes children to respond to similar events differently, and also evokes differing responses from parents. This non-shared environment creates different outcomes, while the shared environment is thought to have little effect.

Theories such as these have given genetics a much more predominant place than previously in explaining behavioural differences between individuals. For example, Scarr's theory implies that children could be reassigned to be raised by different families and they would turn out much the same anyway. Such interpretations lead to profound conclusions. For example, differences in parenting style are seen to matter little – as long as parents are 'good enough' the child will develop as genes dictate. Furthermore, provided the environment is not very deviant, early enrichment programmes for families would be a waste of resources.

Such conclusions have certainly not gone unchallenged. Baumrind, who undertook seminal research on the effects of parenting styles on children's development, strongly took issue with Scarr's notions of average expectable environments and good enough parenting. Baumrind (1993) maintained that the heritability estimates used by Scarr suffer from implausible basic assumptions, underdeveloped constructs, inadequate measures of family environment and unrepresentative populations. For example, the populations in which heritability estimates have been made are extraordinary, mainly being studies of twins and adoptees. Scarr did not specify what constitutes a 'good enough' environment, which appears to be any environment other than abusive. Baumrind cites evidence to support her counterproposition that 'All nonabusive environments above the poverty line are not equally facilitative of healthy development' (1993: 1299). Scarr accepted that her theory depends on children having a broad range of environments from which to choose, and excluded individuals with disadvantaged circumstances or restricted life choices. Baumrind suggested that such 'excluded' individuals are in fact the norm worldwide, the absence of disadvantage not being the same as having a rich environment. She disputed Scarr's assumption that the same ontological principles apply within all cultures: 'What is "normal" or "expectable" in one culture frequently is anathema in another' (1993: 1301). For example, as we will discuss in Chapter 9, parents from different cultural backgrounds rear their children very differently because of different cultural values; this necessarily limits the generalizability of heritability indices. Baumrind maintained that negative social or genetic factors can be attenuated by parents, but that parents will not be open to interventions if they accept Scarr's position and believe the situation is genetic and unmodifiable.

More recently, a detailed critique of the interpretations of behaviour genetics research has been produced (Vreeke, 2000). In particular, the assumption that behaviour genetics studies are relevant for questions of development has been questioned. Echoing the critiques of sociobiology, Vreeke observes that the main statistical technique used by behaviour geneticists is analysis of variance, a correlational technique. Although, as every undergraduate psychology student knows, correlation does not imply causation, in the field of behaviour genetics, providing developmental interpretations of analysis of variance is standard practice. If, say, the heritability of IQ in a population is 80 per cent, this is understood to mean that genetics play a major causal role in intellectual ability (although how this happens is not made explicit). Vreeke argues that there are a number of weaknesses in this logic. For example, as in Baumrind's earlier critique, the nature of the sample is seen as crucial – if the study participants were from a selected background (e.g. college students) one might find a very different heritability estimate than if they were from a sample representative of the broader population. Assuming one does, in fact, succeed in taking such population effects into account, an assumption of analysis of variance is that the variables are additive, whereas the evidence is that developmental processes are interactive, and analysis of variance is arguably not sensitive enough to detect this.

This critique has, in turn, been critiqued by behaviour geneticists who argue, on the basis of Mendel's laws of inheritance, that additivity is the biological reality, as reflected by additive effects of different genes to produce those phenotypes that are determined by multiple genes. However, Vreeke argues that Mendel's laws mention interaction, as well as additivity, between genes, so that taking multiple genes as a model for gene/environment relationships is not a basis for supporting the additivity assumption. A further argument made in support of additivity is that it is adaptive. Yet, using evolutionary theory in this way can be seen as inappropriate: it relies on a consideration of the *outcomes* of development (phenotypes) upon

which evolutionary processes operate, and ignores the actual gene/
environment relationships that determine the phenotypes of individuals.
Although various researchers have come to the defence of the additivity
principle, this stance flies in the face of evidence from molecular biology
and animal research that genotypes are translated into phenotypes by
'complex, dynamic and nonlinear' processes (Vreeke, 2000: 40). Wahlsten
(2000) acknowledges the importance of interaction between genes and
environment, but does not accept that analysis of variance is necessarily an
inappropriate analytic method: rather, the sample sizes must be large
enough to enable the interactions to be detected (but, in practice, are often
not).

Vreeke maintains that Scarr's and Baumrind's interpretations can be
reconciled if we accept that genes and the environment have an interactive
relationship: shared environmental effects that are demonstrated in experimental social research may not show up in a behaviour genetics study if
the research design does not allow for the possibility that individuals with
different genotypes may respond differently to the same environment.
Thus 'it cannot be deduced from percentages of explained variance that an
intervention cannot be successful. An interactive logic predicts that it is a
matter of finding the right key to the right lock, the environment that fits
an individual genotype' (Vreeke, 2000: 43).

Others have also criticized behaviour genetics as placing too much
importance on genetic influences on behaviour, an extreme view being that
the role of genes ceases at conception, with epigenetic processes then taking over, so that phylogeny and genetics add little of significance to an
understanding of phenotypes. The neuroscientist Rose maintains that
'heritability estimates are simply meaningless when applied to complex
human behavioural traits' leading to 'implausible claims such as a significant heritability for "religiosity" or "job satisfaction"' (2001: 144).

A newer framework for understanding gene–environment interactions,
which gives a more important place to environmental influences on development is the bioecological model (Bronfenbrenner and Ceci, 1994;
Bronfenbrenner and Morris, 1998). Bronfenbrenner's (1979) earlier ecological model was highly influential in drawing attention to the multiple
and interacting social and environmental systems influencing children's
development (see Chapter 8). The more recent bioecological model takes
issue with the view that individual and group differences in developmental
outcomes are mainly genetically driven, proposing instead that it is appropriate and ongoing interactions with the environment that enable genes to
exert their potential to a greater or lesser degree (see Chapter 11). It is,
thus, these interactions – known as proximal processes – that drive development, and their quality will affect heritability estimates.

Brain and behaviour in development

Brain–behaviour relations were relatively neglected by developmental psychologists during most of the twentieth century, but we are witnessing the beginnings of an explosion of new information since the development of non-invasive technologies for studying brain functioning (van der Molen and Ridderinkhof, 1998). It is impossible in the space available here to cover this field adequately, so we will restrict ourselves to a few very basic theoretical issues and illustrate these with one particular theory concerned with how abuse early in life can change behaviour permanently.

It is often assumed, and promulgated in populist literature, that genes determine brain structure, which in turn determines behaviour. Differences in brain structure – for example, between males and females, or between those diagnosed and not diagnosed with Attention Deficit Hyperactivity Disorder (ADHD) – may be interpreted as providing evidence of fundamental, inherited individual differences in neurology that underlie observed behavioural differences. It has been proposed that such findings may be favoured for publication over failures to replicate them or over cultural explanations for the observed behavioural differences, so that the evidence for such differences may be much weaker and more contradictory than at first apparent (e.g. Gilbert and Gilbert, 1998: 37). Thus, the nature/nurture controversy is again evident in the field of brain–behaviour relations.

In fact, there is strong evidence that the structure of the human brain is determined by epigenetic processes. The young human child has many more synaptic connections in the cerebral cortex than in adulthood, therefore it can be argued that experience determines which of these are retained and which lost; furthermore, it is difficult to explain the great complexity of interconnections in the human brain as being determined purely by a limited number of genes (van der Molen and Ridderinkhof, 1998).

Animal studies have also established that brain structures can be changed as a result of early experience with environments that are especially stimulating (e.g. Rosenzweig, 1996) or that deprive the young animal of normal experience, such as normal visual experience (e.g. Tees, 1986). The latter studies in particular have shown the existence of sensitive periods for such changes (as for imprinting, mentioned previously). This is also apparent in human infants with uncorrected squints (strabismus), whereby a lack of normal visual input in the early months of life affects neurological functioning permanently, resulting in low acuity in the affected eye and a failure to develop normal binocular vision (e.g. Westall and Shute, 1992). Human and animal studies therefore indicate that while the young brain is plastic, this plasticity is constrained by external factors such as exposure to a normal environment, and internal factors such as the progressive development of the brain from deeper to more superficial areas (van der Molen and Ridderinkhof, 1998).

These issues are illustrated by Perry's (1997) theory of the neurodevelopmental aspects of violence. Perry, whose background is in medicine, acknowledges evolutionary theory, stressing that humans evolved as social animals, with the survival of the individual dependent upon nurturing by the clan. The majority of the brain has evolved to subserve necessary social relationships, and the early caretaking experience is instrumental in determining how the brain becomes organized, from the more primitive brain stem and mid-brain, through the limbic system and up to the complex cortex. The cortex becomes increasingly able to modulate the functions of the more primitive parts of the brain. However, certain experiences in the early years disrupt the development of the lower parts of the brain, which in turn influence the development of the higher parts, given the brain's hierarchical structure. The result of disruption to early nurturing (such as exposure to neglect or violence) can be that the modulating effect of the higher influences is reduced, resulting in effects such as increased anxiety and a predisposition to violence.

Perry argues that biological markers (such as certain blood chemicals) associated with violent behaviours should not mislead us into assuming that these must reflect the genetic differences between individuals that are causing the behaviours. Rather, they reflect the biochemical *outcomes* of brain structures and processes determined by early experience. This view is compatible with the hierarchical nature of Geary's evolutionary theory of development (outlined previously) and incorporates the notion of sensitive periods emphasized by ethologists, and demonstrated by human and animal studies of brain development.

Van der Molen and Ridderinkhof (1998: 89) note the importance of brain plasticity studies in particular for our future developmental theorizing about what they call 'the developmental psychology evergreens "nature/nurture" and "critical periods"', as well as addressing a very basic question: 'Where does development stop and ageing begin?'

The medical model

In a book on psychological theories of child and adolescent development, why are we including an (albeit brief) consideration of a perspective on children's behaviour, which is arguably not a theory, not developmental in nature and not based in the psychological tradition? We consider it essential that this approach be addressed, given the real impact a medical perspective has on the lives of many children whose behaviour is considered to be problematic in some way. Both undergraduate and postgraduate students may be introduced to a medical diagnostic approach to children's behavioural and emotional problems, and indeed clinical psychology course accreditation may require that students learn psychiatric diagnosis. However, in our experience, the specific issue of how such an approach accords (or otherwise) with psychological theories of child development (and indeed, with the scientist-practitioner model frequently espoused by professional psychology courses – see Chapter 12) is rarely addressed. Students and beginning practitioners (and perhaps many not-so-beginning practitioners!) are left to try and make sense of the professional dilemmas this can cause. For example, a psychologist working in a hospital setting in Australia may conceptualize a child-client's difficult behaviour in terms of scientifically well-established principles of learning theory. S/he would devise an intervention accordingly, considering issues such as antecedents and reinforcers. However, the official hospital records may not reflect this theoretical orientation at all, but require the psychologist to record the case in terms of a medical (psychiatric) diagnosis, which may be irrelevant to how the case was actually conceptualized and managed.

The pervasiveness of the medical model in industrialized societies may also *cause* behaviours to become seen as problematic. Imagine, for example, an overstretched mother struggling to cope with many demands including a lively toddler; if she sees a TV programme about ADHD it will not be surprising if she decides that her child must have this condition and so visits her doctor to request psychostimulant medication. There is, indeed, evidence that parents frequently present their children (and even themselves) as suffering from ADHD (Searight and McLaren, 1998). ADHD illustrates the application of medical diagnoses to children's (and adults') behaviour, as laid out in various editions of the *Diagnostic and Statistical Manual of Mental Disorders (DSM)* of the American Psychiatric Association (APA, 1994) – another example of Pepper's (1942) 'formism' metaphor.

When this manual was drawn up, it was done so as a descriptive taxonomic system, which was explicitly claimed to be atheoretical, to enable it to be used by practitioners favouring different theoretical orientations. However, it is not possible to devise an explanatory system devoid of underlying theoretical assumptions. Those underlying the *DSM* project include viewing mental disorder as a subset of medical disorder, with each illness defined by certain behavioural criteria that are endowed with biological significance, removing them from any broader contextual considerations. Butler claims that 'despite the cool neutrality of its language, the diagnostic project was *intended* from its inception to lead to a progressive exclusion of non-biologically focused systems of explanation (psychological, psychosocial, psychoanalytic) from authoritative psychiatric discourse' (Butler, 1999: 21). Butler and others have argued that successive changes to *DSM* classifications, rather than being driven by scientific evidence, as claimed, have been heavily influenced by sociocultural factors – the modification and eventual removal of homosexuality as a mental disorder, in the face of the gay liberation movement, being a prime example.

To return to the example of ADHD, this provides perhaps the best illustration of the current trend to view children's problematic behaviours through a medical lens. ADHD is often 'uncritically accepted as a neurobiological condition' (Reid and Maag, 1997: 13), with children's problematic behaviours in the areas of attention, impulsivity and high activity levels attracting a medical label and a drug-based solution (usually methylphenidate). In fact, three-quarters of children diagnosed with ADHD are seen solely by general medical practitioners, without any psychological evaluation occurring (Searight and McLaren, 1998). The wide acceptance of this medical perspective has sidelined the expertise of other professionals, including child psychologists, whose very area of expertise is children's behaviour (Atkinson and Shute, 1999). Furthermore, the increased demands that industrialized countries place upon children for educational achievement, together with declining education and mental health budgets, increase the pressure for children's behaviour problems to be treated medically (Searight and McLaren, 1998). Consequently, children are more likely to receive drugs than a careful assessment and intervention in terms of the contextual factors maintaining the behaviours or for consideration to be given to the role of broader public policy and funding issues (Prosser *et al.*, 2002); see also Box 2.2.

Even ADHD policy documents in which psychologists have played a leading role use the medical term 'diagnosis' rather than the psychological term 'assessment', and may grant precedence to the medical profession in assessment and intervention (Atkinson and Shute, 1999). In fact, some psychologists argue strongly that it is vital for psychologists to be excellent diagnosticians. On the other hand, expert psychological evidence has been ruled inadmissible in court with regard to behaviours codified within the *DSM* since such behaviours are judged as within the domain of medicine (Australian Psychological Society, 1998). This is part of a general pattern that has been identified in western societies of 'medicalization' of non-disease states, with relief sought for discomforts and distress that would have been tolerated in the past (Searight and McLaren, 1998). For example, it can be questioned whether it is really appropriate for as many as 12 per cent of boys in the USA to be taking methylphenidate for ADHD (Searight and McLaren, 1998). If indeed the very intention of the *DSM* project was to sideline alternative theoretical perspectives on mental and behavioural problems, it has succeeded very well, with those raising voices in protest such as Butler (1999), Pilgrim (2000a; 2000b) and critical psychologists (Bendle, 2001) being in a minority to date.

Thus it can be seen that a document that purports to be atheoretical in fact has underlying theoretical assumptions and has been claimed to further certain professional interests to the detriment of others, even those with genuine expertise in the area at hand. It can therefore be difficult in practice for the alternative perspectives on child development

Box 2.2 ADHD: the social context of biological explanations

The labelling phenomenon represents a powerful social force in the United States which supports and maintains the perspective of ADHD being a neurobiological condition. ADHD is a potent and desirable label of forgiveness because it attributes troubling behaviour to physiological forms (i.e. neurobiological) outside an individual's control. ... the ADHD label legitimizes parents' concerns that children do, in fact, manifest problems and that those problems are recognized, common, and socially palatable. Problem behaviour now can be portrayed as an inability to respond appropriately to an underlying disorder, rather than unwillingness, lack of motivation, or poor parenting. ... the ADHD label allows parents to 'externalize the disorder' thereby separating the 'good' child from the 'bad' behaviour ... a diagnosis of ADHD may be the most powerful route for parents to secure services for children.

(Reid and Maag, 1997: 15)

considered in this book to be brought to bear effectively to address children's behaviour problems, in accord with melioristic values as noted previously.

Conclusions

Biological influences on child development theorizing have been apparent ever since the discipline emerged. With the advent of new technologies for studying genes and brain function, biological approaches to development are gaining further credence, as is a tendency to conceptualize children's behaviour problems from a medical perspective.

While it is generally accepted that genes and the environment interact to produce developmental change, controversies continue about the relative role of each and how far development can be modified by environmental change. A major attraction of evolutionary and other biological approaches to behavioural development may be that they provide psychology with a yearned-for basis in the physical sciences (Miller, 1999). Miller notes that such approaches sideline cultural issues. Culture is seen as an aspect of the environment that *contributes* to a greater or lesser degree in psychological processes, but not as a qualitative *determinant of the patterning* of those processes. She presents a theoretical argument for why culture must be viewed as an integral part of theorizing in psychology. We take up this theme in Chapters 7 and 9. Other aspects of biological approaches we discuss or revisit elsewhere include Pavlov's research on conditioned reflexes (see Chapter 6), the current tendency to view neurological explanations as superior to cognitive or behavioural ones (see Chapter 7), the attempt to develop a systems theory of development that is biologically valid (see Chapter 11) and the notion that evolutionary theory has the potential to play an integrative role in developmental theorizing (see Chapter 11).

3 A rainbow is more than the sum of its colours: beginnings of organicism

Introduction

Organicism, as described by Pepper (1942), draws heavily upon the image of the growing organism whose development is significantly shaped by mutual influence and the patterning of its parts. What is important is not the 'uniqueness' of the individual child but rather the universal features of children. Theories in this tradition emphasize internal regulation and organization, and the ability of the organism to organize and reorganize itself at different levels.

A number of different features underpinning development have been commented upon by organismic theorists. First, it has been noted that children generally share some common features in relation to behaviours and capabilities; for example, children crawl before they walk. Second, there is some commonality in the timing of the emergence of behaviours and abilities; for example, most children will start to crawl at around the same time. Third, while deviations from the general path of development may occur, such deviations tend to be short-lived. Fourth, new abilities and capabilities of quite a different nature emerge out of early behaviours; thus walking is a very different activity from crawling.

The organismic tradition has drawn heavily upon biological writings including evolutionary theory (see Chapters 2 and 11). Human development is conceptualized in terms of the interaction involving genetic maturation and experience. Development unfolds according to a purpose or design – a teleological view. As part of this unfolding, development is frequently conceptualized discontinuously, in terms of stages. The human organism is understood to be relatively active in terms of seeking out and responding to a more or less passive environment. Generally, organismic theories espouse that the organism is different from the sum of its parts, and the structural arrangement of the parts is quite significant.

The nature of organismic thinking is better understood in the light of some historically influential ideas. We will outline these before considering the views of a number of early organismic theorists.

Background ideas

Gestalt psychology was one field that influenced organismic theorizing. Prompted by the thinking of the German scientists Kohler (1927) and Koffka (1925), Gestalt psychology holds that the whole experience of a person is more than just the sum of its parts: it is a phenomenon in its own right. The Gestaltists pointed out, for example, that red, green and blue light combine to produce white, but experiencing the colours red, green and blue is not the same as experiencing white. Using the results of his famous experiments with apes, Kohler (1927) argued that animals and humans learn through 'insight' (and not just through trial and error, as maintained by behaviourists). That is, in Kohler's terms there is a tendency to focus on the relationships between parts and not just the parts themselves. Gestaltists argued for the study of relationships, form and pattern. Gestaltist thinking was vehemently opposed to the reductionist claims of physiological psychology and to the structuralist psychology of E.B. Titchener, which claimed that mental experiences could be analysed into elementary units such as sensations, feelings and thoughts; as such, it was argued that if we could only just objectively examine our experience we would discover that what come to the forefront are sensations (strong), images (fainter than sensations) and affect. Gestaltists were passionately opposed to such a view, arguing that the basic units of consciousness are 'things', not sensations. Thus, we see cars and people and buildings because of the innate perceptual equipment we have, and we do not construct them from sensations, images and affects and the laws of association.

Another influence on organismic theorizing was 'functionalism', a school of thought in psychology founded by the American William James (1890). James was severely critical of 'structuralism' (behaviourism) because he considered its outlook on human behaviour to be narrow and artificial. James had been influenced by the thinking of Charles Darwin, who emphasized, through the mechanism of natural selection, the functional nature of the characteristics of animals. Darwin argued that characteristics such as eyes, ears and hands, for example, had a function that through natural selection ensured their survival. In a similar vein, James argued that human consciousness also had a function, namely to enable people to make rational choices. In the 1940s, the views and research of a number of psychologists belonging to the functionalist school (such as Ames, 1951) began to gain attention. Ames had been experimenting with striking visual illusions (the best known of which is the Ames window – see Figure 3.1) that trick the human visual system into misapplying shape and size constancy.

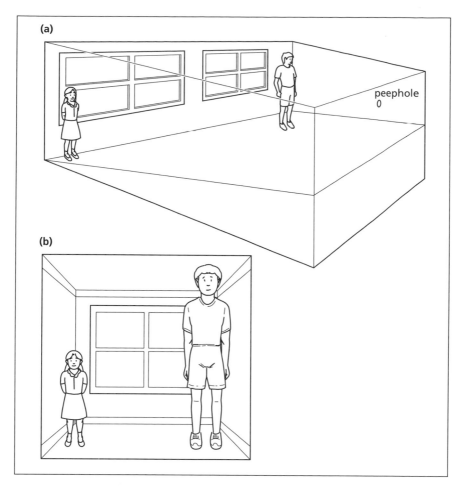

Figure 3.1 The visual illusion of the Ames window

Because the left-hand corner of the room shown in (a) is almost twice as far away from the viewer as the right-hand corner, the girl standing in the left-hand corner projects a smaller retinal image than the boy in the right even though they are both the same height in reality. When viewing the room through a peephole (b), we assume that we are looking at a normal room and that both children are at the same distance: hence the illusion of the impossibly different relative sizes of the children.

Source: adapted from Slee, 2002

From the perspective of psychologists such as Ames, perception is seen to occur as a result of the relationship between the observing person and the observed object. Context is the critical functional factor in helping us interpret the world around us. Ames and other functionalists argued against the idea that we can ever know anything as it 'really is'. We can know things only in their relationship to us.

The work of Eleanor J. Gibson also provides a number of key concepts that will broaden our understanding of cognitive development. Gibson is well known for a range of elegant experimental studies examining perception. For example, most undergraduate psychology students will be familiar with the 'visual cliff' studies conducted by Gibson and Walk (1960). This experiment basically tested whether depth perception is an innate ability or whether it is learned. Another of the classical experiments conducted by Gibson and her partner James Gibson (Gibson and Gibson, 1955) provided a foundation for the introduction of a different way to understand learning. The study involved the opportunity to compare and contrast a series of graphic 'scribbles' against a standard 'scribble'. By simply having the opportunity to make such comparisons, viewers became aware of variations in the nature of the scribbles, their performance improving with the number of trials allowed. Unlike the associationism described in Chapter 6, whereby learning is seen to involve the forming of associations, the Gibsons' experimental studies suggested that the simple opportunity to improve perception (by examining the scribbles) allowed learning to occur. Furthermore, the learning occurred in the absence of any reinforcement (Pick, 1992). A key concept in the Gibsons' research is that of 'differentiation': 'Our perception improves because we come to detect or differentiate more of the aspects, features, and nuances of the tremendously complex stimulation that impinges upon us' (Pick, 1992: 788).

Another key element associated with the research of James Gibson is that of 'affordances'. Gibson (1979) used this term to apply to the particular perceptual arrangements an organism possesses in order to perceive properties of the environment in a certain way. The idea is that the properties of any sensed object are perceived in a way to optimize the species' survival. Thus, how objects are perceived depends on their meaning to the organism (Johansson et al., 1980). Box 3.1 addresses the child's search for meaning in stories.

Another prominent thinker influencing later versions of organicism was the biologist von Bertalanffy. Psychology in the first half of the twentieth century was dominated by a positivistic-mechanistic-reductionistic approach, which can be epitomized as the 'robot model of man' (von Bertalanffy, 1968: 5–6). Von Bertalanffy was particularly interested in the application of systems theory to biological processes. He defined a system as a 'complex of interacting elements' (1968: 55). He was particularly interested in the relationship between the parts and the whole. An important contribution that he made to systems theory was to identify 'open' and 'closed' systems. A closed system was defined as one in which there is no interaction with the surrounding environment (such as a chemical reaction in a closed container). An open system (such as a family) is one that interacts with the surrounding environment. As Minuchin (1985) noted, systems theory is a twentieth-century scientific paradigm that has been used in conjunction with physical, biological and social systems. (Systems thinking will be further described in Chapters 4 and 11.)

Box 3.1 The child's search for meaning in stories

The idea that perception involves 'meaning-making' was an important element of Eleanor Gibson's thinking and research. This idea is well demonstrated in the process by which children learn to read. Various theories have been proposed to account for children's language acquisition. One challenge faced by the various theories is their ability to explain the very rapid growth in word learning such that, by six years of age, an English-speaking child will have a vocabulary of approximately 6000 words (Anglin, 1993). It appears that direct teaching cannot easily account for such a rapid rate of word acquisition, so attention has been given to the means by which children learn words incidentally from their environment. Reading storybooks to children has been researched to understand whether children learn from this. Reviews of research (e.g. Bus *et al.*, 1995) suggest there is a positive correlation between storybook reading and vocabulary development. It has also been established that the style of storybook reading is associated with a child's word acquisition such that a more interactive adult storybook reading style using open-ended questions and praise can positively influence language development. Research by Senechal (1997) indicates that pre-school children make more gains in vocabulary after repeated readings of a storybook than after a single reading. Repeated exposure to the storyline and pictures appeared to facilitate their memory search for novel labels. Senechal (1997) also found that asking labelling questions during repeated readings of a book was a very powerful means for encouraging the acquisition of expressive language.

Having outlined a number of influences shaping an organicist approach to the study of human development, we now turn to a number of prominent early theories that highlighted the 'stage-like' aspect of development, beginning with the work of Stanley Hall.

Gerald Stanley Hall and adolescence

Hall was born in 1844 in a small town in Massachusetts in the United States of America. After graduating from high school in 1867 he went to a theological seminary and later studied theology and philosophy in Europe. In 1884 Hall was appointed as Professor in Psychology and Pedagogy at Johns Hopkins University and as the new professor identified that the psychology he would teach consisted of the three branches of comparative, experimental and historical psychology. Underpinning his psychology was a profound religious belief:

The bible is being slowly revealed as man's greatest text book in psychology – dealing with him as a whole, his body, mind, and will, in all the larger relations to nature, society – which has been misappreciated simply because it is so deeply divine.

(Hall, 1985: 247-8)

After moving to Clark University in Massachusetts, Hall focused on the use of questionnaires to gather data regarding a number of matters: instincts and attitudes; child development, including children's activities and feelings; emotions and will; the moral and religious development of children; individual differences; school processes and practice; and church processes and practice.

Hall is probably best known for his writings regarding adolescent development. Influenced by the writings of Charles Darwin, Hall developed a social-biological framework to explain human development. An important idea was that of 'recapitulation'. Here, Hall drew upon the work of Haeckel (1834–1919), who argued that an embryo's ontogenetic progression mirrored phylogenetic history – the evolution of its species.

As an aside, it is interesting to note that the British philosopher Herbert Spencer (1820–1903) also adopted the idea of evolution, advocating the idea that there takes place in the universe a continuous redistribution of matter and motion. Evolution occurs when the integration of matter and motion are predominant, and devolution when the opposite occurs. Spencer had interpreted Darwin's theory to mean survival of the strongest individuals, although Darwin argued for species, not individual, survival. Spencer's 'social Darwinism' has been interpreted as an argument for the justification of the use of force in the struggle for existence, but this was not the underlying feature of Darwin's theory. Hall's interpretation of Darwin's theory differed from that of Spencer: he argued that during childhood and until adolescence the child repeats through play and fear the evolution of human society. Environmental factors come to have a greater influence at adolescence (Hall, 1904).

In an account of Hall's contribution to psychology, White (1992) noted that it was in 1891 that Hall initiated his child development research at Clark University. His publication in 1891, entitled *The Content of Children's Minds on Entering School*, established a tradition for measuring and observing children, and summarizing the findings in terms of averages for different age levels. Normative descriptive investigations were used to highlight similarities and differences in development. White noted that Hall's two-volume *Adolescence: its psychology and its relations to physiology, anthropology, sociology, sex, crime religion and education* (1904) is largely unread today. The volumes are most often noted for popularizing views on three issues: recapitulation; the idea that adolescence is a time of 'storm and stress' (*Sturm und Drang*); and the claim for the twentieth century's invention of 'adolescence'.

The term adolescence is derived from the Latin *adolescere*, which means 'to grow up' or 'to grow to maturity'. Demos and Demos (1969: 273) argued that 'the concept of adolescence, as generally understood and applied, did not exist before the last two decades of the nineteenth century', indicating that it was Hall's writing that promoted this view. The change, storm and stress in adolescence, as seen by Hall, are characterized by

> lack of emotional steadiness, violent impulses, unreasonable conduct, lack of enthusiasm and sympathy ... previous selfhood is broken up ... and a new individual is in the process of being born. All is solvent, plastic, peculiarly susceptible to external influences.
>
> (Hall, 1904: 26)

However, examination of some early writings indicates that, in fact, the idea commonly attributed to Hall that adolescence is a time of change is not at all new. Early writers noted in particular the impetuosity of youth. The eighth-century BC Greek poet Hesiod's opinion would not be out of place today:

> I can see no hope for the future of our people if they are dependent on the frivolous youth of today for certainly all youth are reckless beyond words ... When I was a boy, we were taught to be discreet and respectful of elders, but the present youth are exceedingly wise and impatient of restraint.
>
> (Hesiod, eighth century BC)

Aristotle (quoted in Demos and Demos, 1969: 633) noted that:

> The young are in character prone to desire and ready to carry any desire they may have formed into action. Of bodily desires it is the sexual to which they are most disposed to give way, and in regard to sexual desire they exercise no self restraint. They are changeful too and fickle in their desires, which are transitory as they are vehement: for their wishes are keen without being permanent. ... They are passionate, irascible, and apt to be carried away by their impulses.

Novelists have been particularly adept at picking up on the 'storm and stress' of adolescence, and such references certainly predate Hall. Violato and Wiley (1990) reviewed the images of adolescence in English literature through the ages from Geoffrey Chaucer (1342–1400) to Charles Dickens (1812–1870). They concluded that, in the main, literary works portray adolescence as 'a time of turbulence, excess and passion, which is consonant with Hall's (1904) depictions' (Violato and Wiley, 1990: 263). For example, in William Shakespeare's *The Merchant of Venice* and *Romeo and Juliet,* youth is depicted as a time of excess, passion and sensuality. In *Romeo and Juliet* the exuberant Romeo kills Tybalt during some irresponsible swordplay. The impetuous, passionate nature of youth is shown in the betrothal of Romeo and Juliet in one night, and in their respective suicides upon believing each other dead. A more contemporary point of view regarding the heightened sensitivity of adolescents is vividly portrayed in the fiction writing of Sue Townsend in *The Secret Diary of Adrian Mole Aged 13¾*:

> The spot on my chin is getting bigger. It's my mother's fault for not having known about vitamins. I pointed out to my mother that I hadn't had my vitamin C today. She said 'Go buy an orange'. So typical! Nigel came around today. He hasn't got a single spot yet. My grandma came by today. She squeezed my pimple. It has made it worse. I will go to the doctors on Saturday if the spot is still there. I can't live like this with everybody staring.
>
> (Townsend, 1982)

Galambos and Leadbeater (2000), in a review of trends in adolescent research, have noted that current views of adolescence continue to think of it in terms of 'risks and opportunities'. They identify 'challenges' in terms of adolescents' engagement in risky behaviours, and issues with poverty, homelessness and unemployment.

Despite the popular conception of adolescence as a period of storm and stress, other points of view are also found among psychological researchers. The Australian writers Connell, Stroobant, Sinclair, Connell and Rogers (1975) argue on the basis of their research that adolescence is *not* an especially stormy period, and that for many individuals it is a fairly undramatic and uneventful time. Others have suggested that current concerns with the problems of adolescence are culturally biased, and are largely a reflection of particular circumstances within North American society. Box 3.2 discusses how theories of adolescence vary in relation to prevailing economic conditions.

White (1992) has emphasized the very significant contribution Hall made to child development, although it is apparent that his work is largely not referred to today in relation to developmental theory.

Heinz Werner and the orthogenetic principle

Werner arrived from Germany to teach at Clark University some 50 years after Hall had begun his work there. Glick noted that Werner published in a diverse range of areas and argued that 'Werner was a very modern thinker whose theoretical views were so at variance with normal professional practices that his message is yet to be heard' (1992: 558). While the work of his contemporaries, such as Piaget and Vygotsky, continues to be evaluated and interpreted (see Chapters 4 and 7), the writings of Werner have largely been overlooked.

Box 3.2 Economic conditions and theorists' views

Enright *et al.* (1987) draw our attention to the need to consider the sociohistorical context when evaluating child development issues. In a major review of the theoretical literature regarding the nature of adolescence, they observed a number of important trends. They discovered that psychological theories of adolescent development are strongly associated with the economic conditions of the time. Thus, during periods of depression or economic retraction 'theories of adolescence emerge that portray teenagers as immature, psychologically unstable and in need of prolonged participation in the educational system' (1987: 553). Quite the reverse applies during periods of economic boom, when theories of adolescence reflect adolescents' competences and downplay the need for further education. Enright *et al.* make the point that developmental psychology may play an important ideological role in society. This role may be directed at maintaining the status quo in society, even when there is some cost to optimal personal development.

Heinz Werner's views of development were influenced by Gestalt psychology and more narrowly by a particular school of Gestalt thinking emphasizing the 'developmental process of formation' (Glick, 1992: 559). Werner, with his strong background in biology and anthropology, argued that development was directional, underpinned by a basic survival drive and a desire to 'know'. While Werner shared an interest with Piaget in providing 'a developmental account of the a priori' his unit of analysis was 'the concept of development itself' rather than focusing on the cognitive functions themselves, as Piaget did (1992: 559). That is, he was more concerned with identifying growth principles or directions than with describing or discovering the nature of growth stages.

Werner elaborated the 'orthogenetic principle' (1948) as follows: 'Man, destined to conquer the world through knowing, starts out with confusion, disorientation, and chaos, which he struggles to overcome ...' (Werner and Kaplan, 1963: 5). While Werner's outlook in some ways reflects the recapitulation theory of G.S. Hall and the views of earlier philosophers such as Herbert Spencer, suggesting a move from a primitive to an advanced state, his theorizing was more sophisticated in many ways. The view presented by Werner was that there was some 'directiveness' associated with development; the organism is motivated by a drive to survive and master his/her fate such that there is a movement toward ever greater differentiation. His research into human perception led him to conclude: 'We assume that organisms are naturally directed toward a series of transformations – reflecting a tendency to move from a state of relative globality and undifferentiatedness towards states of increasing differentiation and hierarchic integration' (Werner and Kaplan, 1963: 7).

The orthogenetic principle refers to establishing the correct ('ortho') development ('genetic') in both physical and psychological development. The orthogenetic principle 'has radical implications that served to make Wernerian psychology fundamentally different from other developmental views' (Glick, 1992: 560). Significantly, it resulted in greater confusion regarding the topic of study because, as Glick noted, Werner did not begin with a topic of development such as language, but rather focused on the entity of development itself.

Hierarchical integration captures the increasing organization of responses and skills into hierarchies. For example, a baby's development of eating skills captures this element. First, the baby needs to be able to sit and focus on the food. Werner used the term 'syncresis' to refer to 'global actions or ideas'. As the child develops there is a move from the syncretic to the discrete as the child is increasingly able to separate out the various components. Perception is combined with physical reaching skills to grasp the biscuit and then bring the biscuit to her mouth. Lewin's notion of 'articulation' refers to the hierachical integration whereby various behaviours are interlinked in the service of other outcomes such as eating the biscuit. Two further orthogenetic principles were that of development moving from a state of rigidity to greater flexibility in order to influence the environment (as when the older child is able to reach inside a box of biscuits) and that of 'stability' such that the older child can concentrate for ever greater periods of time.

There is some confusion regarding the status of Werner's theory, which may be better understood as a 'grand scale' theory (Glick, 1992). In this regard, it is not unlike dynamic systems theory, which also focuses on developmental processes in general rather than specific areas of development, as discussed in Chapter 11.

Arnold Gesell and maturation

Arnold Lucius Gesell (1880–1961) is a very significant figure in the history of developmental psychology. Trained at Clark University under G.S. Hall, Gesell later went on to use innovative techniques in cinephotography to chart the course of normal human development.

Gesell was relieved to find Darwinian views of development superseding theological ideas such as original sin, thus rescuing children from 'gloomier ideas of fixity and fate' (Thelen and Adolph, 1992: 369). Drawing on Darwin's emphasis upon the maturational component of development (Darwin 1959), Gesell did much to advance the charting of the growth of children. Working in the United States during the early part of the twentieth century, Gesell embarked on the task of mapping the foetal, infant and early childhood behaviour of thousands of children. In the course of his work he established and standardized stages of development. His maturational view of development emphasized the natural unfolding of patterns of growth, which he believed was largely predetermined and self-regulated. His theory emphasized the 'lawfulness' of growth and consequently the ability to predict: 'Behavior is rooted in the brain and in the sensory and motor systems. The timing, smoothness and integration at one stage foretell behavior at a later age' (Gesell, cited in Knobloch and Pasamanick, 1974: 3). Gesell was well aware, however, of the multitude of factors impinging on a child that make accurate prediction a risky venture.

Gesell identified the following four major fields of behaviour.

1. **Adaptive.** The most important field concerns the organizational component of behaviour, such as coordinating eye movements and reaching with the hand. Adaptive behaviour is the forerunner of later intelligence.
2. **Gross and fine motor behaviour.** This includes sitting, standing, walking, using fingers and manipulating objects.
3. **Language.** Gesell maintained that language also assumes distinct behaviour patterns and unfolds in a predetermined fashion. For example, inarticulate vocalizations precede words.
4. **Personal and social behaviour.** This incorporates the reaction of children to the social world in which they live. However, according to Gesell, personal and social behaviour patterns are determined by intrinsic growth patterns. Thus, while toileting is a cultural requirement shaped by social demands, the child's attainment of bladder and bowel control depends upon neuro-motor maturation.

According to Gesell, then, 'a child's development proceeds stage by stage in orderly sequence, each stage representing a degree or level of maturity' (cited in Knobloch and Pasamanick, 1974: 7). The view that body growth is strongly influenced by physical maturation is generally accepted (but see our discussion of dynamic systems theory in Chapter 11). However, the assertion that other important aspects of human development, such as personality, are similarly determined has attracted (and continues to attract) criticism. Thelen and Adolph (1992) conclude their overview of Gesell's work by noting the lasting contribution his research has made to developmental theory, while noting the contradictions in his theorizing – for example, in his emphasizing the importance of genetics in determining development and at the same time acknowledging the importance of the environment.

Gesell was an extraordinary stage theorist: 'Who before or since has had the tenacity to describe 58 stages of pellet behavior, 53 stages of rattle behavior, and so on ...?' (Thelen and Adolph, 1992: 376). Gesell's maturational approach fell out of favour with the rise of Piaget, behaviourism and information-processing theories, but he probably laid the groundwork for the acceptance of Piaget's stage theory. The maturational approach to development is still apparent today in clinical work with young children, where scales of developmental norms, based on work that Nancy Bayley began in the 1920s, continue to be used (Rosenblith, 1992).

R.J. Havighurst and developmental tasks

One theorist who has made an important, if underrated, contribution to our contemporary understanding of child and adolescent development is Robert Havighurst (born in 1900). Havighurst described development in terms of 'developmental tasks', or 'those things that constitute healthy and satisfactory growth in our society' (1953: 2). In Havighurst's (1953) view, development is not one long slow uphill climb, but consists of both steep gradients where learning is difficult and plateaux where the individual can coast in terms of development. One example of this is a child who must work hard to master the art of catching a cricket ball, but who, having mastered the skill, can then 'coast' for years. Havighurst's theory addresses the issue of children's cognitive development as well as other aspects of development. His views provide some contrast to cognitive-developmental and information-processing theories.

A question often asked by parents is 'How well is my child doing?' This is often answered in relation to developmental tasks. Slee (2002) noted that evaluations of how a child is doing generally reflect expectations based on pooled knowledge about child development that are transmitted from one generation to the next. The expectations and concerns are often reflected in popular culture such as the milestones provided in child-rearing books. A recent example is an Australian list of developmental tasks presented in *The National Mental Health Strategy Monograph* (2000) (Figure 3.2).

Havighurst explained developmental tasks thus:

> A developmental task is a task which arises at or about a certain period in the life of the individual, successful achievement of which leads to happiness and to success with later tasks, while failure leads to unhappiness in the individual, disapproval by society, and difficulty with later tasks.
>
> (Havighurst, 1953: 2)

Havighurst proposed that inner and outer forces set up certain developmental tasks for the individual. He identified three such forces:

1. The biology of the individual, involving physical maturation, such as learning to walk or learning to relate to the opposite sex during adolescence.

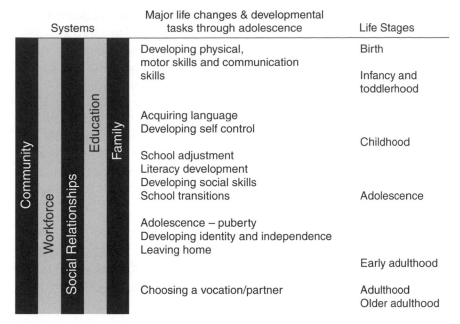

Figure 3.2 Examples of Developmental tasks
*Adapted from P.T. Slee (2002) (2nd Ed.) Child, Adolescent and Family Development.
Cambridge University Press: Melbourne.

2. Cultural forces, such as learning to read and write.
3. The personal values and aspirations of the individual, such as aspiring to become a doctor or engineer.

Havighurst identified nine key tasks to be accomplished during early childhood, such as learning to walk, to eat solid food and to distinguish right from wrong. Nine tasks for middle childhood are delineated, including learning the physical skills to play ordinary games and achieving personal independence. Havighurst identified ten developmental tasks during adolescence, including achieving mature relations with the opposite sex, achieving some economic independence, and selecting and preparing for an occupation.

In a more contemporary development of Havighurst's theory, Selverstone (1989) proposed that the ten developmental tasks during adolescence may be clustered into four main categories:

1. identity, which involves the determination of the question 'Who am I?'
2. connectedness, which includes establishing relationships with peers
3. power – the development of a sense of control and power
4. hope/joy, which is achieved via the accomplishment of the previous three tasks.

According to Havighurst (1953), there is a right moment for teaching or developing a task. That is, there is a moment or time in the individual's life when it is most opportune to be exposed to the learning involved in a task. Havighurst also adopted a broad outlook about the nature of tasks, believing that they extend beyond the individual to the cultural-historical context in which the individual is growing or developing.

At this point it is worthwhile revisiting the usefulness and validity of the concept of developmental stages such as 'adolescence' or 'youth'. As discussed earlier, organicism emphasizes the stages that help us identify and appreciate the nature of the challenges facing us as we grow and develop. However, serious debate is now being engaged in to consider alternatives to simple linear classification of the developmental process identified by normative transitions. Present discussion emphasizes that

> ... the focus on youth is not on the inherent characteristics of young people themselves, but on the construction of youth through social processes (such as schooling, families or the labor market). Young people engage with these institutions in specific ways, in relation to historical circumstances.

> (Wyn and White, 1997: 9)

Thus, for example, historians such as Enright *et al.* (1987) have specifically argued that adolescence is a life stage created to meet the demands of industry for a skilled labour force. Furthermore, the notion of developmental tasks has been criticized as being merely descriptive. However, overall, it provides a means of understanding human development in a way that reflects a popular understanding: at particular times in our lives, we must address important developmental issues, and how effectively we fulfil these tasks has implications for current and future functioning.

Conclusions

In this chapter we have provided some important background to the root metaphor identified as 'organicism' (Pepper, 1942). Reese and Overton (1970: 132) noted that the basic metaphor for organicism is 'the organism, the living, organized system presented to experience in multiple forms'. The emergence of new phenomena at each new level of organization that is not commensurate with a reduction to a lower level of organization is a feature of organicism. Lerner (1983: 53) referred to the idea of 'epigenetic viewpoint' which

> ... denotes that at each higher level of complexity there emerges a new characteristic, one that simply was not present at the lower organizational level and thus whose presence is what establishes a new level as just that – a stage of organization qualitatively different from a preceding one.

To that end, organismic theorists would generally agree with the Gestalt position that the whole is greater than the sum of the parts. Moreover, the whole is not only greater but 'different' in the sense that when one is experiencing a rainbow one is experiencing more than the sum of the various colours. Lerner (1983) has summarized the organicist outlook as comprising viewpoints that are:

- epigenetic
- anti-reductionist
- qualitative
- discontinuous
- multiple and interactionist in nature.

The organicist outlook also emphasizes that the individual's world moves through increasing levels of integration, that individuals are agents in constructing their reality and that there is some structural interdependence to the parts of development. One key feature of the organicist view concerns the universal features of human development.

In the following chapter we continue to pursue the organicism metaphor in considering constructivist theories of development.

4 The child as philosopher

Introduction

In this chapter we continue the presentation of theories associated with organicism. The previous chapter began with some background ideas relevant to this viewpoint, including Gestalt psychology, functionalism, the search for meaning, and general systems theory. In introducing here the field of thinking broadly referred to as 'constructivism', we add some further background ideas, including the philosophical notion of the 'world of ideas', George Kelly's theory and the psychological construct of 'cognition'. We then address in particular the theoretical contributions of Piaget, Maccoby and Bruner, and also consider the significant contributions that 'connectionism' and 'theory of mind' are making to our theorizing about human development.

Background ideas

Popper (1972) proposed that the task of philosophy is to enrich our image of the world, arguing that the generally accepted picture involves a variation of mind–body dualism. Popper suggested that there are, in fact, the following three worlds.

> The first is the physical world or the world of physical states; the second is the mental world or the world of mental states; and the third is the world of intelligibles, or of *ideas in the objective sense*; it is the world of possible objects of thought: the world of theories in themselves, and their logical relations; of arguments in themselves; and of problem situations in themselves.
>
> (Popper, 1972: 154)

In World 1 we have physical reality, which we relate to with our five senses. World 2 is the inner world of thoughts, feelings and emotions, accessible through introspection. In World 3 we have the world that can be examined using the objective methods of logic and mathematics (similar to the Platonic realm of 'Ideas', to be described briefly in Chapter 6). Writers such as Tonnessen (1999) argue that cognitive psychology is located in World 3, and in this chapter we will see the emergence of information-processing theory and connectionism as reflecting mental structures and models derived from logical and mathematical reasoning.

As reference to the 'milestones' in Appendix 1 indicates, the 1960s and 1970s were witness to a significant shift toward cognitive psychology. Behaviourism had been the dominant influence in the 1940s and 1950s, particularly in North America. As we will describe in Chapter 6, the early psychologists, including William James and Wilhelm Wundt, were certainly interested in aspects of cognition, including attention and memory, but the dominance of behaviourism discredited the study of the 'mind'. In his critical 1913 paper, the behaviourist John Watson confidently wrote that after psychology accepted behaviourism, psychology could then be equated with the physical sciences: 'The findings of psychology ... lend themselves to explanation in physico-chemical terms' (Watson, 1913: 177).

Despite Watson's prediction, the mid-twentieth century was witness to the emergence of a strong interest in cognitive processes, including an increasing interest in children's cognitive development, social cognition and cognitive therapy. Significant influences bearing on this shift in influence included the work of George Kelly and his personal construct theory. Kelly (1963: 12) posited two notions, namely '(1) that viewed in the perspective of the centuries, man might be seen as an incipient scientist, and (2) that each individual man formulates in his own way constructs through which he views the world of events'. This indicated that the personal constructs people hold lead them to understand and explain events in different ways, which in turn leads to different action. Personal construct psychology as developed by George Kelly argued that individuals develop bi-polar dimensions of meaning. These personal constructs are used to make sense of experience and anticipate the future. Each person psychologically constructs understandings of self, others and relationships, and continually evaluates whether these constructs effectively account for the world around them. (Readers are particularly encouraged to read further regarding the work of George Kelly to better understand the point being made here.)

Apart from the writings of Kelly, methodological advances in the middle part of the twentieth century meant that it also became possible to study cognition without resort to introspectionism. For example, bar-pressing in the context of a certain stimulus, such as a green light, would indicate that the subject was attending to the stimulus. All in all, there was an increasing research effort directed toward the understanding of cognitive development.

Kreitler and Kreitler (1976: 4) noted rather sceptically that 'the term "cognitive" has been used so widely that one might wonder whether there is anything in psychology that is not cognitive'. We would suggest that cognitive psychology is concerned with mental representations, symbols and computations. A number of the theoretical developments described in this chapter have received some significant input from the field of artificial intelligence. As Newell and Simon (1972: 282) noted, 'There is a growing body of evidence that the elementary information processes used by the human brain in thinking are highly similar to a subset of the elementary information processes that are incorporated in the instruction codes of ... computers'. In fact, cognitive psychologists have used the metaphor of the computer to compare with cognitive processes, highlighting at the same time the objectivity of their research (Tonnessen, 1999).

Jean Piaget's cognitive developmental theory

We will now provide a brief description of the theory developed by Jean Piaget (1897–1980), one of the most significant figures in twentieth-century developmental psychology. For interested readers, Slee (2002) has described the basic tenets of Piaget's theory in more detail, and a number of major reviews of Piaget's theory have been provided by Beilin (1992), van Geert (1998) and Flavell (1992a).

Piaget's theory of children's cognitive development was at heart an epistemological one – that is, a theory of how we know what we know. In providing an overview of his work, Elkind (1974) has identified three main phases in Piaget's theory.

1. During the first period (1922–28), Piaget was concerned with the ideas that children held about the physical world. In working with Alfred Binet on routine intelligence testing, Piaget's attention was caught by the incorrect answers children gave on such tests. During this period Piaget developed and refined his clinical interview technique (*la méthode clinique*). Piaget discovered that children reasoned differently from adults and they had literally different philosophies about the nature of the world (Elkind, 1971). Observations that occupied Piaget's attention during this period included young children's 'animistic' beliefs (for example, that sticks and stones are imbued with life and purpose). Piaget was also concerned with the apparent egocentrism of young children and their often observed inability to take in another's perspective.

2. The second period of Piaget's investigations began in 1929 when he undertook the study of children's mental growth, prompted primarily by curiosity about his own children's development (Elkind, 1971). As a result of his acute observations he published a number of books. Issues such as object permanence were addressed by Piaget during this period of his work.

3. The third period of Piaget's studies began during the 1940s when he dealt with the child's understanding of concepts such as number, quantity and speed.

As described by Honstead (1968) there are two components to Piaget's theory, namely a stage-independent component and a stage-dependent component. In developing his theory incorporating the two components, Piaget emphasized that the child is actively involved in development. In Piagetian theory the child's mind is not a blank slate (Elkind 1971). On the contrary, the child has a multitude of ideas about the world, which may be quite different from an adult's understanding of it. The child in the course of his or her education is always learning and unlearning ideas about the world such as the concepts of space, time, quantity and number. Finally, 'the child is by nature a knowing creature' and as such 'the child is trying to construct a world view of his own, and is limited only by his abilities and experience' (Elkind, 1971: 108).

In the stage-independent component of his theory, Piaget addressed the issue of how cognitive development proceeds. He listed four factors to account for cognitive development: maturation or organic growth, experience, social transmission and equilibration (Honstead, 1968). Further details of these are given below.

1. **Maturation.** From a biological perspective, the developing child is maturing. At birth the immaturity of the infant's brain is a factor limiting cognition, but brain development (most rapid before birth) proceeds rapidly in the first two years after birth and continues to some extent for much longer. Understanding of the links between brain development and cognition has begun only recently (Fischer, 1987).
2. **Experience.** Piaget has argued that experience is of two kinds:
   (a) direct physical experience, such as playing with water and generally using the five senses to experience the world
   (b) mathematical experience, which occurs when the child reflects on the structure of experience and particularly on its logical and mathematical structure; according to Piaget and Inhelder (1969), logico-mathematical experience comes from the child's acting on the world rather than from the experience itself.
3. **Social transmission.** The concept of social transmission is the least developed part of Piaget's model: 'Piaget placed his main emphasis on the dialectic between the child and the physical world, but included social interaction as a motivator of development, particularly through conflict of ideas between peers' (Meadows, 1986: 108). That is, in the process of interacting with other children or adults, a child is challenged and forced to 'decentre' in order to deal with the multitude of conflicting ideas with which she or he is presented.
4. **Equilibration.** This is probably the most basic of the four factors:

   It is the process of achieving equilibrium, of finding a balance between those things that were previously understood and those that are yet to be understood. A child, encountering something new to him, actively works at relating it to something he knows. As the new object in its turn becomes familiar to him, he reaches a new level of equilibrium. He has thus gone through the process of equilibration of self regulation.

(Honstead, 1968: 135)

Piaget's theory is well known as a 'stage' theory of development. Four criteria for such theories were described by Inhelder (1975):

1. a period of formation and progressive organization of mental operations
2. the progressive hierarchical development of one stage upon another
3. relative similarity on the attainment of each stage
4. a directional and hierarchical nature.

As our readers will doubtless be aware, the stage-dependent component of Piaget's theory is made up of four major stages (as described below): sensori-motor; pre-operational; concrete operational; and formal operational. Each of Piaget's stages is identified in terms of the child's principal method of knowing.

1. **Sensori-motor period (0–2 years).** The child's primary method of knowing during the sensori-motor period is through the actions he or she performs on the world in terms of the five senses. Initially the child's behaviour is governed by simple reflexes but this situation changes rapidly during the next few years.
2. **Pre-operational period (3–7 years).** The emergence of language, modelling and memory are key features of the pre-operational period. It is the time when, according to McGurk (1975: 36–7), 'the child's internal, cognitive representation of the external world is gradually developing and differentiating but many serious limitations are also in evidence'. The child's thinking is dominated by perception rather than concepts (McGurk, 1975). For example, the child makes judgements in terms of how things look to her or him, not how they actually are. If shown two balls of clay of equal size and weight, and if one is then squeezed into a sausage shape and the child is asked if there is as much clay in the sausage as the ball, he or she is likely to say that the sausage has more clay because it looks longer. The child's acquisition of language signals the beginning of symbolic thought. Thus a child sees a hairy animal with four legs, a tail, ears and making a barking sound, and calls the animal a dog. The animal is the reality; the word dog is the symbol. Egocentrism is another element of the child's thinking; thus a girl may tell you she has a sister but deny that her sister has a sister.
3. **Concrete operations period (7–11 years).** During this period, children's thinking attains greater flexibility:

   He can understand, easily and naturally, the concept of conservation. 'Grouping' of ideas thus comes about; logical deductive reasoning is possible. However, concrete operations are limited in that they are capable of operational groupings only with concrete objects such as blocks, sticks, clay, liquids and marbles. Logical thought does not yet extend to verbal stimuli.

(Honstead, 1968: 139)

4. **Formal operations period (11+ years).** In Piaget's theory this is the final period of cognitive development. McGurk (1975: 39) notes that 'The hallmark of this stage is the child's ability to reason abstractly without relying upon concrete situations or events'.

Piaget's view of cognitive development is that in the process of development the individual moves from a less to a more mature level of functioning. The child is actively involved in pursuing information and attempting to understand the world. Piaget's theory has been labelled 'constructivist' (Gelcer and Schwartzbein, 1989) inasmuch as the child actively constructs the external world in acting upon it. Such a view contrasts with behavioural theories that emphasize the passivity of the child who is acted upon and shaped by the external world. From a biological perspective, though, Piaget viewed development as progressive and directional. The invariant feature of his theory emphasized a stage-like development, in which the child's manner of thinking at one level is qualitatively different from the way of thinking at a later stage.

A critique of Piaget's theory

Gardner (1969: 73–4) acknowledged the tremendous contribution that Piaget has made to our understanding of the child's cognitive development as follows:

Whatever its ultimate scientific fate, Piaget's contribution has over the past few decades provided a major impetus for research in developmental psychology. Before Piaget began research into the child's special cognitive and conceptual powers most work consisted of either sheer descriptions of objective features of the child's existence (physical milestones, preferred activities, motoric activities), anecdotal accounts of individual children, including ones displaying unusual abilities or difficulties, or broadly speculative interpretations of the course of growth.

The rise to prominence of Piagetian psychology coincided with the declining influence of behaviourism (Halford, 1989). At the same time the writings of cognitivists such as Bruner and Vygotsky were gaining ascendance. Halford observed that if the 1960s represented a period of optimism regarding the application of Piagetian psychology to understanding children's cognitive development, then the 1970s produced a reassessment resulting in some disillusionment with the theory. According to Halford, the disillusionment can be attributed to research that challenged many of Piaget's assumptions regarding the nature of cognitive development and to the failure of Piaget's research to reap the anticipated rewards in some applied areas. The following represents an overview of some of the major criticisms of Piagetian theory.

A feature of Piaget's experimental method, *la méthode clinique*, was his careful interviewing of the child. His child-centred approach in his earliest work consisted of an open-ended discussion with the child. From an empirical perspective, as outlined in Chapter 1, Piaget's interview technique has been criticized as too subjective and value-laden. Criticism has also been directed at the reliance on verbal introspection of immature minds. Phillips (1969: 4) described Piaget's interview methods thus:

> He observes the child's surroundings and his behaviour, formulates a hypothesis concerning the structure that underlies and includes them both, and then tests that hypothesis by altering the surroundings slightly – by rearranging the materials, by posing the problem in a different way, or even by overtly suggesting to the subject a response different from the one predicted by the theory.

For example, in a simple conservation task the format might be as follows. Arrange two rows of objects (such as one cent pieces or buttons), about ten in each row so that there is a one-to-one correspondence and the two rows are of equal length. Ask the child 'Are there the same number of buttons in each row?' If he or she agrees, say 'Watch me now' as you lengthen one of the rows, and then repeat the question, 'Are there the same number of buttons in each row?' Depending upon the child's answer, you might ask the child about the reason for the answer, rephrase the question or reset the experiment to repeat it.

Thus language was a very significant element that Piaget used to try to discover the course of children's cognitive functioning. McGarrigle and Donaldson (1974) and Donaldson (1978) are critical of the language used in such experiments. A child may take the repetition of the question as a cue to alter his or her first judgement, reasoning along the lines that if the researcher has altered the experimental set-up then perhaps a different answer is warranted. Donaldson also argues that sometimes the language used will carry so much weight that it will override the meaning of the situation, leading the young child to make errors in judgement. This is exemplified by the following:

> 'So here's a question for you. How old did you say you were?'
> Alice made a short calculation, and said 'Seven years and six months.'
> 'Wrong!' Humpty Dumpty exclaimed triumphantly. 'You never said a word like it!'
> 'I thought you meant "How old are you?" ' Alice explained.

'If I'd meant that I'd have said it', said Humpty Dumpty.

(Carroll, 1982)

Another trenchant criticism of Piagetian theory is directed at the sequence of stages and the nature of children's behaviour within the stages (Gardner, 1979). Major concerns have been expressed that a universal age/stage approach overlooks the part played by differences in mental and environmental factors in shaping a child's behaviour.

A further criticism is that Piaget tended to treat other people in the child's life as objects. This neglects the social competence of infants and the role of others as *social partners*, with such partnerships promoting cognitive development (Eibl-Eibesfeldt, 1989).

Piaget's theory has been said to fit 'the orderliness of development on a large scale' (Thelen and Smith, 1994: 21). To that extent, while Piaget's theory of cognitive development and the conclusions drawn from it have come under increasing scrutiny, the fact remains that few viable alternative frameworks have been developed (Halford, 1989). Piaget's writings have helped 'psychologists to think of development as transformation in the direction of greater epistemological adequacy, or as a construction of more adequate forms of knowing' (Bassecher, 1989: 189).

However, Thelen and Smith argue that on a more detailed scale the theory fails to capture the 'complexity and messiness of cognitive development in detail' (1994: 21–2). Donaldson's (1978) work, among others, indicates that when variations are made to Piagetian tasks there are confusing and contradictory findings. In particular, some central tenets of Piagetian theory have been challenged, as follows (Thelen and Smith, 1994).

1. Children develop from an impoverished beginning state. Research suggests that, in fact, the young infant is highly competent.
2. There are global discontinuities in cognition across stages. In fact, there is evidence of early precursors to abilities.
3. Cognitive growth is monolithic. In fact, there is wide individual variation in development and competences.

Thelen and Smith (1994: 22) conclude that 'Cognitive development does not look like a marching band; it looks more like a teeming mob'.

Despite such criticisms, Piaget's theory remains influential educationally and has become one of the best-known theories of child development. It has also triggered much further research, one of the best-known neo-Piagetian theorists being Robbie Case (see, e.g. 1998), who has combined a Piagetian approach with an information-processing one (see Chapter 6). According to his theory, as the brain develops and schemes become more automatic with practice, working memory capacity increases, allowing more advanced processing of information. Thus, children become able to undertake more complex cognitive tasks. The uneven nature of cognitive development noted by Thelen and Smith is accounted for in this formulation, as practice in one domain more than another would lead to uneven development across domains. For example, as we will see in Chapter 9, children who are 'supposed' to be in the concrete operational stage may display abstract reasoning in areas to which their culture exposes them.

Connectionism

Connectionism first emerged as a force in the early 1980s and is today a significant influence relating to research in language development, categorization and decision-making (Mahoney, 1993). Clark (1993: ix) has written optimistically of connectionism that it 'promises to be not just one new tool in the cognitive scientist's toolkit but, rather, the catalyst for a more fruitful conception of the whole project of cognitive science'. In reading the research it is clear that connectionism is generally identified as a form of cognitive psychology, but there is no doubt that it also shares a great deal in common with behaviourism. Thus, neither approach distinguishes between the cognitive and the biological: 'Both emphasize that learning occurs primarily through changes to the nervous system' (Tonnessen, 1999: 391). Both are also able to explain gradual improvement through drill and repetition, trial and error and gradual adjustment. Connectionism is linked to Popper's 'World 3' (Popper, 1972) inasmuch as it is linked to mathematical reasoning and the world of logic. The emergence of connectionism was associated with the development of supercomputers. A number of models have been developed to account for developments in perception and cognition.

Connectionist models have also been influenced significantly by research relating to brain processing structures. Connectionist models, often termed neural networks, attempt to explain how the brain works. At the most basic level, the connectionist network contains many 'simple processing units, interconnected by unidirectional links that transmit activation' (Smith, 1996: 895). As explained by Eliot, the units are usually assumed to perform some simple computation. Athanassios (1999: 414) has observed that the 'neural network comprises a number of interconnected units, or nodes, each of which is characterized by an activation value'. As such, it is possible to identify the positive or negative sign of the input or output from a weighted algebraic sum of the units. The learning process is hypothesized to shape the weights on the interconnections among the units.

The description of neural networks in terms of 'units' and 'activation' 'leaves unanswered the question of what a unit represents semantically' (Smith, 1996: 898). A traditional conceptualization of memory invokes the metaphor of a filing cabinet wherein 'storage', 'search' and 'retrieval' represent 'inscriptions' that can be accessed (Eliot, 1996). Connectionist models use a very different representation: 'There is no discrete location for each representation. Instead, the whole network of connection weights is a single representation that contains information derived from many past experiences' (Smith, 1996: 898).

In relation to cognitive development Ramsay *et al.* (1991) have noted that it is unquestionable that connectionism has already fostered major changes in how cognitive scientists conceive of cognition. Thelen and Smith (1994) see it as intimately related to dynamic systems theory (mentioned later in this chapter), but observe that connectionist models fail as developmental theories in not seriously considering a number of issues, including how biology (including the brain) really works and how complex development actually is.

Theory of mind

Premack and Woodruff (1978) introduced the idea of 'theory of mind' as part of their efforts to understand the cognitive and language abilities of chimpanzees: 'An individual has a theory of mind if he imputes mental states to himself and others' (1978: 515). As we spend time with others we take into account their feelings, thoughts and behaviour in order to try and understand why individuals behave as they do. Indications of the existence of theory of mind awareness are found in everyday language usage such as 'I think she was upset' or 'I'm sure you will like this'. To understand that children have a developing sense of another, researchers must first rule out the possibility that the child is: (a) not behaving egocentrically (e.g. indicating that another child wants something based not on their knowledge of the other's desire but on their own desire) or (b) not simply using past experience to infer something about another child.

In a major review of the field Flavell (1999) has identified three main waves of research relating to children's knowledge about the mind. The first wave, as described earlier in this chapter, largely involved Piaget's theory and research. Piaget's argument concerning the essentially egocentric nature of children in the early stages of development indicated that children were restricted in their ability to appreciate the perspectives of others. Research studies confirm a gradual increase in children's perspective-taking abilities (Flavell, 1992).

A second wave of research related to children's metacognitive development. Research into metacognitive development concerns knowledge relating to 'people as cognizers, about the nature of different cognitive tasks, and about possible strategies that can be applied to the solution of different tasks' (Flavell, 1999: 22).

The third, and now dominant, wave of research relates to theory of mind development. A virtual avalanche of research beginning in the 1980s presently almost dominates the field of cognitive development. Readers are referred to the following publications for major reviews of research relating to this field: Astington (1993); Flavell (1999); Flavell and Miller (1998). Flavell (1999) is very optimistic that theory of mind research holds much promise for increasing our understanding of children's cognitive development. An interesting application of theory of mind to the issue of school bullying has been presented by Sutton *et al.* (1999) (Box 4.1).

Box 4.1 Bullying and theory of mind

As noted in this chapter, theory of mind is enjoying wide application to explain various aspects of child development; one example is school bullying. A common portrayal of students who bully others, particularly in fiction writing, is of the bully as a rather 'powerful, but "oafish" person with little understanding of others' (Sutton *et al.*, 1999: 117). Such a view is consistent with a social skills-processing view, suggesting that individuals might be deficient at any one of the five stages of information processing, including (a) social perception, (b) interpretation of cues, (c) goal selection, (d) response strategy generation, and (e) response decision. A bully might be thought of as lacking one or more of these 'social skills'. In contrast, Sutton *et al.* (1999) suggest that some bullies at least might be very adept at using a theory of mind and understanding other individuals in order to manipulate and organize them. This particular theoretical viewpoint has attracted some debate (e.g. Crick and Dodge, 1999).

Eleanor Maccoby: adding the 'social' to cognitive development

The extensive research interests of Eleanor Maccoby (born in 1917) place her at a particular advantage in psychology to integrate the thinking of various theoretical influences and interpret contemporary research findings in child development. In developing her own theoretical beliefs Maccoby acknowledges the influence of cognitive-developmental theory in shaping her views (Maccoby, 1980), hence her inclusion in the present chapter. However, she has expressed a concern echoed by others, that 'the theory is too "cold" and does not give enough weight to the role of emotions in social development' (Maccoby, 1980: 31). She has also been critical of stage theory, arguing instead that there are 'decision points' in children's lives and at such points various influences, such as the family, can lead any two children to follow different developmental patterns.

Eleanor Maccoby was born in Tacoma, Washington. Her mother was a folk singer and believed in astrology, while both parents were vegetarian and followed metaphysical thinking including ideas such as reincarnation

(Stevens and Gardner, 1982). Maccoby's adolescent rebellion against her parents' values was possibly reflected in an early interest in psychology and in her belief that human behaviour could be studied empirically according to the objective methods developed by positivist sciences. In 1950 she began her teaching at Harvard University, but according to Stevens and Gardner (1982) she suffered some gender discrimination in the rather patriarchal setting of the university (for instance, women were not permitted to enter the Faculty Club by the front door) and she was unhappy in this university setting (in Chapter 10 we will take a slightly more contemporary look at the lives of women in academia). She subsequently moved to Stanford University.

From an early stage in her career she was interested in studying children, including the effects of television on children. At various times her eclectic research interests have also encompassed mother–child interaction, women's studies, gender, moral values, aggression, attachment and the relationship between intelligence and non-cognitive abilities. Maccoby's focus on the complex topic of the socialization of children has drawn upon a wide range of theory and research. In outlining her views of children's socialization she acknowledges the influence of behaviourism and the particular contributions that the concepts of reinforcement and contingency have made to our understanding of how children's social behaviour is influenced. According to Maccoby, Freudian theory has also contributed to our understanding of the socialization process, particularly in relation to sex-role development. Perhaps most importantly, however, Maccoby has identified those contemporary influences that have shaped children's social development, including:

- research involving trait theory, which has highlighted the inconsistency of children's behaviour in various situations
- cognitive-developmental theory, which has alerted us to the manner in which children's thinking shapes their perception of events
- ethological theory and the associated concept of instincts, which raises the possibility of the predisposition of children to learn certain things – for example, attachment
- temperament research, which has made us aware of the dissimilarity of infants at birth
- cross-cultural research, which has alerted us to the influence of social structures such as the nature of the family unit, the economic basis of a society (e.g. agricultural or industrial), the role of men and women, and how a culture educates its members.

Maccoby's view of the socialization process is particularly far-reaching, drawing as it does on various theoretical influences, and she has made a significant contribution to our current understanding of socialization. Broadly speaking, though, her views reflect an awareness that the biology of the child should also be taken into account, and that the child actively participates in the socialization process and also moves through various phases in developing a concept of the social self.

One important feature of Maccoby's thinking (Maccoby, 1980) concerns the parents' role in aiding the child's social development. She believes that children's social-psychological development will be fostered if parents:

- are interested in and responsive to their children's needs
- have realistic age-appropriate expectations of their children's behaviour
- provide their children with some structure and predictability in their daily lives
- are democratic in decision-making within the family
- listen to their children's views
- allow their children the opportunity to solve their own problems
- are warm and affectionate towards their children
- work at developing a set of values with their children.

In regarding the environment provided by parents as making a real difference to children's development, her perspective is more consistent with that of Baumrind than Scarr (see Chapter 2).

Jerome Bruner and constructivist theory

Constructivism has its philosophical roots in the European tradition of thinking drawn from the philosophy of Berkeley and Kant, who emphasized the subjectivity of our perception. More recently, the links with constructivism have been made with the thinking of Piaget. Gelcer and Schwartzbein (1989) have summarized two important assumptions of Piaget's theory: that there are different levels of knowing the same experience, and that the higher or greater the level of abstraction, the more flexible is the individual's approach to problem-solving.

Key writers who have contributed to theory relating to constructivism include the Chilean biologist Maturana and his colleague Varela (1988), and the cybernetician von Foerster (1973). The systems thinking of Gregory Bateson, discussed later in this chapter, also had an impact on constructivism.

The important assertion of constructivism is that reality cannot be revealed to us in only one true way. It is through the process of construing that we come to know reality, as in Kelly's theory, which we mentioned previously: 'each organism creatively constructs its world within the limits of whatever biological or environmental context it encounters' (Gelcer and Schwartzbein, 1989: 440). Constructivism emphasizes a proactive view of the individual, who as an observer participates actively in the process of observation. It is through this process of active participation that the co-creation of meaning occurs. Such a proactive view of the person contrasts with much of mainstream psychology, which views the individual as reactive.

The theory of the North American psychologist Jerome Bruner (born in 1915) reflects a constructivist approach, and has been greatly influenced by the thinking of Piaget and the Russian psychologist Lev Vygotsky (see Chapter 7). While Bruner's theory is similar to that of Piaget in many respects, it also differs in crucial aspects. For Bruner, language is intimately related to a child's cognitive growth. In his view, thinking would not be possible without language. Bruner (1987) has also argued that the competences of children are greater than Piaget's theory leads us to believe. He places great emphasis on the child as a social being whose competences 'are interwoven with the competences of others' (Bruner, 1987: 11).

Bruner (1966) has identified three major themes in understanding cognitive growth and the conditions that shape it. The first relates to how humans organize and represent their experience of the world. Bruner argues that as children develop they pass through three stages, or three modes, of representing their world: enactive, iconic and symbolic. Each of these three modes enables the child to represent the world in unique ways (Bruner, 1987).

A second theme in his theory relates to the impact of culture on growth. Bruner notes that cognitive growth is shaped as much 'from the outside in as the inside out' (Bruner, 1966: 13). We will take this idea further in later chapters.

A third major theme relates to the evolutionary history of humans. Bruner believes that humans are particularly suited to adapting to their environment by social means rather than by morphological means (Bruner, 1986).

In reading Bruner's work, several key assumptions are evident. One of these is that reality is constructed. Bruner places a great deal more emphasis than Piaget on the notion that humans actively construct meaning from the world. In *Actual Minds, Possible Worlds* (1986) Bruner cites Goodman's notion of a constructivist philosophy:

> Contrary to common sense there is no unique 'real world' that preexists and is independent of human mental activity and human symbolic language; that which we call the world is a product of some mind whose symbolic procedures construct the world.
>
> (Bruner, 1986: 95)

As such, the world we live in is 'created' by the mind, an idea consistent with the postmodern philosopical ideas we encounter elsewhere in this book. Bruner argues that the idea that we construct the world should be quite congenial to developmental or clinical psychologists, who observe that humans can attach quite different meanings to the same event.

Another of Bruner's key assumptions is that development is culturally and historically embedded (Bruner, 1986; Bruner and Haste, 1987). In Bruner's words (1986: 67), 'It can never be the case that there is a "self" independent of one's cultural-historical context'. In this way Bruner's outlook is closely aligned with that of Vygotsky (see Chapter 7). Culture is the means by which 'instructions' about how humans should grow are carried from one generation to the next (Bruner, 1987). That is, culture helps transmit knowledge and understanding.

Bruner also assumes that the child is a social being. Bruner and Haste (1987: 11) observe that 'we are now able to focus on the child as a social being whose competencies are interwoven with the competencies of others'. Bruner and Haste are critical of the legacy bequeathed by Piaget, suggesting that while the child is active in the construction of the world, the picture that emerges from Piagetian theory is one of a rather isolated child working alone at problem-solving tasks. They emphasize that the child is in fact a social operator, who through a social life 'acquires a framework for interpreting experience, and learns how to negotiate meaning in a manner congruent with the requirements of a culture' (Bruner and Haste 1987: 1).

Bruner (1966) proposes that children pass through a number of stages in their cognitive development. The first is enactive representation, equivalent to Piaget's sensori-motor period. Bruner argues, as does Piaget, that the infant gains knowledge about the world not from mental images but rather from action. Comparing his enactive stage with Piaget's sensori-motor stage, Bruner notes that Piaget regards the 'first part in sensori-motor intelligence as one in which things are lived rather than thought' (Bruner, 1966: 17; Piaget, 1954). Bruner likens this type of intelligence to an irreversible and fixed succession of static images, each connected to an action. The child seems able to 'hold an object in mind by less and less direct manual prehension of it' (Bruner, 1966: 17). During the enactive stage infants can perform actions but do not know how they perform them. To this extent, Bruner agrees with Piaget that the infant's intelligence is one in which things are 'lived rather than thought' (Piaget, 1954).

Bruner's second stage of knowing, that of iconic representation, involves using a mental image or picture in the mind: 'A second stage in representation emerges when a child is finally able to represent the world to himself by an image or spatial schema that is relatively independent of action' (Bruner, 1966: 21). The word 'iconic' comes from the word 'icon' (from the ancient Greek word for likeness or image). A mental image is a genuine cognitive representation. It is representative of a body of information but takes a different form from that which it represents. In Bruner's (1966) view, iconic knowledge has a number of identifiable characteristics.

- It is inflexible.
- It focuses upon small details.

- It is self-centred in relation to having central reference to the child as an observer.
- It is subject to distortion because of the child's needs or feelings.
- Perception is closely tied to action or doing.
- Perception is unsteady in terms of the young child's unsteadiness of concentration.

Bruner and Piaget disagreed about the role of iconic representation in a child's thinking. In Bruner's theory the role of iconic knowledge is crucial to the explanation of conservation or the ability to understand that the physical attributes of objects (for example, mass) do not vary when the object's shape is changed.

Bruner's third stage of knowing, symbolic representation, refers to the ability to represent our experience of the world by using symbols. Bruner writes (1966: 31): 'The idea that there is a name that goes with things and that the name is arbitrary is generally taken as the essence of symbolism'. Thus, a written sentence describing a beautiful landscape does not look like a landscape, whereas a picture of a landscape looks like a landscape. The landscape is symbolized in the language describing it. In Bruner's (1966) theory, symbolic representation is enhanced through language acquisition in particular. Without the ability to symbolize, the child will grow into adulthood dependent upon the enactive and iconic modes of representing and organizing knowledge of the world.

Bruner's writing could be considered as not receiving the attention it deserves in the mainstream developmental psychology and educational psychology fields. Nonetheless his research and writing have important implications for psychologists' understanding of the developing child. By emphasizing the constructive nature of cognitive development and the influence of cultural factors, Bruner has added a richer dimension to our contemporary understanding of the nature of children's thinking.

Systems thinking and dynamic systems theory

In the previous chapter we mentioned that general systems theory is one of a number of influences on organismic developmental theories. Here, we develop this further in considering the contributions of Bateson and Prigonine.

During the 1950s Gregory Bateson and colleagues developed and applied the ideas associated with general systems theory, in connection with research on families whose members had schizophrenia. They conceived of families as systems having properties that are more than the sum of the properties of their parts. Furthermore, they saw families as open systems, which none the less are governed by rules, and as cybernetic systems, incorporating the important notion of feedback to family members.

Bateson contributed a number of significant concepts to contemporary systems thinking, including ideas about levels of communication and 'patterns that connect'. Bateson maintained that communication can occur across different levels: 'unhealthy' communication may contain 'double messages', which confuse one of the communicators regarding just what is being conveyed. Also, with a consuming interest in biology as well as human behaviour, Bateson was interested in 'patterns that connect'. As he wrote in *Mind and Nature* (1979: 16–17):

> What pattern connects the crab to the lobster and the orchid to the primrose and all four of them to me? And me to you? And all six of us to the amoeba in one direction and to the backward schizophrenic in another?

In the same book, Bateson went on to describe the patterns that connect as metapatterns – patterns of patterns. In this regard Bateson's thinking highlights the organicist concept of structural interdependence in development, as described in Chapter 3.

Another significant contributor to the development of systems thinking was the 1997 Nobel Prize-winning Belgian chemist Ilya Prigogine. His research into dissipative structures arising out of the non-linear processes in non-equilibrium systems provided a comprehensive theory of change (see Chapter 1 regarding the nature of development as 'change'). The theory incorporates some key concepts, as outlined below.

- **Systems and subsystems.** All systems are composed of subsystems, which are in a continual state of fluctuation or change. At any one time the fluctuation may be so strong as to shatter the pre-existing order.
- **Chaos and order.** At any 'singular moment' or 'bifurcation' the system may descend into 'chaos' or transcend to a higher level of organization or 'order' known as a 'dissipative structure'. Such structures are called 'dissipative' because they require more energy to sustain them than the previous structures.
- **Equilibrium.** In Newtonian thermodynamics all systems run down to disorder with energy dissipating over time. In the natural world there are 'closed systems' that do operate like machines. However, many systems are 'open', exchanging energy, matter or information with the environment.

While systems thinking, with its notions of self-organization, has clear connections with the organismic metaphor described by Pepper (1942), its novel emphasis on holism and non-linear causality suggests that it should be considered a new developmental metaphor in itself. In a developmental psychology context there is a growing interest in the application of systems theory to the study of children and the family (Kaye, 1985; Scarr, 1985;

Tolan, 1990; Wachtel, 1990). For example, a number of developmentalists, including Sameroff (1982), recognized the implications of Prigonine's theorizing: 'Adoption of such a systems model, with its assumptions of wholeness, self-stabilization, self-organization, and hierarchical organization, has implications for every aspect of developmental psychology' (Thelen and Smith, 1998: 575). To illustrate this point Thelen and Smith cite the need for development to be contextualized because the concept of 'open systems' necessitates an interchange between the organism and the environment. Ideas of non-linearity may be used to explain how apparently small transformations result in significant changes in the organism.

In the fifth edition of the *Handbook of Child Psychology*, edited by Damon and Lerner (1998), Lerner (1998: 1) notes that the current focus in theoretical development is 'a burgeoning interest not in structure, function, or content per se, but in change, in the process through which change occurs, and thus in the means through which structures transform and functions evolve over the course of human life'. In many ways this understanding captures significant features of a new developmental theory – dynamic systems theory.

Dynamic systems theory draws on the insights provided by systems thinking in the physical, biological and psychological sciences. It draws upon principles related to the global properties of complex systems (Thelen and Smith, 1994):

> The new science that can extract common principles in the behaviour of chemical reactions, clouds, forests, and embryos is variously called the study of dynamic, synergetic, dissipative, nonlinear, self-organizing, or chaotic theories. (We adopt here dynamic systems as the descriptor to emphasize that these are systems that change continuously over time.)
>
> (Thelen and Smith, 1994: 50)

Increasingly, dynamic systems theory is being applied to various areas of developmental psychology (Pepler and Craig and O'Connell, 2000; Slee, 2001; Thelen and Smith, 1984; Thelen and Smith, 1994) (Box 4.2). We will discuss it further in Chapter 11, in considering recent moves towards more integrative theories of child development.

Conclusions

In this chapter we have continued to examine theories based upon the organismic metaphor. One of the significant features of developmental psychology is the richness of its theoretical development. Presently, new and exciting breakthroughs are occurring in this theorizing and in this chapter we have attempted to capture some of the vibrancy of the current debate in relation to organicism. Generally, the organismic worldview (Pepper, 1942)

Box 4.2 The application of systems thinking to school bullying

In terms of the view that 'Bullying is collective in its nature, based on social relationships in the group' (Sutton and Smith, 1999: 97) one can apply many of the principles of systemic thinking described in this chapter. Thus, it can be argued that an identified problem such as bullying is not located solely within a particular individual. Conventional western mechanistic ways of thinking, with a strong causal component, direct us to search for the faulty or broken part or problematic individual in order to fix or cure the 'problem'. Much is known about how such a mechanistic person-centred approach works. Schools are, however, also based around systems, and systems within systems (e.g. community, home, school, year level, classroom and peer groups). The various systems interact with each other, and within the systems individuals are viewed as active agents in construing their own world. From a systemic perspective, people are viewed in terms of their relationships with one another, rather than simply being understood principally on the basis of their individual development. A child's misconduct in school (e.g. bullying others) is understood to serve some purpose within the system or reflects something about the system itself. The behaviour is not just the result of some inner psychic disturbance or carried out for some reward. The student's behaviour is, in a sense, a window through which we can look to understand his or her place in the system, and provides an important insight into the various roles and relationships within the system (Slee, 2002).

---

highlights the directional movement of the organism towards ever-increasing integration against the backdrop of a dynamic, evolving context. All phenomena are interdependent. In this situation the child is an active constructor of reality and not merely responding passively. As an active individual, the child constructs interpretations of environmental events, and continually acts and interacts with his or her environment in order to construct and reconstruct experience. The child is viewed as a spontaneously active organism, and because some activities are not simply a response to external events it is not theoretically possible to predict all of an individual's behaviour. Acting like lay theorists, children are continually adapting their theories to fit ever-changing events in their world, altering the world in the process. However, the lay theories are by no means as neat and consistent as we might like to imagine (Basseches, 1989) and it is the very inconsistencies in children's theorizing that force them to act to resolve them.

While this approach takes into account the uniqueness of the individual and the active participation of the individual in his or her own development, two key limitations to organismic theories must be observed. One relates to the structural stage conceptions of development, which 'fail to reflect the complexity and diversity of individuals' meaning making' (Basseches, 1989: 189). The second limitation associated with this approach includes a lack of explanation of how internal regulation, organization and self-organization relate to the developmental process.

5 From Oedipus to attachment: the Freudian legacy

Introduction

Freudian theory is something about which beginning psychology students often expect to hear a great deal, given the great impact it has had on western psychology and its popular image. However, they may find Freud's work given only a minor place in psychology curricula that emphasize the scientific method and evidence-based psychology practice. Freud's ideas were indeed developed in the absence of scientific support, during the first part of the twentieth century. Despite – and possibly because of – this lack of scientific support, Freud's concepts had a great influence upon social science and the practice of psychiatry at the time. Freud may have tapped into ongoing desires to study subjective experience, which was being rejected by psychologists at the time as being inappropriate for scientific study (Fisher and Greenberg, 1996). More recently, too, Freudian ideas have been said to have 'penetrated into the matrix of modern psychology and continue to exert formidable influence' (Fisher and Greenberg, 1996: 6–7).

With the benefit of hindsight, we can say today that Freud's psychosexual theory of child development, derived from his reflections on the early childhood recollections of his adult psychiatric patients, has to be seriously questioned. Nevertheless, empirical support has been found for some aspects of Freudian theory, and his thinking was inspirational to others who have in turn greatly influenced our understanding of children's development, especially in infancy. Such workers include Melanie Klein, Erik Erikson, John Bowlby, René Spitz, Mary Ainsworth and Michael Rutter. They were in no way Freud's disciples, but reflected upon certain of his key insights and developed them in their own ways. In this chapter, we provide a brief reminder of Freud's Oedipal theory of child development, examine the scientific evidence for it and describe some of the later work in child development theory that built upon the Freudian tradition.

Freud's theory of child development

Sigmund Freud (1856–1939) took a biological approach to development, seeing the child as coming into the world already equipped with basic instincts to survive and reproduce. These basic drives constituted the aspect of the psyche that he called the id. The ego was the part of the psyche in touch with reality, mediating between the id and the superego, or conscience. We noted in Chapter 1 that Darwinian theory has been taken as a common influence on several schools of thought in developmental psychology, although the directness and strength of this influence has been questioned (see Chapter 2). A continuity of Freud with earlier Darwinian theory can be observed in that Freud applied notions of phylogenetic evolution to intrapsychic development (ontogeny) (Emde, 1992). He proposed that the functions of current actions could be understood in terms of past history, placing great emphasis on early experience as laying the foundations for a series of developmental stages – a notion later developed much further by Piaget.

The stages of development delineated by Freud were the oral, anal, phallic, latency and genital. His theory is psychosexual, in that each stage is defined by the zone of the body that is the focus of pleasure for the child (the exception being the latency stage, when sexual instincts lie dormant): 'A child has its sexual instincts and activities from the first; it comes into the world with them; and after an important course of development passing through many stages, they lead to what is known as the normal sexuality of the adult' (Freud, 1974: 71). His emphasis upon the sexual nature of children was considered outrageous at the time. Although one of Freud's most enduring legacies is the recognition of the importance of early experiences for later development, it is important not to lose sight of the fact that Freud was a medical man who also emphasized the importance of hereditary and constitutional factors in development. It should be noted, however, that the word 'genetic' as used by Freud means ontogenetic or epigenetic rather than gene-controlled (Hilgard, 1962).

Although there are various aspects of Freudian theory with implications for child development, the one we will concentrate on here is the Oedipal theory, which has been described as 'the skeleton of the psychoanalytic model' (Fisher and Greenberg, 1996: 118). In fact, Fisher and Greenberg conceive of Oedipal theory itself (like other aspects of Freudian theory) as a collection of mini-theories about a range of developmental issues, such as family dynamics, identification with parents, moral development and sexual development. Freud doubtless saw his theory as a 'grand theory', and the tendency to look back on it as a collection of mini-theories is perhaps reflective of the modern trend towards mini-theories rather than grand systems. (In Chapter 11 we note the beginnings of a reversal of this trend.)

From the vantage point of today's scientific psychology, it seems remarkable that a man who proposed a theory of child development undertook very little research or clinical work with children. Rather, he built his theory on the basis of the recollections of his (mainly female) middle-class patients, diagnosed with psychological disorders such as hysteria.

Descriptions of childhood sexual experiences by such women were originally taken at face value by Freud, and he initially attributed their adult psychological symptoms to repressed sexual trauma. However, Freud veered away from his original ('seduction theory') interpretation that these women had suffered early abuse. He renounced his seduction theory in 1897, and came to see these women as expressing childhood sexual fantasies. Although he worked mainly with women, Freud took the development of male children as the prototype for development (a reflection of his historical times), although we know today that, biologically speaking, the reverse is actually the case (Emde, 1992).

In describing the phallic stage of development, Freud drew upon the Greek myth of King Oedipus, who killed his father and married his mother. Freud theorized that the young boy, around the age of four or five, harbours sexual impulses toward his mother. This places him in direct competition with his father for her affections, and he fears that his father will castrate him as a punishment. To overcome this Oedipal conflict, the boy identifies with his father, in the course of which he internalizes his father's moral values and develops his own superego. Freud postulated that, for girls, a parallel but necessarily somewhat different process occurs (Electra complex), with the girl believing she has already been castrated by her mother and moving towards her father as a love object; he has the potential to give her a baby in compensation for the presumed loss of her penis (the 'penis–baby equation'). Freud was less clear about how the female's conflict is resolved, but maintained that it is more gradual and results in a weaker superego for girls than boys. Freud saw normal adult psychological development as dependent upon the resolution of these early psychosexual conflicts, and theorized that adult neuroses and sexual dysfunctions result from a failure to resolve them adequately.

As we have noted, this theory was based on Freud's assumption that when his female patients described early sexual encounters with adult men, they were fantasies. John Bowlby later placed the emphasis back on reality, rather than fantasy, in early childhood experiences (Andrews and Brewin, 2000), and writers increasingly began to suggest that Freud's earlier interpretations of his patients' recollections as actual abuse were correct (e.g. Masson, 1984). With today's understanding of the prevalence and impact of sexual abuse of children, many agree with this assessment, even though debates continue to rage about the accuracy of memories of childhood recovered in adult therapy.

Putting aside the point that the Oedipal theory was probably based upon a false premise, it is nevertheless possible to examine how it stands up to scientific scrutiny. Fisher and Greenberg (1996) undertook two very detailed reviews of the scientific literature (first in 1977 and again in 1996) to determine how much empirical support there was for various aspects of Freudian theory. They addressed the issue of whether it is in fact appropriate to apply scientific standards to test Freudian theories or whether, as some have argued, it is more appropriate to apply alternative methods of inquiry such as those in a more relativist-subjectivist vein. Freud, as a scientist himself, was ambivalent about this issue; he was pleased when science seemed to support his theories, but did not apply scientific principles to his clinical data collection. Fisher and Greenberg adopted the position that it is appropriate to evaluate support for Freud's theories from a scientific perspective, but to avoid trivial critique of studies and look instead for overall trends across multiple studies.

Many studies were, in fact, undertaken by experimental psychologists during the twentieth century to directly test propositions derived from Freudian theory. For example, the very basic proposition that infant experiences have enduring effects on adult behaviour was examined and supported by experiments during the 1940s and 1950s, demonstrating that adult rats' food-hoarding behaviour is influenced by early food deprivation (e.g. Albino and Long, 1951). With specific regard to Oedipal theory, Fisher and Greenberg concluded that there is a considerable body of evidence supporting the basic notion of the 'Oedipal triangle' (the child favouring the opposite-sex over the same-sex parent). They also found evidence for children's concern about body experiences around the age at which Freud identified castration anxiety as occurring. They even found evidence supporting predictions derived from the controversial penis–baby equation theory – for example, an increase in phallic imagery during pregnancy. However, they found no evidence for the proposition that a boy identifies with his father and adopts his values as a result of fearing him. On the contrary, boys identify most strongly with fathers who are warm and nurturing. Evidence linking later sexual functioning with Oedipal notions is also lacking. Neither is there any evidence for the Freudian notion that boys develop a stronger superego than do girls (in this respect, Freudian ideas of morality development can be seen as male-centric, as was also the case with Piaget and Kohlberg – see Chapter 10); also, moral development has been found to be influenced by a range of factors other than the father–child relationship.

Although they found support for particular aspects of the Oedipal theory, Fisher and Greenberg concluded overall that the empirical evidence for Freud's attempt to produce a grand theory of children's sexual and moral development was not strong. In a similar vein, Emde (1992) has pointed out that both gender identity and moral development can be observed well before the time when Freud saw the Oedipus complex as becoming resolved; also, rather than having an attachment to one parent disrupted later by the other, children usually develop ties of affection with both parents from an early age. Emde also makes the more general theoretical point that Freud, in keeping with understandings of physics at the time, saw mental processes in terms of entropy (tending towards lower levels of organization, as in drive reduction), which contrasts with modern notions that development tends towards *greater* levels of complexity (see Chapter 11).

Despite its shortcomings, the influence of Freudian theory upon more recent developmental theories can easily be detected. A range of observations by Freud is echoed in later developmental theories (or, perhaps more appropriately, mini-theories), such as mirror play in a young child (development of self-awareness), peek-a-boo games (maternal 'scaffolding' of development – see Chapter 7) and ego development through separation from caregivers (attachment theory, as discussed below) (Emde, 1992). Such ideas were reflected in the work of later major developmental theorists such as Spitz, Bowlby and Ainsworth (attachment and loss), and in the development of the psychoanalytic approach to child therapy (e.g. Klein, Winnicott and the object relations school). Also, Piaget learned from Freud's open-ended approach to inquiry and, in particular, his attention to what an individual's errors can reveal about their cognitions, as Freud discussed in *The Psychopathology of Everyday Life* (1914/1940). We will now consider a number of important twentieth-century child development theorists upon whom Freudian ideas had a particular influence.

Erik Erikson and lifespan development

Erikson (1902–94) built upon Freud's theory, accepting his basic psychosexual framework, but developing the theory into further stages in adulthood, thus promoting the notion of lifespan development. Similarly to Freud, he saw development as resulting from conflicts; at each stage, the nature of their resolution could be more or less adaptive. Erikson's theory was a psychosocial one, which saw the ego not just as a mediator within the individual's psyche, but as an active promoter of development, under cultural influence. Erikson's influential works included *Childhood and Society* (1968) and *Identity, Youth and Crisis* (1968). We will say a little more about Erikson in Chapter 9.

Object relations

Melanie Klein (1882–1960) was an influential figure from the 1920s to the mid-twentieth century in the object relations school of psychoanalysis. She was involved in training therapists at the British Psychoanalytic Institute, and emphasized the potential of early loss for later psychopathology. An 'object', in the Kleinian sense, is a loved thing or, especially, person. Unlike Freud, she saw fear of death as being primary, not learned, and as the underlying cause of anxiety. However, she provided few observations of how infants actually behave in separation situations (Bowlby, 1975). She saw anxiety as being apparent right from the initial traumatic experience of birth, and internal conflict as the source of childhood emotional problems.

Others, such as Winnicott, later developed Klein's approach but gave more emphasis to external factors. Winnicott (1953) discussed the fact that young children often become attached to inanimate objects. For instance, the niece of one of the present authors carried around a blue toy rabbit for several years until all that was left of it was a small piece of blue cloth. Linus's blanket in the *Peanuts* cartoon strip is another example. Winnicott termed such objects 'transitional objects', maintaining that they demonstrated the beginnings of symbolic thought. In representing a love object, such as the mother or her breast, they characterize the infant's journey from subjectivity to objectivity.

Object relations theory has been described as forming a bridge between Freudian theory, with its intrapsychic emphasis, and family therapy, which emphasizes interrelationships between family members (Gladding, 1998). The influence of early object relations and the unconscious influence they may have on current relationships is recognized; these may lead to repeated dysfunctional patterns of interaction. Therapy aims to break these through assisting the family members to gain insight into them.

Maternal deprivation

As we have observed, Freud's legacy can be traced through other theorists whom he influenced, and important among these was René Spitz (1887–1974). Spitz's work is known through his research into 'maternal deprivation' of babies in orphanages in the middle of the twentieth century. Spitz was directly influenced by Freud, meeting him in 1911 and regarding him as a mentor (Emde, 1992). However, in contrast with Freud, his theorizing arose from direct observations of infants, and his (for the time) innovative use of film strengthened the impact of his work. Spitz also stressed a Darwinian influence on his work, was a friend of the ethologist Lorenz, and told Emde that he wanted his final words to be remembered as 'survival, adaptation, and evolution' (Emde, 1992: 354). Thus we could perhaps equally well have placed Spitz's contribution in Chapter 2 – a reminder of the multiple influences that impinge on any theorist's work – although it is certainly for his work on infant socialization that he remains recognized.

Spitz overturned notions that the institutionalized infants of unmarried mothers were sickly because their mothers were constitutionally morally inferior beings, and maintained instead that the infants had failed to thrive because of a lack of mothering. His work on infant social smiling and on fear (more often now called wariness) of strangers around eight months of age remains well known. He also laid the foundations for a more recent thriving area of inquiry in proposing that reciprocity exists between infants and their caregivers – he recognized that a two-way flow of interaction occurs long before the child develops speech. In comparison with Freud, Spitz's research methods were exemplary, but in keeping with refinements in scientific methodology he was criticized even in his own time for poor reporting of experimental detail and lack of evidence for the reliability and validity of his measures. Nevertheless, his theory that maternal deprivation causes depression and apathy in infants was upheld by later work such as that of Bowlby, although further refinements remained to be made, such as the recognition that infants are typically attached not only to the mother (Emde, 1992).

Goldfarb, a New York psychologist, was another researcher whose work was influential in this area (cited in Bowlby, 1953). He compared the development of two groups of adolescents, all of whom had been surrendered by their mothers in infancy. Those who had spent their first three years in institutions were delayed in development in comparison with those who had been taken straight to foster homes in infancy. For example, their speech and social skills were poorly developed. These findings demonstrated that early deprivation could have long-lasting effects, and suggested that there was a critical period for the development of such skills.

Spitz, Goldfarb and, as discussed below, Bowlby, are credited with establishing notions of infant institutionalization and maternal deprivation as developmentally damaging. Yet, in the nineteenth century, this issue was well recognized in South Australia, as recorded by a Scottish-Australian pioneer of women's rights and children's welfare, Catherine Helen Spence (1825–1910). She wrote a book in honour of Miss C.E. Clark, who had worked to establish a system of care for destitute children in family homes rather than institutions (Spence, 1907). At a time when unmarried mothers were vilified, legislation was enacted in 1881 to try and keep infants with their mothers: women entering the Destitute Asylum to have their babies were contracted to stay with their babies for six months, 'giving it the natural nourishment', and Spence noted that 'affection grows strong during these six months' (Spence, 1907: 59). Where an infant could not be kept with its mother, rather than being institutionalized, it was boarded out to a foster mother: 'It is wonderful the love that grows up in the house where there is only one child placed' (1907: 62). Efforts were also made to maintain the child's relationship with its natural mother: 'the foster mother shows to the real mother all its pretty ways, encourages it to crow and laugh ... and sometimes is the means of reconciling the mother to her relatives' (1907: 63). These images of happily attached nineteenth-century infants present a very different picture from those of the sickly infants observed in orphanages elsewhere in the world well into the twentieth century. It is also interesting that Spence's writings on these matters have been overlooked historically in the maternal deprivation literature. It does appear that one needed to be in the right place at the right time (and generally of a certain gender) in order to have one's work recognized (see Chapters 9 and 10).

Attachment theory

The following sections, on attachment theory, draw upon a review by Bretherton (1992). As noted in Chapter 3, readers are also referred to Susan Goldberg's (2000) book *Attachment and Development.* John Bowlby (1907–91), one of the originators of attachment theory, studied medicine and psychiatry, and also trained at the London Child Guidance Clinic and the British Psychoanalytic Institute. He disagreed with Klein's approach to child psychopathology, which emphasized internal conflict rather than external influences as the source of children's emotional problems. The later object relations theorists, such as Winnicott, were more in accord with Bowlby's views of the importance of early family relationships, although Bowlby preferred the term 'affectional bonds' to 'object relations' (Bowlby, 1975: 15) (Box 5.1).

Box 5.1 Did Bowlby's ideas anticipate Vygotskian theory?

As we discuss in Chapter 7, the Soviet psychologist Vygotsky and later workers such as Bruner maintained that children develop through interaction with more capable individuals, who gradually withdraw support for activities as the child becomes independently capable of them. Vygotsky's work had not been translated into English at the time Bowlby wrote the following passage. While the language is Freudian, the notion is distinctly Vygotskian (Bretherton, 1992).

> It is not surprising that during infancy and early childhood these functions are either not operating at all or are doing so most imperfectly. During this phase of life, the child is therefore dependent on his mother performing them for him. She orients him in space and time, provides his environment, permits the satisfaction of some impulses, restricts others. She is his ego and his super-ego. Gradually he learns these arts himself, and as he does, the skilled parent transfers the roles to him. This is a slow, subtle and continuous process, beginning when he first learns to walk and feed himself, and not ending completely until maturity is reached. ... Ego and super-ego development are thus inextricably bound up with the child's primary human relationships.
>
> (Bowlby, 1951, cited in Bretherton, 1992: 761)

Bowlby's interest in the importance of early attachment and loss developed originally from a couple of specific cases of children with emotional problems who had experienced early maternal loss (one of these used to follow him around the clinic and was known as his shadow). Later, he analysed over 40 case studies, concluding that the children's problems (including thieving) resulted from maternal deprivation. During the 1940s he began to put this area of research on a more scientific footing when he developed some expertise in statistical analyses, which enabled him to add some numerical support to his case study approach. After the Second World War he became director of London's Tavistock Clinic's Children's Department. Significantly, he renamed it as the Department for Children and Parents and, in 1949, wrote a paper on a form of family therapy he had devised.

Bowlby was commissioned by the World Health Organization (WHO) to write a report on children displaced by the war, which appeared in 1951, and a later version of this report appeared as the well-known book *Child Care and the Growth of Love* in 1953. It is interesting to observe that in Bowlby's WHO report, a Freudian influence is obvious in the language used, but certainly not in the concepts expounded (Bretherton, 1992). His basic tenet was that healthy mental development of the young child was dependent upon an ongoing warm, intimate relationship with the mother (or permanent mother substitute). The mother acts as the child's ego and superego, the child gradually taking over such functions as s/he becomes capable – a very different scenario from the internal and interpersonal conflicts that characterize the Oedipal processes described by Freud.

Bowlby's thinking was influenced by biological considerations and ethology, fruitful exchanges of ideas occurring between himself and Robert Hinde. He saw the organism's behaviour as controlled by a hierarchy of action plans which, in more complex organisms, are determined by a combination of innate factors and those that are flexible in the light of environmental circumstances. This theorizing reflected a movement towards cybernetic, rather than drive-reduction, models of behavioural control (Bretherton, 1992). He likened the psychological development of the infant to that of an embryo: just as early interference in embryonic development will have widespread ill effects, so the failure to establish an attachment relationship to a single individual in the first year of life will be very difficult to make good, as 'the character of the psychic tissue has become fixed' (Bowlby: 1953: 59). Thus the notions of imprinting and critical periods in mother–infant relationships began to supplant the Freudian idea that the child is attached to the mother because she gratifies its oral needs. These ideas were later supported through animal research, such as Harlow's well-known research with infant rhesus monkeys, who preferred to cling to a terry-cloth 'mother' than to a wire one that provided milk (Harlow and Harlow, 1966); however, as pointed out by Robinson (1999), it is possible that the terry-cloth mother assisted temperature regulation and was thus still meeting the infant's physical needs. Bowlby cited Harlow's research in his later discussions of attachment (Bowlby, 1969).

Like Winnicott, Bowlby discussed infants' attachment to inanimate objects, but took issue with Winnicott's explanation in terms of a symbolic shift from subjective to objective existence. He maintained that a more parsimonious explanation is simply that certain components of attachment behaviour become directed towards such objects because the 'natural' object, such as the breast, is unavailable. Thus he suggested the term 'substitute object' rather than 'transitional object'. Bowlby's interpretation has been supported by more recent research, which has shown that in Mayan society in Guatemala, where infants sleep with their mothers and feed at will during the night, such objects are almost unknown (Morelli *et al.*, 1992).

Bowlby later expanded upon the notions of separation from and loss of attachment figures (Bowlby, 1975), drawing upon the work of Ainsworth, discussed below. An important theoretical advance in this connection was the introduction of the notion of 'working models' of the self and attachment figures. In other words, the child develops internal representations of the self and others, which guide his/her expectations about how others are likely to respond should he/she seek support from them. Bowlby suggested that this theory, taken together with Piagetian theory, provides a framework for understanding the psychoanalytic phenomenon of transference: the analyst is assimilated to the patient's pre-existing model, which has not yet accommodated to incorporate the way the therapist has actually behaved towards the patient.

In contrast with Freud, Bowlby's theorizing was supported through empirical observations of mothers and children. However, his ideas were very critically received by influential members of the psychoanalytic movement at the time. Nevertheless, Bowlby's work has supplanted that of psychoanalysis in its influence on modern child development theory, and his ideas about attachment have deeply influenced broader theorizing about grief and loss (Archer, 1999). Bowlby was concerned about the public policy implications of attachment and loss for children's welfare, and addressed issues such as adoption and the importance of mothers maintaining contact with their hospitalized children.

Someone else who proved to be an important figure in the development of attachment theory was James Robertson. He learned child observation skills working as a boilerman at a residential London nursery for children displaced by the Second World War, run by Freud's daughter Anna. In fact, Bretherton (1992) sees the training of Robertson as being Anna Freud's enduring contribution to attachment theory. The skills Robertson developed were later used to good effect when he worked for Bowlby collecting data about the hospitalization of young children. Observing the plight of these children separated from their mothers, Robertson (1953, and later with his wife) made films that had the desired impact of bringing to public attention the hitherto unrecognized distress caused to young children through being separated from their parents – for example, through hospitalization or absence of the mother to give birth to another child.

Another person who joined Bowlby's unit a little later was Mary Ainsworth (born in 1913), whose name has become almost synonymous with attachment theory. As Mary Salter, she had completed a dissertation on secure dependence of the young child on parents, and moved from Canada to London in 1950, where she became familiar with Bowlby's work. She first studied mother–infant attachment in Uganda in the early 1950s, but did not publish the data for several more years, after moving to the United States and also renewing her intellectual collaboration with Bowlby.

Mary Ainsworth made a very important contribution to attachment theory in two respects. She introduced the notion that the mother, or other attachment figure, provides a secure base from which the young child can explore the world. Second, she introduced the notion of parental sensitivity to child signals, paving the way for a later body of research on parent–infant communication. Ainsworth (e.g. Ainsworth *et al.*, 1978) is famed for developing an experimental protocol for examining infants' attachment to their mothers, known as the Strange Situation. The child is examined around the age of a year. She or he is first observed playing with her/his caregiver, usually the mother. The child's behaviour is then observed in several different situations: when a stranger enters the room; when the mother leaves the room; when the mother returns and the stranger leaves; when the mother leaves; when the stranger returns; and when the mother returns. On the basis of studies using this procedure, Ainsworth proposed that infants vary in the degree of security of their attachment relationship. 'Securely attached' infants explore the room freely in their mother's presence, protest at her absence and reunite joyfully with her; this is regarded as the optimum type of attachment relationship, resulting from sensitive parenting. 'Insecure-avoidant' infants are less distressed at separation and avoid the mother on her return, while 'insecure-resistant' babies are distressed throughout the procedure and respond to the mother with a mixture of relief and anger on her return.

The sharing of ideas between those interested in infant development and attachment issues was not limited to Bowlby and Ainsworth: Bowlby was also influential in bringing together in regular meetings other researchers from various backgrounds, including those interested in comparative psychology, such as Harlow and Hinde. The proceedings of these meetings appeared in *Determinants of Infant Behaviour* – a series of volumes edited throughout the 1960s by Brian Foss, whose own research interests lay in imitation and ethology. The second author of the present book (RS) was, as an undergraduate, lectured in ethology by Foss; on social occasions he would accompany himself on the piano and sing his own ditties on ethological themes, such as 'I'm a little fish' celebrating Tinbergen's famous stickleback research.

Work by the psychiatrist Michael Rutter was later very influential in examining more closely the mechanisms involved in 'maternal deprivation'. In a close examination of the evidence, in his 1972 book, he concluded that there were two separate aspects to the reported ill effects of separation: disruption of bonding with an attachment figure (not necessarily the mother) and privation of social, perceptual and linguistic stimulation. The former might occur in short-term situations, such as hospitalization, while the latter was a crucial factor in the case of the institutionalized infants studied by Spitz and Goldfarb. A particularly important aspect of Rutter's work was to point out that not all children are similarly affected by separations from attachment figures. Variables modifying the long-term reponse include the child's age, the length of separation, whether there are other attachment figures available, whether the separation is a result of family discord, and the temperament of the child. Thus, it was becoming apparent that the developmental implications of attachment were much more complicated than previously supposed.

Modern developments in attachment theory

Attachment theory became controversial as the twentieth century progressed, with increasing numbers of western women maintaining both careers and motherhood. The issue was raised as to whether separation from their mothers would damage young children's development. Bowlby had always maintained that the attachment figure need not be the mother, but could be a mother substitute. Later research indicated that infants could be satisfactorily attached to a wider circle of caregivers, including fathers, grandparents and others (e.g. Schaffer and Emerson, 1964). Some researchers who have examined children's social support have viewed it from an attachment framework, and studies have indicated correlations between children's satisfaction with the social support they receive from a range of providers and their psychological adjustment (e.g. Shute *et al.*, 2002).

Scarr and Dunn (1987), like Rutter, concluded that the psychological disturbance of children raised in institutions was due to a lack of human contact and stimulation, not the lack of a mother *per se*. Despite the early reports of horrified outside observers of children raised communally in Israeli *kibbutzim*, systematic research indicated that they were no more disturbed than children raised by their parents in the USA. Nevertheless, Aviezer *et al.* (1994) concluded, on the basis of assessments of attachment with the Strange Situation, that communal sleeping arrangements were problematic, and too far removed from 'natural' parenting behaviour.

With regard to alternative child care to mother care, Scarr and Dunn concluded that what matters is the quality of alternative – or, rather, supplementary – care to mother care (after all, most working parents still spend a good deal of time with their children). Good-quality care means that the parents and other carers should collaborate to provide a 'consistent and agreeable world for the child' (1987: 187). Consistency involves having routines and not too many changes of carer. Children cared for consistently by others outside the family who are sensitive to their needs develop attachment relationships with them. As noted by Robinson (1999), research that indicates harmful effects of day care on infants, such as that by Belsky, mainly comes from the USA, where the quality of such centres is not well regulated and is highly variable in comparison with that available in some countries, such as Australia; even so, most US infants in day care display secure attachment, and for those who do not, this may be a passing phenomenon when they begin day care. As Schaffer (1996) has commented, 'Children no doubt differ in the quality of the attachment relationships they form; however, the issue of the antecedents of such differences and their consequences is nowhere near as straightforward as has been suggested by many attachment enthusiasts'.

Ochiltree (1994), in reviewing 40 years of research on child care, reached similar conclusions to those of Scarr and Dunn. She raised various methodological criticisms of studies claiming negative effects of long hours of non-maternal child care, including questioning the validity of the use of the Strange Situation to examine the attachment of day-care infants to their parents; such children are quite used to being left in the care of others and being comforted by them (the same would apply to communally reared *kibbutz* children). She also observed the tendency in this literature to ignore the overwhelming body of evidence for a lack of harm and to make much of minimal negative findings (and we can add here that *kibbutz*-reared children actually experience benefits, in terms of group skills and close peer relationships). Other methodological issues included the fact that one much-quoted study by Belsky did not even measure child-care status, but assumed that the children of mothers in full-time employment must have been in full-time day care. Even as we write this chapter, the debate continues. A news report on television (22 May 2002) has again placed the emphasis on *time* spent in child care rather than the *quality* of the care, with a new Australian research thesis by Margitts claiming to have demonstrated that four or five days a week in child care, especially in infancy, is detrimental to children's development. There followed a newspaper article (Albrechtsen, 2002) and a subsequent flood of letters to newspapers supporting the notion that babies need care in the home, preferably from their mothers.

Robinson (1999) has attempted to apply the notion of attachment to the 'stolen generation' of Australian indigenous children removed from their families (see Chapter 9). She raises the question as to why many of these people have shown such deep psychological disturbance if it is indeed the case that a child does not need to be attached to a single mother figure, but is capable of multiple attachments. For one thing, such children experienced a range of stressors, such as racist attacks and various forms of abuse, as well as separation. Also, it is highly unusual for a child to simultaneously lose *all* attachment figures, as was usual in these cases. Even when siblings were removed together, it was often a deliberate policy to separate them. As Anna Freud found in studying Second World War orphans, the peer group can provide attachment figures, and the second author has heard indigenous people raised in institutions comment that other children were their lifeline. However, Robinson observes that many children may have received minimal support from peers because they too were psychologically injured. These children also generally experienced multiple placements; even if they had been securely attached to their original family members, if we assume, as Bowlby did, that attachment 'blueprints' can be updated through experience, then we might predict that multiple placements would lead children to develop internal working models of relationships as temporary. It would hardly be surprising, then, if such children grew up to have difficulties in maintaining interpersonal relationships.

Despite various challenges, attachment theory has remained an important guiding concept in developmental psychology. The Strange Situation has continued to be used (with the addition of an extra type of attachment style – disorganized), although alternative, more naturalistic, methods have also been developed. With the growing influence of lifespan approaches to development, attachment theory is also being increasingly adapted and applied to adults as well as young children, under the assumption that early attachment schemas form a blueprint for other relationships. Main *et al.* (1985) developed the Adult Attachment Interview as a means of assessing attachment style in older children and adults. A recent example of attachment research with adults is a study by Allanson and Astbury (2001), which found that insecurely, anxiously attached pregnant women reported a higher incidence of physiologically and psychologically adverse life circumstances, such as violence and emotional problems. Intergenerational links have also been suggested, with abusive mothers having internal working models of relationships in terms of power and hostility (Crittenden, 1988). An obvious problem with such research is that it is questionable how far it actually taps into early attachment relationships as data on this are collected retrospectively, and such studies focus on how the individual expresses attachment memories rather than on actual attachment events.

Freud's theory was that attachment developed *as a result of* the satisfaction of instinctual drives such as hunger, a view still supported by some biologically oriented writers (the 'cupboard love' theory of attachment –

Archer, 1999). Freud's granddaughter, Sophie, has observed that, by contrast (and in line with the object relations school), some modern psychoanalysts have replaced this idea with the notion that seeking attachment is itself the primary motivational force of human beings – 'an essential wired-in human propensity' (Freud, 1998). This is consistent with the ethological tradition, and with the ideas of modern evolutionary psychologists who have proposed that attachment theory can be seen as a major theoretical approach within the broader metatheoretical framework of evolutionary theory (see Chapter 11).

Bowlby saw grief as having evolved in relation to attachment. Attachment theorists today use the term attachment to apply not only to the child's attachment to the caregiving figure, but also the caregiver's attachment to the child – thus the term is used more broadly to apply to any affectional bond (Archer, 1999). Viewed in this way, attachment theory assists in understanding grief reactions to all kinds of losses of affectional relationships. Archer has discussed the puzzling fact that, from an evolutionary perspective, grief appears maladaptive rather than adaptive, resulting, for example, in immunosuppression and increased risk of ill-health. However, it can be argued that temporary losses and separations from loved ones are much more common than permanent ones, and that humans have evolved behaviours that serve the purpose of attempting to become reunited with the missing person – searching, calling, preoccupation, etc. – typical grief reactions. Thus grief becomes a by-product of the adaptive process of seeking to maintain important social relationships, and is the cost to be paid for the benefits of close relationships. As the UKs Queen Elizabeth II said in her condolence message with regard to the loss of life at New York's World Trade Center on September 11 2001, 'Grief is the price we pay for love'.

Attachment theory, like many other developmental theories, is open to the criticism that it has been developed within western societies and thus ignores alternative cultural perspectives (see Chapter 9), although we should recall that Ainsworth's early work was in Uganda. It has been found that Japanese infants are much more likely than US children to show resistance; however, it has been questioned whether the Strange Situation is valid in Japan, as Japanese infants typically spend 24 hours a day with their mothers, so that the situation is especially strange for them (Miyake *et al.* 1985).

As we noted earlier, recent research suggests that attachment to inanimate objects such as blankets may be specific to societies that expect infants to sleep alone, and communally reared *kibbutz* children develop satisfactorily. Ritchie and Ritchie (1979) noted that children's socialization in the West begins with an intense relationship with the mother, from which the child must gradually be 'weaned' to progress towards independence over several decades of life (being expected to sleep alone at an early age is one manifestation of this). In most societies worldwide, this is not the situation. In Polynesia, for example, a child is never required to identify with a single caretaking individual, but has multiple caregivers, including peers, and is expected to match her or his behaviour to various social environments, always having the choice to move from one to another.

The Ritchies suggest that the view of attachment as a necessary and inevitable aspect of child development has arisen from western cultures where the social structure promotes it, and where some suburban mothers are driven to the edge of breakdown by their struggle to fulfil, alone, the mothering role prescribed for them. They observe that '[m]illions of human beings have grown up without [attachment]' and query what western child development experts would make of 'a New Guinea tribe where any lactating female will happily feed a hungry child or even a pig' (1979: 155). Indeed, being attached to a number of caregivers makes good evolutionary sense in case one attachment figure is unavailable for any reason (temporarily or permanently). Nevertheless, findings from attachment research have been used to explain the abandonment of communal sleeping arrangements for children in Israeli *kibbutzim* (Sagi and Aviezer, 2001). A positive aspect of western grief and loss theory for indigenous peoples is that it is being adapted for use by Australian indigenous people to provide a framework for understanding the effects of colonization (Wanganeen, undated).

Finally, Rutter's work has been especially influential in drawing attention to the fact that not all children are affected equally by separations and other adverse situations early in life. Establishing why some children are more resilient than others has become a growing research area. Theories of the risk and resilience of children and families are being developed (e.g. Garmezy, 1985); however, there is considerable confusion in the literature about whether resilience is seen as an inborn, temperamental quality of a child, an outcome variable that results from experience in overcoming adverse circumstances or a moderating variable that influences ultimate developmental outcome in the face of risk. A recent proposal, developed in relation to youth suicide risk, is that resilience is best seen as a *process*, or pathway, that interacts with a risk pathway to determine developmental outcome (Maine, 2001).

Conclusions

The focus group students who advised us on the preparation of this book commented that they felt there was too much emphasis in psychology teaching upon what was wrong with theories, rather than on what was right. While much has been written about what was wrong with Freudian theory – indeed, Farrell (1951), a philosopher, described it as 'unbelievably bad' as a theory – we should not close this chapter without a reminder of some of its enduring legacies for understanding child development. Although there is a lack of evidence to support Freud's central Oedipal theory, his work continues to influence developmental theorizing via some of the paths we have attempted to chart above. In 1962, just over 20 years after Freud's death, Hilgard (1962) suggested that it was possible to extract some influential 'guiding ideas' from the changing writings of Freud over the years. These included the notion of the continuity of development from infancy onwards, the idea that earlier influences on later behaviour occur at an unconscious level, and the suggestion that behaviour often results from attempts to resolve internal conflicts. That these concepts remain broadly taken for granted in psychology today is a measure of the depth of Freud's influence. Freud's influence on the later development of attachment theory also remains as a major contribution to developmental psychology, and we have observed above other areas of developmental theorizing that can trace their heritage back to Freud.

Finally, it is of interest that Freud's granddaughter, Sophie, has made a connection between Freudian theory and postmodernism (Freud, 1998). Similarly to Freud, the overriding concern of constructivist theorists and narrative therapists is with the idiosyncratic meaning that individuals make of their experiences. Thus, while we noted earlier that Freud's theory was in many ways a reflection of its times, in this respect it can be said to have anticipated some modern developments in psychological theorizing.

6   Mechanism: the whole is equal to the sum of its parts

Introduction

In Chapter 3 we gave consideration to functionalism, founded by the American William James (1890). James was severely critical of 'structuralism' (behaviourism), the approach to development that forms the core of the present chapter, because he considered its outlook on human behaviour to be narrow and artificial. It is possible that no other theory of child development has been subject to such scrutiny. As Horowitz (1987: 62) noted,

> It has been declared obsolete, overthrown, and outmoded. Yet, paradoxically, this object of derision, behaviorism, has given us our most unassailable behavioral laws and provided the underlying principles from which our most powerful behavioral technologies have been derived to help the retarded, the handicapped, the dependent and the ill.

In this chapter we will describe the research and theory of a number of influential theorists including Pavlov, Watson, Skinner and Bandura, the root metaphor for whose theories is 'mechanism' (Pepper, 1942). As described by Reese and Overton (1970: 131) the mechanistic model 'represents the universe as a machine, composed of discrete pieces operating in a spatio-temporal field'. In addition, we will address some relevant aspects of information-processing theory. First, however, we provide some philosophical background.

A mechanistic outlook

The philosophical issue of the relationship between the mind and the body is relevant for a consideration of mechanism. Plato ($c.429$–$c.347$ BC) adopted a dualist position, arguing that the two were different entities. In effect he was more interested in the nature of the mind, arguing that the body was temporal whereas the mind has greater permanency with ideas living on through generations. In his book *Utopia* the mind was to be cultivated by education in order to bring some reason and order into what are often seen as chaotic ideas. Plato's theory of 'Ideas' (or 'thoughts') was developed in *The Republic*. Plato was seeking to understand the essence of things – the distinction between reality and appearance. In the seventh book of *The Republic* Plato relates a myth that represents, symbolically, the structure of reality.

> 'And now,' I said, 'let me show in a figure how far our nature is enlightened or unenlightened: Behold! Human beings living in an underground den, which has a mouth open toward the light and reaching all along the den: here they have been from their childhood, and have their legs and necks chained so that they cannot move, and can only see before them, being prevented by the chains from turning round their heads. Above and behind them a fire is blazing at a distance, and between the fire and the prisoners there is a raised way; and you will see, if you look, a low wall built along the way, like the screen which marionette players have in front of them, over which they show the puppets'.
>
> 'I see'.
>
> 'And do you see,' I said, 'men passing along the wall carrying all sorts of vessels, and statues, and figures of animals made of wood and stone and various materials, which appear over the wall? Some of them are talking, others silent'.
>
> 'You have shown me a strange image, and they are strange prisoners'.
>
> 'Like ourselves,' I replied; 'and they see only their own shadows, or the shadows of one another, which the fire throws on the opposite wall of the cave'.

What is being represented in this myth is that the cave is the world perceived by the senses, and its shadows are the things of the world of the senses. The outside world represents the true world, the world perceived by the mind of the world of Ideas. The difference between them is one of appearance and reality. Plato's identification of the mind–body split is indirectly linked to the rise of experimental science in the modern era, since the mechanistic approach rejects introspection as a method appropriate for a behavioural scientist. Subjectivism and speculation regarding entities that cannot be directly observed or measured are believed to have no place in an empirical behavioural science. As a rationalist, Plato sought to solve problems using deductive as opposed to inductive reasoning, with knowledge derived from reason, which he argued to be superior to that derived from sense perceptions alone. As every undergraduate psychology student learns, psychologists rarely call upon concepts like mind or consciousness. Plato enunciated the mind–body split and in doing so set the scene for an ongoing debate regarding the 'proper' subject of study of psychology. One significant branch of this debate will be described in this chapter.

The context in which behaviourism arose

Behaviourism developed in the context of the rise to prominence of Newtonian science in the nineteenth century. Newtonian science replaced the medieval view of the world as a living, organic, spiritual universe with a mechanistic vision of reality. In the Newtonian view of science the earlier interpretation of the world based upon introspection, revelation, reason and ordinary experience was abandoned in favour of rigid determinism and linear causality. Science delimited knowledge to a worldview constrained by statistical probability, value-free research and quantification. The presentation of science as the sole arbiter of knowledge has since come to be labelled scientism (see also Chapter 1).

Another underlying factor associated with the development of behaviourism is called materialism. A key feature of materialism was that scientific principles could be applied to the study of living organisms. To this end, physical and chemical laws were the basis of explanation – for example, physiology was reduced to chemistry. It was in this intellectual climate of scientism and materialism that pioneer psychologists such as Freud (see Chapter 5) and Pavlov were educated.

Ivan Pavlov and the conditioned reflex

Ivan Pavlov (1849–1936) was born in a small town in central Russia. The son of a clergyman, Pavlov attended the local theological seminary where his interest in science was fostered. In 1870 he began attending the University of St Petersburg. Pavlov obtained his medical degree in 1883, after which he travelled in Europe and studied with other scientists. He founded the Institute of Experimental Medicine in St Petersburg in 1890 and continued to be its director for the rest of his life. Pavlov's early research involved the physiological process of digestion, using dogs for his experiments. In 1904 he was the first Russian to be awarded the Nobel Prize for his research.

Pavlov's interest in physiology was prompted by a curiosity about how such a complicated system as the human body functioned. This curiosity fanned his determination to become an experimental physiologist. From 1902 until his death in 1936, Pavlov worked on understanding the functions of the highest nervous system. His discovery of classical conditioning as a way to view the functioning of the nervous system remains his greatest contribution to psychology. In the course of his experiments Pavlov noted certain irregularities in the normal functioning of the digestive glands of dogs. Sometimes dogs would start to secrete digestive juices before food was given – that is, as soon as the dog saw the person who customarily fed it. Pavlov's preliminary experiments were conducted by simply showing the dog bread and then giving the dog bread to eat. Eventually the dog would begin to salivate as soon as it saw the bread. Salivation when the bread was placed in its mouth was a natural reflex of the digestive system. Salivation at the sight of the bread was learned – that is, a conditioned reflex, or CR.

Further experimentation clarified the conditioning process. For example, a bell (conditioned stimulus) was repeatedly sounded before food (unconditioned stimulus) was placed in a dog's mouth to produce salivation (unconditioned reflex) until eventually the sound of a bell alone caused salivation (conditioned reflex). Only the briefest outline to Pavlov's work is provided here and you are referred to child development texts (e.g. Slee, 2002) for further information regarding the concept of the conditioned response.

Pavlov grasped that the importance of his discovery of the CR lay in the potential it provided for reducing complex behaviour to basic elements. Thus, his work lay well within the prevailing empirical paradigm of the time. As Pavlov (1928/1970: 18) wrote:

> We are becoming better acquainted with the fundamental mode of conduct with which the animal is born – with congenital reflexes, heretofore usually called instincts. We observe and intentionally participate in building new reactions on the fundamental conduct in the form of so called habits and associations, which now increase, enlarge, become complicated and refined. According to our analysis these are also reflexes, but conditioned reflexes.

From a scientific, empirical point of view, the significance of the discovery of the CR lay in its potential to explain human behaviour, for 'The conditioned reflexes which accumulate progressively during the individual life of animals and man are formed within the cerebral hemispheres' (Pavlov, 1928/1970: 20). Later in his career Pavlov worked to link the CR to an understanding of human neuroses.

New understandings regarding brain neurology have overriden Pavlov's theory that excitation and inhibition occur on the surface of the cortex: it is now understood that the transmission of neural impulses occurs along neurons and across synapses. Pavlov's theory has also been criticized for suggesting that all behaviour is the sum of accumulated CRs, but it does not appear that Pavlov made such a suggestion (Pavlov, 1932). Others, such as J.B. Watson, were certainly interested in such an idea.

John Broadus Watson and behaviourism

John B. Watson (1878–1958) was born in Greenville, South Carolina, USA. His PhD in psychology was completed at the University of Chicago where he subsequently lectured. Later he took up a position as a professor at Johns Hopkins University. Scandal led to his being dismissed from the post and in 1920 he left for New York, moving out of the academic world to apply his knowledge very successfully to the world of advertising. However, he continued to write psychology articles for popular magazines such as *Harpers* and *Cosmopolitan*. Watson strongly rejected introspection as a method for understanding human behaviour. His method was based upon the principles of objective observation of behaviour, and placed emphasis on the importance of the environment in shaping human development.

The first psychological laboratories set up in Germany and America defined psychology as the study of consciousness. Introspection or the consideration of one's own behaviour was the principal method used to discover the content of consciousness. However, in evaluating the methodology, critics quickly identified that subjects could not agree with any reliability on the description of sensation, images and feelings. At the same time Freud was arguing that important aspects of the mind were not in consciousness. In North America a literal revolution was occurring in the study of human behaviour. A range of researchers was making a significant contribution to the understanding of human development, utilizing basic tenets of the scientific method. J.B. Watson called behaviourism a 'purely American production' (1914: ix).

In brief, Watson's method involved a great deal of emphasis upon objective observation. Drawing upon his experience as a student of animal behavior, Watson claimed that the subject matter of psychology was not consciousness but the behaviour of the person. Thus, he rejected all subjective methods, relying instead solely on what could be observed or recorded:

> Psychology as the behaviorist views it is a purely objective, experimental branch of natural science. Its theoretical goal is the prediction and control of behavior. Introspection forms no essential part of its methods, nor is the scientific value of its data dependent upon the readiness with which they lend themselves to interpretation in terms of consciousness. The behaviorist attempts to get a unitary scheme of animal response. He recognizes no dividing line between man and brute.
>
> (Watson, 1913: 158)

He emphasized environmental stimuli (such as a loud noise or praise from a teacher) and the response (such as a startled reaction or on-task pupil behaviour). For this reason Watson's view of behaviour is often called stimulus-response (S-R) psychology.

There are two important aspects to Watson's view of psychology. The first is the belief that the environment is all-important. Watson argued that the only inherited features of behaviour were simple physiological reflexes (such as the knee-jerk reflex). Watson credited all else to learning, hence his claim:

Give me a dozen healthy infants, well formed and my own specified world to bring them up in and I'll guarantee to take anyone at random and train him to become any kind of specialist I might select – doctor, lawyer, artist, merchant-chief, and yes even beggar-man and thief, regardless of his talents, penchants, abilities, vocation and race of his ancestors.

(Watson, 1930: 104)

Second, Watson was heavily influenced by the work of Pavlov on the conditioned reflex. Watson wanted to explain how all complex behaviours of both animals and humans were the result of conditioning by their environment.

One of the most frequently cited learning theory experiments in psychological literature was conducted in 1920 by John Watson and his research assistant Rosalie Rayner (who was implicated in the scandal that led to his dismissal from Johns Hopkins University). They had already tested an infant, Little Albert, at nine months, and had found that he did not show any fear reactions when confronted suddenly with a white rat, rabbit, dog, monkey masks, cotton wool and so on. That is, in learning theory terms, the stimuli were neutral. The unconditioned stimulus was to be a loud sound made by striking a hammer upon a steel bar. They discovered that when the iron bar was struck behind Albert he would cry. When Albert was 11 months and 3 days old, a white rat was presented to him and as he reached for the rat the iron bar was struck immediately behind his head. Little Albert jumped and fell forward with his face in the mattress. When he reached for the rat again and his hand touched it, the iron bar was struck and once more he fell forward and began to whimper. The experiment was stopped at this point. One week later, when the rat was presented he would not reach for it. When the rat was pushed nearer he reached for it very tentatively. Thus, Watson and Rayner demonstrated learning in infancy through a process of conditioning.

An interesting aside in Watson's biography is that he reported suffering from an anxiety attack while at the University of Chicago. He observed that this experience 'in a way prepared me to accept a large part of Freud when I first began to get really acquainted with him around 1910' (Watson, 1936: 274). Watson first used William James' habit theory to explain psychoanalysis and later used Pavlov's notion of classical conditioning. He hoped ultimately to assimilate psychoanalysis with behaviourism (Rilling, 2000) as exemplified in Box 6.1.

Horowitz (1992: 360) has noted that evaluating Watson's contribution to developmental psychology is problematic given that many psychologists suggest that 'he was, at best, a psychologist concerned only with defining psychology as a natural science and, at worst, a dogmatist who went far beyond his data to popularize his beliefs about development'. Watson certainly acknowledged the biological functions of the human organism (Horowitz, 1992), but his theory focused on learning as almost entirely responsible for behavioural development. In sum,

> Watson's developmental model was exceedingly simple, containing no discussion of stages and little of sequences; there was no consideration that learning principles were in any way influenced by the age of the child. Furthermore, the developmental progression, despite the nod to structural change as variable, was linear and cumulative.
>
> (Horowitz, 1992: 361)

John Watson's theory provided a basis for shaping the nature of psychological thought in the early 1900s, particularly in North America. In fact, he was hailed as a 'second Moses' for achieving the 'promised land' of behaviourism (Magai and McFadden, 1995: 98). He also influenced parenting at the time, providing the following advice in a book on child care:

> There is a sensible way of treating children. Treat them as though they were young adults. Dress them, bathe them with care and circumspection. Let your behavior always be objective and kindly firm. Never hug and kiss them, never let them sit in your lap. If you must, kiss them once on the forehead when they say goodnight. Shake hands with them in the morning. Give them a pat on the head if they have made an extraordinarily good job of a difficult task. Try it out. In a week's time you will be utterly ashamed of the mawkish, sentimental way you have been handling it.
>
> (Watson, 1928: 81–2)

Watson himself was rather ambivalent towards parenthood, and did not display physical affection towards his own children. In Chapter 9 we will see a suggestion that Watson's cultural and personal background influenced his attitude to emotions. However, he did compare children favourably with the subjects of his comparative psychology experiments, commenting that a baby could be 'more fun to the square inch than all the frogs and rats in creation' (Buckley, 1989, cited in Magai and McFadden, 1995). Box 6.1 describes Watson's views about introspectionism and psychoanalysis.

Mary Cover Jones and behaviour therapy

Like Rosalie Raynor, Mary Cover Jones worked for Watson as a research assistant. She was not comfortable with the ethical aspects of Watson's work with Little Albert (although Watson had some reservations about it himself, this did not prevent him from joking that if Albert had problems later in life, some psychoanalyst would probably attribute it to a sexual

---

Box 6.1 Watson takes aim at Freud and introspectionism

Watson wanted no competitors and took aim at his rivals. Both Freudian psychoanalysis and introspectionism came under his fire. He regarded psychoanalysis as a rather occult enterprise, and berated its reliance on untestable hypothetical constructs and mystical notions such as the 'unconscious'. Many of Freud's observations, he felt, could be rendered in more behavioral terms. For example, affection could be restated as an 'organic sensory response', and transference as 'stimulus generalization'. Introspectionism, which was more deeply entrenched in American psychology, had to be more forcibly rooted out. In a letter to Robert Yerkes, Watson wrote that he had been experimenting with conditioning in humans and was elated to find that 'it works so beautifully in place of introspection ... that it deserves to be driven home; we can work on the human being as we can on animals and from the same point of view.

(Magai and McFadden, 1995: 98)

---

neurosis) (Magai and McFadden, 1995). Jones was more interested in the question of whether Watson's procedure could be reversed – whether a child with a phobia could be cured using conditioning principles. Jones' work in this area was seminal, representing the establishment of behaviour therapy, and yet she is hardly known today in comparison with Watson (Magai and McFadden, 1995).

John Burrhus Skinner and operant conditioning

Behaviourism as developed by Skinner has come to be known as operant conditioning. One of the most basic differences between operant conditioning and classical conditioning is that the former applies to reflexes while the latter relates to voluntary behaviour. Reflexes are called respondent behaviour, in contrast with voluntary or operant behaviour. Thus, when a dog salivates in response to food in its mouth the salivation is a reflex or a 'respondent'. Operants, in contrast, are said to occur voluntarily – they are emitted rather than elicited. Thus, operants operate on, or have an effect on, the environment, and are not necessarily associated with any particular stimulus. When you see a bird moving around in its cage, it is not necessarily responding to any stimulus. Similarly the babbling of a young baby is operant behaviour. We will not be describing the basic elements of Skinner's theory in any detail; for this the interested reader is referred to such introductory child texts as Slee (2002).

general view of information-processing theorists is that, over time, a person develops an increasingly more complex and sophisticated 'computer' (mind) for solving problems, a computer that stores more and more knowledge and develops ever better strategies for solving problems.

Dodge *et al.* (1990) have examined children's social adjustment using an information-processing approach. Thus the child is seen as confronting a particular problematic situation, such as solving an interpersonal conflict with another child via serial cognitive processes that allow her to generate effective responses. Dodge proposes five sequential steps: encoding, which refers to the individual's ability to attend to and perceive social cues; interpretation, or understanding the meaning of the cues; response generation, in order to ascertain which is the most applicable response from a repertoire of responses; response evaluation; and enactment of the chosen response.

A number of critical claims by Piaget regarding conservation and transivity problems have to do with the interaction of the *amount* of information a child receives with the *kind* of information (Bryant and Trabasco, 1971; Halford, 1982). For example, the likelihood of a child providing a correct response to a conservation problem is partly a function of how much information there is and how varied it is. The research of Keating and Bobbitt (1978) with children aged 9, 13 and 17 found 'evidence that late childhood and very early adolescence are a prime time for maturation of the information processing system' (Keating, 1980: 242).

In sum, information-processing theories have added another perspective to our understanding of children's cognitive development. In 1982 Keating expressed scepticism about the contribution of the approach, but arguably this has increased in recent years. Apart from its application to social processing, as mentioned above, the information-processing approach has been used to conceptualize how children develop gender schemas (Martin and Halverson, 1981), and to explain reading processes and dyslexia (Snowling, 2001).

Albert Bandura and social learning theory

In terms of learning theory, we have established that an individual may learn through classical conditioning (Pavlov) or operant conditioning (Skinner). Throughout their research, learning theorists have attempted to develop a theory to account for all learning, but to date this goal has proved elusive. A third possibility accounting for learning has been described by Albert Bandura and associates, and is known as social learning theory (Bandura, 1986).

Bandura (1971), and Bandura and Walters (1963) have developed a comprehensive theory to account for learning in terms of imitation. In 1963, Bandura and Walters wrote *Social Learning and Personality*

Development, broadening the scope of social learning theory with the now familiar principles of observational learning and vicarious reinforcement. They argue that not all learning can be accounted for using explanations derived from classical and operant conditioning:

> Learning would be exceedingly laborious, not to mention hazardous, if people had to rely solely on the effects of their own actions to inform them of what to do. Fortunately, most human behavior is learned observationally through modeling: from observing others, one forms an idea of how new behaviors are performed, and on later occasions this coded information serves as a guide for action.
>
> (Bandura, 1977: 22)

Their research has called attention to the importance of imitation and role models in learning. In what some psychologists have described as a classic study, Bandura *et al.* (1963) set up a laboratory study where nursery school children watched a woman model play with toys and a life-size plastic doll (known as a 'Bobo doll'). In the experimental condition, the woman played quietly with the toys for a minute and then approached the doll and began to hit, kick and sit on it along with accompanying vocalizations such as 'Pow' and 'Sock him in the nose'. In the control condition she played quietly with the toys for the entire period. During both conditions neither the model nor the watching children were directly reinforced at any time. Later, after the model had left the room, each child in turn was left alone with the toys (including the doll). It was discovered that children who had observed the aggressive model were more likely than the control group of children to act aggressively in imitation of the model's aggressive behaviour. These results could not be predicted by operant conditioning theories since there was no apparent reinforcement for the children's behaviour.

Generally, Bandura believed that existing models of learning theory were too mechanistic in outlook: 'Much of the early psychological theorizing was founded on behavioristic principles that embraced an input–output model linked by an internal conduit that makes behavior possible but exerts no influence of its own on behavior' (Bandura, 2001: 2). In this view, human behaviour is shaped and controlled automatically and mechanically by environmental stimuli. That is, behaviourism is seen primarily as a theory of performance control, rather than a theory of learning. While it can explain how learned imitative behaviour can be shaped by the prospect of a reward, it cannot explain how new response structures are developed as a result of observation. As such, mechanism undervalued the potential of individuals to affect their own behaviour. In Bandura's theory, psychological development is neither driven by inner forces nor shaped by external stimuli. Rather, symbolic, vicarious and self-regulatory processes play a significant role. For example, Dodge *et al.* propose that 'Social learning theory posits that the experience of physical abuse will lead to later aggression to the extent that it makes aggressive responses salient in one's response repertoire as efficacious in leading to positive outcomes' (1990: 259).

As reflected in his writings, by the 1970s Bandura was becoming aware that a key element was missing not only from the prevalent learning theories of the day but from his own social learning theory. In 1977 he published *Self-efficacy: toward a unifying theory of behavioral change*, in which he identified the important piece of that missing element – self-belief. With the publication of *Social Foundations of Thought and Action: a social cognitive theory*, Bandura (1986) advanced a view of human functioning that accords a central role to cognitive, vicarious, self-regulatory and self-reflective processes in human adaptation and change. People were viewed as agents who were proactive, self-reflecting, and self-regulating, and not simply reactive organisms shaped by environmental forces or driven by inner psychic impulses. Theoretically, human behaviour was viewed as the product of an interaction among personal, behavioural and environmental influences. For example, how people interpret the results of their own behaviour informs and alters their environments and the personal factors they possess which, in turn, inform and alter subsequent behaviour. This is the foundation of Bandura's (1986) conception of *reciprocal determinism*. This is the view that behaviour, personal factors (in the form of cognition, affect and biological events) and environmental influences create interactions that result in a *triadic reciprocality*. Bandura altered the label of his theory from social learning to social *cognitive* both to distance it from prevalent social learning theories of the day and to emphasize that cognition plays a critical role in people's ability to construct reality, self-regulate, encode information and perform behaviours.

Bandura has continued to develop his work, and has elaborated on the idea of human consciousness: 'Consciousness is the very substance of mental life that not only makes life personally manageable but worth living' (Bandura, 2001: 3). He posits that it is 'functional consciousness' that means the individual is very active in choosing, sorting, storing and accessing the information needed to make choices regulating everyday living.

He has also focused, recently, on the concept of human agency:

> To be an agent is to intentionally make things happen by one's actions. Agency embodies the endowments, belief systems, self regulatory capabilities and distributed structures and functions through which personal influence is exercised, rather than residing as a discrete entity in a particular place.
>
> (Bandura, 2001: 2)

He refers to a substantial body of research, which supports the view that perceived self-efficacy motivates and guides one's actions:

Perceived self-efficacy is defined as people's beliefs about their capabilities to produce designated levels of performance that exercise influence over events that affect their lives. Self-efficacy beliefs determine how people feel, think, motivate themselves and behave. Such beliefs produce these diverse effects through four major processes. They include cognitive, motivational, affective and selection processes.

(Bandura, 2000: 75)

Bandura (2001) is also particularly concerned about what he calls the 'biologizing of psychology' and the overemphasis on evolutionism (see Chapter 2). At the same time he is concerned that, in a similar vein 'the geneticization of human behavior is being promoted more fervently by psychological evolutionists than by biological evolutionists' (Bandura, 2001: 19).

Social learning theory has enjoyed wide application to various fields of the social sciences, such as education. For example, teaching is often a matter of modelling behaviours, and Bandura observed that people learn much more efficiently by the use of cognitive aids rather than by a tedious process of shaping and reinforcement (even though the latter have their place at times) (Bigge, 1982).

Conclusions

As we noted at the beginning of this chapter, mechanism has elicited strong and polarized opinion regarding its contribution to theoretical development and, more particularly, regarding its contribution to understanding and explaining human development. There is certainly little doubt that the writings of various researchers have contributed a significant corpus of knowledge, and that this continues to be applied in areas such as clinical psychology, health and education. However, DeGrandpre (2000) has argued that, presently, behaviourism is being marginalized within the broad field of psychological science. He has argued (DeGrandpre, 2000: 721) that

although principles of operant psychology certainly are constrained in their ability to provide anything resembling a complete picture of psychological experience and action, psychological science has yet to exploit the full implications of basic operant principles, especially for a science of meaning.

While information-processing theories and Bandura's work both have their origins in the mechanistic school of thought, we have seen how these represent a move towards greater organicism. Furthermore, in emphasizing the notion of personal agency, Bandura is attempting to provide a fuller and richer account of human development.

7 Dialecticism: the child developing in a social world

Introduction

As we have seen in previous chapters, organicists such as Piaget viewed development as arising from children's own actions as they experiment with the world, while mechanists saw the child as a passive recipient of environmental influences. In stark contrast, Vygotsky, Rubinstein and Riegel developed *dialectical* theories, based on the notion that development occurs as a result of a tension and interaction between internal and external influences. The most influential of these theorists is Lev Semenovich Vygotsky. He was a Soviet psychologist who developed his ideas over just ten years between the two world wars before he died at an early age from tuberculosis, leaving many unpublished manuscripts. He thus had a very short time in which to elaborate his theoretical framework, in contrast with the long-lived Piaget, who spent decades revising his theory. Vygotsky's focus was upon the development of cognition under social influence. In this chapter, we outline the dialectical approach to development (especially Vygotsky's) and some ways in which it has influenced recent theorizing in development and education.

Dialecticism

The German philosopher Hegel, born in 1770, adopted Socrates' notion of the 'dialectic' (Feibleman, 1973). This is when two people arrive at the truth through a process of debate. Hegel proposed that reality is arrived at through a dialectic between three components: a beginning position is the 'thesis', its opposite the 'antithesis', and the position arrived at in resolving the discrepancy is the 'synthesis'. The synthesis in turn becomes the next thesis, and so the process continues. Thus Hegel's philosophy concerned circular processes, with the whole greater than the sum of the parts. We will see these ideas reflected in the developmental theories of Vygotsky, Rubinstein and Riegel.

Vygotsky's dialectical theory

Although Vygotsky (1896–1934) was a deep thinker, he was also a very practical man who founded and directed a number of research institutes, including the first Russian institute for the study of children with disabilities (Kozulin, 1988). Vygotsky was committed to Marxist doctrine but his interpretation of it led to a suppression of his writings until Khrushchev denounced Stalinism in 1956. Despite this, his work had a great influence on psychological theory and practice in his own country, especially in terms of the education of children with disabilities. The work of the 'Institute of Defectology' in using his principles to foster the development of deaf/blind children – even enabling some to enter university – was beautifully illustrated in the documentary film *The Butterflies of Zagorsk* (BBC, 1990).

In his lifetime he had intellectual exchanges with Piaget, but Vygotsky's main influence on western developmental psychology is much more recent, following from the translation of his works into English. *Thought and Language* was published in English in 1962, with a foreword by the US psychologist Jerome Bruner. By the end of that decade, this text was set by Joan Wynn Reeves for one of the present authors' (RS) undergraduate classes at London University and, without doubt, had Reeves lived to write a second edition of her 1965 book *Thinking about Thinking*, Vygotsky would have featured prominently. It was not until a decade later, when an edited and translated body of his work appeared in 1978 as *Mind in Society*, that the broader psychological community began to take notice of Vygotsky's work. In the past few years, he has gained a place in undergraduate developmental textbooks, where his theory is typically compared and contrasted with that of Piaget. Possible reasons for his increasing influence in the West include republications of his work in Russian and further translations into English, an increasing exchange of ideas between US and former Soviet Union academics, and the relevance of his ideas for education (Wertsch and Tulviste, 1992). Also, his theoretical framework seemed to have come at the 'right time' in western scholars' thinking.

Central to Vygotsky's theory is the notion that human cognition has its beginnings in human social life. This idea seems to have come from previous thinkers such as Marx and Janet (who was in turn influenced by Durkheim, and also George Herbert Mead) (Wertsch and Tulviste, 1992). Vygotsky emphasized that the child develops cognitively through interactions with others, hence his theory is dialectical. He was critical of mainstream western views of education and psychology where the emphasis was on individual development and where collective functioning was generally ignored.

In his preface (1962) to the English-language translation of *Thought and Language*, Bruner observed that Vygotsky's theory represented an enormous step up from understanding development in terms of classical Pavlovian conditioning. Vygotsky built upon Pavlov's notion of the 'second signal system', which 'provides the means whereby man creates a mediator between himself and the world of physical stimulation so that he can react in terms of his own symbolic conception of reality' (Bruner, in Vygotsky, 1962: x).

Vygotsky's theory was instrumental, cultural and genetic (Holaday *et al.* 1994). It was instrumental inasmuch as it claimed that '[p]eople actively modify the stimuli they encounter and use them as instruments to control conditions and regulate their own behavior' (Holaday *et al.*, 1994: 16). As such, a feature of Vygotsky's theory was that individuals are active agents in creating their own development and learning, a feature held in common with Piaget's theory. The cultural aspect of his theory (discussed further below) was expressed through the centrality he granted to language as a cultural tool in the development of thinking. The genetic aspect of his theory (in the same developmental sense we noted in connection with Freudian and Piagetian theory) was that, through interactions with others, higher-order mental functions develop from lower-order ones.

According to Vygotsky, child development is made up of periods of relatively stable growth, crises and transformation, which implies that development passes through qualitatively distinct stages. The development of an individual can come to a standstill or even regress. Based on Vygotsky's work, Van Der Veer (1986: 528) described five stages in child development: infancy, early childhood, the pre-school period, school age and adolescence. Each of these stages is a so-called stable period preceded and concluded by a period of crisis. At around 12 months of age the toddler faces a new period of crisis or transformation which is associated with three new developments – namely walking, speech and emotional reactions. For Vygotsky, the child's language development is paramount, and he made the distinction between thought and speech development in the first two years of life. However, at about two years of age the two curves of development of thought and speech come together to initiate a new form of behaviour. In Vygotsky's view this is a momentous time in the toddler's cognitive development: speech begins to serve intellect and thoughts begin to be spoken. The onset of this stage is indicated by two unmistakable objective symptoms: a sudden active curiosity about words, and questions about every new thing; and the resulting rapid increase in the child's vocabulary.

Vygotsky also articulated a number of stages in children's conceptual development, derived from experimental work on the sorting of blocks varying in colour and shape (Vygotsky, 1934/1962). Initially, objects are sorted into unorganized 'heaps'. Later, objects are grouped in terms of functional, concrete uses, such as knife with fork and spoon (a kind of categorization that adults also use). Then come chain complexes, in which groups of objects are sorted consecutively according to certain criteria (such as shape or colour), but the decisive criterion changes over time. Then come diffuse complexes, in which the criteria for selection are fluid, and based on unreal attributes that would surprise an adult. These are followed by pseudo-concepts, which predominate in the thinking of the pre-school child: superficially, the child appears to be using true concepts, but deeper probing reveals 'flawed' reasoning; the development of pseudo-concepts is very much directed by adult language, which enables an adult and a pre-school child to communicate, but the underlying understandings may be quite different. True, abstract thought appears in adolescence, but earlier, more concrete, forms of thinking continue to operate. This latter point – that adolescents (and even adults) do not always, or even usually, operate at the highest level of abstraction, has also been demonstrated through studies designed to test Piagetian ideas about intellectual development.

Piaget's stage theory of intellectual development has very much over-shadowed the stage aspects of Vygotskian theory, which is acknowledged most for its emphasis on the social, language-driven nature of children's cognitive development, and is identified by some (e.g. Berk, 2000) as a continuity theory.

Particularly influential has been Vygotsky's discussion of *egocentric speech*. Initially, the child's behaviour is controlled by verbal instructions from others, then at a later stage the child talks aloud, especially when difficulties arise – in effect, instructing the self. Finally, these instructions 'go underground' (to use Vygotsky's phrase) and become internalized as thought. Vygotsky gave an example to illustrate how the child's self-directed speech performs a controlling function: a child was drawing a streetcar when his pencil broke; he said 'It's broken' and, using another pencil, proceeded to draw a *broken* streetcar after an accident (Vygotsky, 1934/1962). Thus egocentric speech (which Piaget saw as a by-product of thought) becomes an integral part of the developmental process in Vygotsky's theory. Vygotsky's pupil Luria and more recent researchers have experimentally demonstrated the shift in children's development from speaking aloud while performing tasks, to muttering, to silence (e.g. Frauenglass and Diaz, 1985). Today, the terms private speech or inner speech are preferred. A summary of Vygotsky's view of the relationship between thought and language is presented in Box 7.1.

Although Vygotsky placed much emphasis on language, research has indicated that some activities (especially in certain cultures) are better learned by observation (Rogoff, 1990). Imagine, for example, trying to teach someone to knit through verbal instruction alone! It is certainly the case that Vygotsky placed enormous importance on language, but his theory encompassed all forms of cultural signs and symbols. Furthermore, he made special mention of the ability to imitate as being an important sign that the child is developmentally ready to understand the task at hand (Vygotsky, 1978).

This notion of 'developmental readiness' brings us to another of the main features of Vygotsky's theory: the notion of the *zone of proximal development*. He defined this as 'the distance between actual developmental level

---

Box 7.1 Vygotsky and the relationship between thought, word and action

The relation between thought and word is a living process; thought is born through words. A word devoid of thought is a dead thing, and a thought unembodied in words remains a shadow. The connection between them, however, is not a pre-formed and constant one. It emerges in the course of development, and itself evolves. To the Biblical 'In the beginning was the word', Goethe makes Faust reply, 'In the beginning was the deed'. The intent here is to detract from the value of the word, but we can accept this version if we emphasize it differently: in the *beginning* was the deed. The word was not the beginning – action was there first; it is the end of development, crowning the deed.

(Vygotsky, 1934/1962: 153)

---

as determined by independent problem solving and the level of potential development through problem solving under adult guidance or in collaboration with more capable peers' (Vygotsky, 1978: 86). Thus, a standard mental test, such as an IQ test, is a measure of independent problem-solving (completed development), but does not capture the entirety of a child's ability: two children with the same IQ might be able to reach different levels of performance under adult guidance. Furthermore, Vygotsky's perspective implies that a child's capacity to learn is not just a property of the child, but a shared property between the child and a particular guide (socially shared cognition). Thus, a child's zone of proximal development (ZPD) might be greater with a guide who is more sensitive to the child's developmental needs.

Two important dimensions of the ZPD are 'joint collaboration' and 'transfer of responsibility'. 'Joint collaboration' is best viewed as active, shared participation for the purpose of solving a problem. The adult or peer, by virtue of greater understanding of the problem, actively facilitates or encourages the child in his or her own definition and redefinition of the problem to promote the achievement of a solution. 'Transfer of responsibility' refers to the adult's decreasing role in regulating and managing behaviour or task performance, with the child being given more opportunities to perform the task independently (Holaday *et al.*, 1994; Rogoff, 1986). While the notion of the ZPD has become influential in child development theory and education, it has also been criticized as circular; in other words, it cannot be defined a priori, but only in relation to the child's performance (it is not alone in this, however, with the behaviourist term 'stimulus' being criticized as only definable in relation to a response).

It is often said that the Vygotskian child is a 'little apprentice', in contrast with the solitary 'little scientist' of Piaget. From a Piagetian perspective, while procedures can be learned from others, this does not represent true understanding, which is demonstrated by unassisted performance (Wood, 1998). However, as we observed in Chapter 4, Piaget did maintain that social interactions between equals could be important for cognitive growth, especially with regard to the development of moral understanding. The European social psychologist Doise (1990) took up the notion that social interaction can promote cognitive development under some circumstances, but based this on Piaget's theory, not Vygotsky's. He proposed (and demonstrated experimentally) that a child can develop cognitively if her/his schema comes into conflict with an alternative schema proposed by another person, provided circumstances permit the successful resolution of the cognitive conflict to produce a more advanced schema. For this to happen, the child must already have a certain level of competence; to translate this into Vygotskian terms, this would mean the task must be in the zone of proximal development. Also, the nature of the social relationship must be one in which the cognitive conflict can be explored and resolved. Drawing upon ideas of Durkheim, Doise maintained that this can only happen in 'relations of cooperation' rather than 'relations of constraint'. In other words, if the other person uses their authority to impose their perspective on the child, cognitive growth will not occur. It is often peer relationships that permit the necessary cooperation, rather than the relationships with adults that Vygotsky saw as important for cognitive development. There is no real antagonism between the view of Piaget/Doise and the Vygotskian perspective if we take into account that an adult who uses authority to impose their view upon a child would also be an adult who, in Vygotsky's view, was not operating within the child's zone of proximal development – and, again, no cognitive progress would be expected. A crucial difference between Piaget and Vygotsky remains, however. While Piaget acknowledged that the speech of another person could spark thoughts leading to cognitive growth, the real driver of that growth is the child's own activity. For Vygotsky, however, cognitive processes are directly derived from speech.

Scaffolding

The concept of sensitive guidance for development was taken up and developed by a number of workers, who applied the term *scaffolding* to this (Bruner and Haste, 1987; Wood, 1988; Wood *et al.*, 1976; Wood *et al.*, 1978). These researchers were inspired by Vygotsky's theory to examine the tutoring of young children by adults on tasks the children were unable to perform alone. They discovered, for example, that mothers provided different levels of support for the children's performance on a block construction task, ranging from full demonstration of the task, through verbal instruction on how to do it, to simply encouraging the child to perform the task. Not all such tutoring was equally effective: for example, children often became frustrated with full demonstration (an example of adult imposition of a solution) or were given verbal instructions that were too difficult. It was found that children's learning was best promoted by providing assistance as soon as the child became stuck, and refraining from intrusive assistance when the child was making progress. Wood called such an instructional style 'contingent teaching': 'These mothers ensured that the child was not left alone when he was overwhelmed by the task, and also guaranteed him greater scope for initiative when he showed signs of success' (Wood, 1988: 79). Rogoff and Gardner (1984: 109) describe scaffolding as occurring when 'a more competent or able adult or peer adjusts the learning situation or task conditions ... to produce appropriate understanding of a particular problem for a learner at a particular level of ability'.

Rogoff has suggested that the term 'guided participation' is more inclusive than scaffolding. This term was used earlier by Bandura and others to refer to assistance provided by a trusted and encouraging companion to help children and adolescents to overcome fears, such as the fear of snakes (Bowlby, 1975: 226). As Rogoff uses the term, it involves children with 'multiple companions and caregivers in organized, flexible webs of relationships that focus on shared cultural activities' (Rogoff, 1990: 98). This acknowledges that it is not just parents who participate in the process: Vygotsky drew attention to the role of more capable peers and, in some societies, young children spend more time with older siblings and peers than with adults. Older siblings and peers can thus play a particularly powerful role in younger children's development (indeed it has recently been proposed that in all societies it is peers, rather than parents, who mainly influence children's development (Harris, 1995)).

In general terms, Rogoff suggests that the characteristics of guided participation are: the provision of a bridge between existing skills and knowledge, and those needed to perform tasks requiring new skills and knowledge; the provision of structure by the tutor; active learning; and transfer of responsibility to the learner. There need not be an intention on the part of the tutor to teach: learning can occur in this way whenever children participate in helping more capable companions to perform everyday tasks (Rogoff, 1990).

These ideas have been applied educationally and, indeed, Bruner has observed that Vygotsky's theory is as much a theory of education as of cognitive development. We noted above how Doise has used Piagetian theory as a basis for understanding how peer collaboration on a task can lead to cognitive growth. By contrast, Vygotsky's theory provides a theoretical framework for understanding peer tutoring, in which a more expert child tutors another (Foot *et al.*, 1990). Children are certainly able to teach one another in this way, and there may be social, as well as cognitive, advantages to peer tutoring. However, children's ability to provide sensitive scaffolding, such as their ability to detect misunderstandings by their tutees, is limited by their own level of cognitive development (Foot *et al.*, 1997; Shute *et al.*, 1992). The notion of scaffolding has also been used to examine how well computer programs are able to support children's learning. For example, Shute and Miksad (1997) showed that computers were as effective as teachers in promoting pre-schoolers' cognitive development, but only if the program was structured to scaffold learning appropriately.

Wood (1998) has cited research by Van Lehn, Jones and Chi in which experts' and novices' problem-solving strategies were examined. Experts, but not novices, report self-monitoring, self-correction and so forth – known as 'self-explanations'. These researchers constructed computer problem-solving simulations including both task knowledge and self-explanations, and found that when the self-explanation aspect was switched off, the computer model lost flexibility and some powers of generalizability. Wood suggests that this supports the Vygotskian notion that self-talk (aloud or silent) plays a vital role in enabling individuals to solve tasks that tax their capabilities. As Wood observes, 'Language is not simply *what* we think about but part of the thinking process itself' (1998: 108).

The notion of scaffolding has been applied to the social as well as the cognitive sphere (e.g. Kaye, 1977). An interactive social relationship exists between parents and infants from a young age, but initially it tends to be the parent who 'does most of the work'. Later, there is a sharing of responsibility, while as infants grow older they increasingly initiate and manage social interactions. In the course of such interactions, 'shared meaning' develops between adults and infants (Schaffer, 1989).

Cognition and culture

An important feature of Vygotsky's theory, as the earlier quotation from Rogoff illustrates, is that it offers a link between individual cognitive development and the culture in which the individual develops. Whereas the Soviet system was supposed to provide equal chances for everyone's development, Vygotsky and his pupil Luria found individual differences in cognitive performance between young adults, and between those varying in ethnic group and geographical location, requiring explanation (Meacham, 1999). Although Vygotsky did not provide an extensive account of the notion of culture, in broad terms he saw culture as being a product of human social activity over historical time. Such activity produces cultural 'tools' consisting of sign systems such as language, writing, numerical systems and art. Through social interactions, these sign systems mediate between the culture and the developing individual, becoming incorporated into individual mental functioning.

Vygotsky and Luria had a view that various cultures could be ranked in terms of how 'developed' they were. As we shall see in Chapter 9, it has been common practice for western psychologists to perceive their own culture as superior to others. This is illustrated by Glick's (1975) research with the Kpelle people, in which individuals were asked to classify objects such as an orange, a potato, a hoe and a knife. They classified them functionally (potato and hoe, orange and knife – in the way Vygotsky described children as classifying objects early in development). The western, abstract, response (classifying the tools together and the food items together) – which would gain more points on a typical IQ test – the Kpelle people said was how a fool would classify them. More recent theorists have developed ideas apparent in Vygotsky's own writings to argue that such differences in mental activity are better seen as characteristic of the specific setting in which they develop, and are qualitative differences rather than inherently 'better' or 'worse'. Along these lines, workers such as Wertsch and Tulviste propose that individual mental functioning can best be seen as consisting of a 'cultural toolkit' of mental processes. The link Vygotsky's theory creates between individual development and culture means that his theory has become especially popular with cross-cultural psychologists (Rogoff and Morelli, 1989).

Although Vygotsky's theory is based on a *dialogue* between the individual and the social world, he placed most emphasis on how social processes shape individual development. More recent researchers have also emphasized the role of the developing individual in influencing the world. Wertsch and Tulviste do not believe the notion of individual agency to be in conflict with Vygotsky's concepts, and unite the two perspectives by proposing that the individual uses culturally derived tools to operate upon the world in new ways. Nevertheless, creativity is necessarily constrained by culture to be 'a new use for an old tool' (1992: 555).

An aspect of Vygotsky's work that has been challenged by more recent work is his view that the cultural aspects of development initially operate separately from 'natural' development, with these two aspects only uniting around the age of two. As Wertsch and Tulviste (1992) point out, much research has clearly demonstrated that, from the earliest days, infants develop under the influence of adult speech. Vygotsky, of course, did not have the benefit of such empirical findings in devising his theory.

Another aspect of Vygotskian theory that is being given attention is the question of how far he saw development as being mechanistic rather than organismic. Despite occasional phrases in Vygotsky's writings that suggest a mechanical influence of the social environment on the child's development, Wertsch and Tulviste are in no doubt that Vygotsky did not intend this. Rather, individual agency and social influence are intimately linked in the sense that individual actions are carried out by socially determined means. This issue is one that can be illuminated by considering the theory of Rubinstein.

Rubinstein and constitutive relationalism

Rubinstein is not a name that is likely to be found in standard textbooks of developmental psychology, yet he was another prominent twentieth-century Soviet psychologist who played an important part in the development of dialectical theory. Particularly influential were books he wrote in 1940 and 1959, which addressed some of the basic questions of psychology, especially the mind–body relationship (Meacham, 1999). He drew together Marxist-Leninist and Pavlovian ideas to create the notion that the mind develops as a result of links between historical/cultural and biological aspects of development. As Meacham (1999) explains, Rubinstein did not envision this in terms of a mechanistic *interaction* between the separate entities of the brain and the sociohistorical world. Rather, the mind is a reflection of both nervous system activity and the material world, and is always in a *transactional* state with them. Thus, the mind exists only in mutual relationship to these entities. This was his theory of *constitutive relationalism*. In other words, it is the *relation* that is primary, and the entities in transaction cannot be understood – indeed, do not exist – in the absence of the relationship.

There are some present-day echoes of Rubinstein's ideas (although not attributed to him or any other dialectical psychologist) in a discussion by Herlihy and Gandy (2002) about reductionism. In line with our discussion in Chapter 2, they observe that the modern tendency is to consider neuro-biological explanations of phenomena as the 'real' explanations, with an implicit belief that 'to rely on anything but the tangible, like brain matter, somehow implies unworldly and mystical thinking' (2002: 248). Drawing upon the ideas of Marr and Rose, they raise the issue that explanations for any particular phenomenon can be given at different levels, such as bio-chemical, cognitive or behavioural. However, they suggest, it is wrong to imply that a neurological event *causes* a cognition or behaviour, and it is even misleading to speak of the relationship in terms of correlation. They propose that the biology and the psychology are only separable in the abstract, and are actually two pieces of information about the same event. They conclude that psychologists should not, nor lead the public to, consider neurological explanations as superior to cognitive or behavioural ones; rather, we should think of human beings as 'moving from one psychophysical state to another, describable on different levels by different specialists. Causation flows between these states and not between the levels of description' (2002: 251). Their concerns reflect those of others we have mentioned, such as Bandura, about the current tendency to 'biologize' behaviour.

Riegel: transactions in historical context

Klaus Riegel's contribution to dialectical developmental theorizing has been described by his associate Meacham (1999). Riegel (1925–77) was born in Berlin but later worked as an academic psychologist in the USA. In the years leading up to his early death in the 1970s he developed a form of dialecticism, disseminated through his university lectures, publications and conferences. Precursors of his theory included the work of Spranger (who proposed that individuals could only be understood in relation to their historical times), and it was Rubinstein, rather than Vygotsky, who influenced his thinking (*Thought and Language* but not *Mind in Society* appeared in English translation in Riegel's lifetime). Riegel's psychological theory was in stark contrast to traditional psychology's concern with stability and the maintenance of equilibrium. Rather, his theory was specifically developmental in nature. Drawing upon Rubinstein's transactional theory, he proposed that aspects of the individual (biological, psychological and sociocultural/historical) are in transactional relationships – each being defined in relation to all the others. A change in one aspect produces a crisis, the resolution of which results in development (which may be positive or negative). His theory was reflexive, in that he recognized that the theory should be applied to theorizing itself, which is therefore influenced by its historical times. Riegel's own times encompassed the Holocaust, the birth of the civil rights movement in America, and the publication of Jensen's controversial work on genetics and intelligence; in fact, Riegel presented what was probably the first university course in black psychology. Riegel's concern was therefore not with individuals' stability, but with their development in relation to sociocultural change.

We will take up and expand on the sociocultural theme in Chapter 9, and also mention the place of Riegel's theory in relation to integrative theories of development, in Chapter 11. It is of interest that his work is now much less well known than that of Vygotsky. This might be because his emphasis on relativism is more explicit than that of Vygotsky, and thus presents a greater challenge to traditional positivist developmental psychology. Indeed, Broughton (1987) suggested that the critical perspective on developmental psychology offered by Riegel's dialecticism has been lost in its application to lifespan psychology. He maintained that this field has 'trivialized history ... reducing it positivistically to a variable confounded with psychological change' (1987: 11).

Conclusions

A dialectical approach to children's development was proposed by Vygotsky in the early twentieth century, but not taken up beyond the Soviet Union until much later. The contributions of Rubinstein and Riegel also deserve mention, although it is Vygotsky's theory that has become the best known. Van Der Veer (1986) argued that Vygotsky made three original contributions to our understanding of human development: in his description of the crisis-like character of development, the importance he placed on the role of speech, and his emphasis on the social nature of the young child. Vygotsky's work has inspired research on the crucial role of adults and older peers in cognitive development, with a focus on process rather than structure, and has become influential in education.

Dialectical theory, in providing a link between individual development and the social world, paves the way for a greater consideration of the role of culture and history in individual development, and represents a move in the direction of more holistic and systemic views of development. In this respect, Rubinstein's and Riegel's notion of constitutive relationalism is worthy of fresh consideration. These issues will be taken up in Chapters 9 and 11.

8 The historic event: contextualism

Introduction

In Chapter 1 we gave consideration to influences that shape child development theory, including history and culture. In this chapter we examine the basic tenets of contextualism, adopting the argument advanced by Kalbaugh (1989: 4) that 'contextualism is based on assumptions fundamentally distinct from those of the dialectical (organismic) paradigm'. We can address this issue by considering the work of Pepper, which we introduced in Chapter 1 and further elaborate in the final chapter. Pepper's work embraced the idea that different theoretical positions adopted by scientists are related to different philosophical positions that they hold, which can be represented in terms of root metaphors (Pepper, 1942), including organicism and contextualism. There is some commonality between these two metaphors, in particular, the idea that 'reality is in constant flux' (Kramer and Bopp, 1989: 4). They also share an emphasis on placing activity in a given time and place. The difference is that for organicism the emphasis is on the developmental process of the organism, whereas contextualism includes the subjective context of the observer and the observed in a certain social context.

We have taken Pepper's idea that the root metaphor for contextualism is 'The real historic event' (Pepper, 1942: 232). Pepper (1942) maintained that contextualism (pragmatism) is generally associated with the writings of William James, John Dewey and Margaret Mead.

These theorists are covered in this chapter, as is Urie Bronfenbrenner, and we will also give consideration to lifespan developmental psychology. Using a contextualist approach, it will be argued that developmental change involves reciprocal or bi-directional influence (Bell, 1978), whereby an active organism is relating to a responsive context. The bi-directional nature of influence emphasizes that just as the individual is changed by the context, so the context is changed by the individual. Thus individuals are both products and producers of their contexts (Lerner, 1986).

Essentially, contextualism is based on the idea of the unique historical event. Rosnow and Georgoudi (1986) have identified four themes that are especially important in considering contextualism.

1. The historic event is the basic unit of analysis with a consequent focus on change and development.
2. The context consists of all the conditions surrounding the event. The sociocultural context in which the event takes place provides meaning to the event.
3. Variability and chance are an integral part of contextualism because contexts themselves are ultimately developing and impermanent realities. This point alone differentiates contextualism from mechanism and organicism, which are based on the assumption that the true order and unity of events can be determined probabilistically (Thayer, 1968).
4. Action and knowledge. The purposive and intentional nature of human action is emphasized in contextualism. Development, then, is an active participation in the construction of contexts that in turn impact on any future action.

William James and functionalism

Whether William James (1842–1910) was a true contextualist is open to debate, but his work certainly provides some relevant background. As we observed in Chapter 3, James, under the influence of Darwin, was the founder of the school of thought in psychology known as 'functionalism'.

The brother of the novelist Henry James, he was profoundly influenced by his father, a theologian, particularly in relation to his indifference to worldly success and his focus on addressing some of the fundamental problems of life. He rejected the idea of becoming a painter and entered Harvard University at the age of 19. After graduating he spent time in Germany, experiencing bouts of ill-health and depression, contemplating suicide at times. It seems that this was a turning point in his life, confirming for James his deep and abiding interest in philosophy. When he returned to Harvard he completed his medical degree and had a Harvard academic career that spanned the years 1872 to 1907. In 1878 he began the 12-year task of writing his *Principles of Psychology*, which was finally published in 1890 and was a significant marker in the history of psychology.

An undergradute friend was the American philosopher Charles S. Peirce (1839–1914). The writings of Peirce focused strongly on the link between theory and practice and particularly the application of philosophy to everyday life. According to Peirce, truth was discovered using the scientific method and then the next step was to apply it to solve everyday problems. Philosophical pragmatism embraced the idea that what is true will work, and highlighted the practical usefulness of discovered truth. James endeavoured to understand and apply Peirce's philosophy and in doing so refined and developed his own version of pragmatism. The pragmatic outlook appealed to the 'practical-minded' – those interested in using science to solve everyday problems. This outlook appealed to the frontier mentality of some developing western nations, such as the United States, in the early twentieth century.

Also influenced by Darwinian thought, James argued for adaptive function. According to James, the mind is revealed in habits, knowledge and perceptions:

> Sow an action and you reap a habit;
> Sow a habit and you reap a character;
> Sow a character and you reap a destiny.
>
> (James, 1890/1982)

The mind is seen as constantly engaged in interaction with adaptation to the environment. James emphasized the selective function of consciousness, holding that the 'stream of consciousness' includes ideas as well as relations among them. As a pragmatist, James argued that 'thoughts and feelings exist' (James, 1890, Vol. 1: vi).

A significant component of his *Principles of Psychology* was its trenchant criticism of the structuralist psychology originating in Germany (see Chapter 6). As elaborated by James, his main purpose was the development of a functional psychology whereby the aim was not to reduce psychology to its constituent elements, but rather to study consciousness as an ongoing process or stream. In Chapter 6 of his book James critiqued the 'mind-stuff' theory that 'our mental states are composite in structure, made up of smaller states conjoined' (1890, Vol. 1: 145). Mind-stuff theory attempted to explain higher mental states by viewing them as the sum of lower ones:

> All the 'combinations' which we actually know are effects, wrought by the units said to be 'combined', upon some entity other than themselves ... no possible number of entities (call them as you like, whether forces, material particles, or mental elements) can sum themselves together. Each remains in a sum, what it always was; and the sum itself exists only for a bystander who happens to overlook the units and to apprehend the sum as such.
>
> (James, 1890, Vol 1: 160–1)

As noted by Flanagan (1984: 42) 'Thus the mind cannot be identical to the sum of its parts because we need the mind to do the summing and to acknowledge the addition'.

Both mechanism and organicism assume some connection between events across some dimension, either temporal or spatial; there is a causal connection: 'Events are assumed to be systematically related such that each new state is both an improvement over and a transformation of the previous one' (Kahlbaugh, 1989: 77). James, however, did not advocate a theory of progress, but proposed that history was simply a collection of unrelated facts, without any assumption about what the end state would be, or that it would represent an improvement. In this respect, we can see a connection with dynamic systems theory, as discussed in Chapter 11.

In the 1940s, the views and research of a number of psychologists belonging to the functionalist school (such as Ames, 1951) began to gain attention. As we described in Chapter 3, on the basis of the research of psychologists such as Ames, perception came to be seen as resulting from the relationship between the observing person and the observed object, with context as the critical functional factor in helping us interpret the world around us.

John Dewey: active minds in cultural settings

In her review of Dewey's work, Cahan (1992: 213) concluded that 'Dewey is not well known to contemporary psychologists, nor did he exert a strong influence on the emergence of a disciplinary psychology'. With psychology's current reflections on the role of history, culture and values redressing some of the preoccupation with the collation of fact, there is a significant place for a greater understanding of Dewey's thinking. Kliebard (1995: xvi) noted that Dewey did not quite belong to any particular movement 'somehow hovering over the struggle'.

Studying under G.S. Hall (see Chapter 3) Dewey developed a rather idealist philosophy, perhaps influenced by the writings of Rousseau (see Chapter 1). This idealist philosophy was somewhat tempered by G.S. Hall who counselled against the excesses of idealism. Cahan (1992: 206) noted Dewey's 'personal craving for a philosophical system in which parts related to a whole in a manner consistent with the new evolutionary biology with its emphasis on the organism in interaction with the environment'. To that end Dewey shared a great deal in common with William James. Dewey's thinking capitalized on two significant achievements of his time, namely biology's concepts of the 'organism in the environment' and social psychology's emphasis on observing 'active minds in cultural settings'. Dewey's writings provide a counterbalance to much of the laboratory-based psychology of the time: 'folk-lore and primitive culture, ethnology and anthropology, all render their contributions of matter and press upon us the necessity of explanation' (Dewey, 1884: 57).

In his 1896 article, 'The reflex arc concept in psychology', Dewey argued against the suggestion that human beings are mechanisms made up of separate parts. Dewey also argued against those who viewed consciousness as the simple additive sum of discrete elements such as sensations. In a functional manner Dewey did not believe that stimulus and response were separate, unrelated entities, instead arguing that they were 'functionally related to each other through purposeful activity' (Cahan, 1992: 208).

For example, a behavioural interpretation of a child learning not to put her or his hand in a flame would be presented as follows. The sight of the flame would entice the child to reach for it out of curiosity, and the burning sensation of touching the flame would have the child withdrawing her hand. Any further encounter with the flame would call up the idea of the painful burn and result in the child avoiding the flame. That is, a simple association has formed between the sight of the flame and the burn. Dewey would explain the child's behaviour in a more functional manner. The child would see the attractive dancing flame in a curiosity-arousing way and the flame would not be a passive thing at all. After touching the flame and the resultant burning it would not be correct to say that the sight of the flame is associated with the pain of the burn. Rather, in a holistic way, the experience has literally changed the flame to a shining hot painful object. It is our interaction with objects as a whole that gives them their meaning. Development, then, is an active partici-pation in the construction of contexts that in turn impact on any future action.

As Schutz (2001: 269) notes, 'Dewey was convinced that understanding something involves seeing how it is connected with other things and events'. Authentic learning occurs in the midst of purposeful activity. In this regard he believed that the best learning occurred when instruction was geared to a student's interests and motivations. His approach to edu-cation involved student interest, student activity, group work and real-life experience. Thus, Dewey took a child-centred approach to education well before the introduction of open classrooms, discovery learning and the idea that there should be an activity-based curriculum.

In 1896 Dewey established and created one of the most important edu-cational experiments of the nineteenth and twentieth centuries – the Laboratory School at the University of Chicago. Dewey believed strongly that it was from our experiences that we develop our theories about the world. As noted by Cahan (1992: 207), 'Dewey warned against the excess-es and indicated the limits to the knowledge' gleaned from laboratories – a view later expounded by Bronfenbrenner, as explained later.

Margaret Mead and cross-cultural research

The American anthropologist Margaret Mead (1901–78) is widely known for her cross-cultural research and writing, heralded by the publication of *Coming of Age in Samoa* in 1928. She was a prolific author and social commentator, and was married to Gregory Bateson, anthropologist and social historian (see Chapter 4), after they met on a field trip in New Guinea.

Mead's ideas help us to appreciate the role played by culture in shaping our views of children and the family. In her book *Culture and Commitment* (1970) she called upon knowledge she had gleaned from studying children in Manus, Bali and New Guinea, following their lives into adulthood to identify three different kinds of culture: postfigurative, cofigurative and prefigurative.

1. **Postfigurative.** According to Mead, in this type of culture children learn primarily from the collective experience and history of their forebears.
2. **Cofigurative.** People living in this type of culture learn from their peers.
3. **Prefigurative.** In this type of culture adults are also capable of learning from their children, as well as vice versa.

To make a connection here with Vygotsky, we can see that his theory explicitly focused on the first two types of learning. However, his theory could be applied to the third type if we assume that, in some circumstances, children are more capable than adults (for example, one of the present authors, PS, constantly turns to his children for assistance with computing and setting the video recorder).

In her 1970 book, Mead mounted a powerful argument, based on years of anthropological research, to suggest that a number of conditions had combined to bring about the revolt of youth around the world. For the first time, there was the emergence of an identifiable world community characterized by the sharing of knowledge and an awareness of the dangers we face of nuclear annihilation. Second, advances in modern technology, while beneficial in some areas such as food production, were seriously challenging the ecology of the planet. Third, advances in medical knowledge had reduced the pressure for population increase, which in turn freed women from the necessity of devoting themselves entirely to reproduction, thereby changing their role in society and influencing the raising of children. In the light of these momentous changes, which are just as significant in the twenty-first century as they were when she wrote her book in 1970, Mead believes we are living in a present for which our understanding of the past has not prepared us: 'In the past there were always some elders who knew more than any children in terms of their experience of having grown up within a cultural system. Today there are none' (Mead, 1970: 61).

According to Mead, the young generation felt there must be better ways than those offered by the previous generation to deal with society's problems, and that they must find them. They recognized the crucial need for immediate action on world problems. Mead (1970: 73) wrote:

Now, as I see it, the development of a prefigurative culture will depend on the existence of a continuing dialogue in which the young, free to act on their own initiative, can lead their elders in the direction of the unknown. Then the older generation will have access to new experiential knowledge, without which no meaningful plans can be made. It is only with the direct participation of the young who have that knowledge, that we can build a viable future.

Of course, Mead wrote this in an era of student protests (e.g. against the Vietnam War), and it might be questioned whether the young as a whole are still as active in seeking to change the world – for example, cuts to public funding of universities in many countries, such as Australia, mean that many students are obliged to take employment as well as studying, which leaves little time for civic participation – a reminder that Mead's theory, like others, must be historically contextualized.

In summary, Mead added a strong voice and some semblance of balance to the nature/nurture debate, which until that time had favoured nature, although there has been considerable recent debate about the validity of her Samoan research, with suggestions that her adolescent participants 'pulled the wool over her eyes' in describing their sexual adventures (Freeman, 1996). We have included a brief summary of her significant contribution in this chapter because of her strong focus on culture in explaining differences in development. In this regard she shares some commonality with John Dewey, who emphasized the need to study the developing organism in context.

Urie Bronfenbrenner and the ecology of development

During much of the twentieth century, there was an emphasis on childhood as an individual process, to the neglect of social and cultural contexts (Oakley, 1972). During the 1970s, Bronfenbrenner (born in 1917) began to address this neglect. He modestly claimed that the increasing attention paid to such issues was not especially due to his work, but rather that his work represented an idea whose time had come (Bronfenbrenner, 1986). Nevertheless, Bronfenbrenner's name remains the one that developmental psychologists most closely associate with the shift at the end of the twentieth century towards recognizing the influence of environmental contexts on children's development, a shift that can be traced to the publication of Bronfenbrenner's 1979 book *The Ecology of Human Development*. As we have noted elsewhere in this book, Bronfenbrenner had earlier criticized developmental psychology as being 'the study of the strange behavior of children in strange situations for the briefest possible period of time' (Bronfenbrenner, 1974), and argued instead for the importance of studying children in the real contexts within which they develop.

Bronfenbrenner argued (1979: 21) that:

The ecology of human development involves the scientific study of the progressive mutual accommodation between an active, growing human being and the changing properties of the immediate settings in which the developing person lives, as this process is affected by relations between these settings, and by the larger contexts in which the settings are embedded.

He was also advocating a closer connection between child development research and public policy.

He envisaged the child as developing within a nested series of contexts, like a set of Russian dolls, although students of psychology often recall him as 'the man with the circles' – a reference to the two-dimensional visual representations of the interacting layers of the environment surrounding the child as a series of mutually influential concentric circles. The layers of the environment are as follows.

1. **Microsystem.** This is made up of the individual characteristics of the child and the various setttings within which the child is embedded – family, school and neighbourhood, to name but a few.
2. **Exosystem.** These settings do not impinge on the child directly but influence the child because they affect one of the microsystems, e.g. extended social network of friends, neighbours, the media.
3. **Macrosystem.** These settings refer to the much larger cultural or sub-cultural environment in which the child lives. The term refers to the values and mores that are part of the broader environment, e.g. in Australia being raised within the context of a particular ethnic group such as Greek, Italian or Vietnamese.

The role of the individual child in development has been stressed much more strongly in more recent versions of Bronfenbrenner's theory. The individual child possesses various unique characteristics that interact with the child's environment. In terms of these unique characteristics Bronfenbrenner describes the most important as 'developmentally instigative'. That is, these characteristics are capable of influencing other people in ways that are important to or have an impact on the child. For example, a child with poor social skills who irritates and agitates others around him/her will have a different impact in their social milieu than a child who has a more amenable set of social skills.

Bronfenbrenner argues for a transactional view whereby the child and the environment continually influence one another (Bell, 1978). For ex-ample, consider the child mentioned above who irritates and upsets others. The child's behaviour has an impact on the parents' behaviour, leading them to greater degrees of frustration, which means their interaction with the child is increasingly agonistic. In turn, this has an impact on the child's behaviour towards the parents. The parents may seek out the help of a paediatrician. The child may be diagnosed with ADHD, and prescribed medication and psychological treatment. The child's behaviour may now have a less negative impact on those around him/her, which in turn results in others' seeking out the child more and being more positive to him/her. Bronfenbrenner argues that these types of transaction are best studied *in situ* and not in the laboratory environment.

Bronfenbrenner has adopted the notion of the 'developmental niche' (see Chapter 2) in relation to his belief that the child assumes a very active role in his or her development. For example, a child who enjoys reading at school will seek out like-minded individuals who share this developmental niche. In turn, in actively seeking out such individuals the child shapes and selects her or his own experiences.

Bronfenbrenner has also added another system, the 'chronosystem', to take account of history and time, which shape development. For example, over time ideas about ways to discipline children have changed how parents raise their children.

There is no doubt that Bronfenbrenner's model has influenced theorizing and practice concerning children's development within various contexts, e.g. Hart *et al.* (1998) and Box 8.1. We further consider his contribution, especially how it has developed more recently, in Chapters 9 and 11.

Lifespan development

As we identified in Chapter 6, a contrasting view to the idea that the individual is actively involved in his or her development is the idea of the passive organism influenced by the environment. However, the notion of change across the lifespan, and the concept of perfectibility and transformation have a long history dating back to Aristotle's idea of action, to the Renaissance Man ideal and, latterly, to the German 'understanding psychology' of Dilthey (Brandtstadter, 1998). Despite this long history, developmental psychology has not paid great heed to 'the developing individual's contribution to the creation of his or her own developmental

---

Box 8.1. An illustration of Bronfenbrenner's theory

The general principles of Bronfenbrenner's theory of interconnecting systems is illustrated in the following research conducted by Irving (1998) with Australian parents and children. Irving gathered information about four to seven year olds' social networks and peer relations using parental diary reports. Her findings identified that while, as expected, mothers played a central role in the arrangment of their children's peer contacts, other adults, including family friends and relatives, also had a significant role to play. Furthermore, the location and extent of young children's peer contacts was influenced by social and cultural values.

history over the life span' (Brandtstadter, 1998: 807), possibly because of developmental psychology's preoccupation with the formative period from birth to adolescence. Early approaches to infant socialization adopted a uni-directional model, in which emphasis was given to the parents' influence on the child's development.

However, in 1974 Lewis and Rosenblum (1974), in a significant publication, addressed the question of how infants affect their own development. In another important paper by Richard Bell (1978) child development researchers were alerted to consider infant socialization as a bi-directional process. Investigators are now more aware of infants' ability to participate in and influence the outcome of their socialization. Infants are not simply passive creatures who are moulded and changed by their caregivers, any more than caregivers are unresponsive to infant behaviour. In a review of the infant's social world, Lamb (1977) concluded that there is very little support for the belief that infants are passive recipients of socializing stimulation. Not only are there marked individual differences apparent at birth and consistently thereafter; infants are also shown to play an active role in modulating their interaction with the social world. This notion of the active individual, adapting to changing circumstances, is central to lifespan psychology.

Lifespan developmental psychology is a contextually oriented psychology with the core assumption that development is not completed at adulthood. Rather, ontogenesis continues across the entire life course, and the notion of development is adapted and used to encompass the idea of lifelong adaptive learning (Baltes et al., 1998; Harris, 1957; Wohlwill, 1973). The scene was set for lifespan theory by Baltes (1979: 1) when he wrote, 'There can be no strong field of lifespan developmental psychology without a solid foundation in and connection to childhood. By the same token, the study of child development does not exist in a vacuum, but is vitally enriched by considering the aftermath of childhood'.

The contextual model developed by a number of authors draws on the work of Pepper (1942) discussed earlier in this chapter. The twin notions of 'constant change' and 'embeddedness' emphasize change as promoting change. As Lerner (1983) notes, the organism is conceived of in relation to, or in transaction with, its context.

Recent research into infant neurobiological development has emphasized plasticity in development. By contrast with other organisms with a lower ratio of association-to-sensory fibres (Hebb, 1949), which results in a higher correlation between sensory input and behavioural output, human behaviour is less stereotyped in nature. That is, human behaviour bears a lower correlation between stimulus input and behavioural output. This situation means that the individual and social system have high regulatory requirements. Lerner and Stefanis (2000: 476) have argued that 'the regulation by individuals of their relations with their complex and changing context is the process involved in successful development across life'.

Conclusions

In this chapter we have focused on contextualism as a means for under-standing human development. Contextualism is significantly different from either mechanistic or organismic views of development. We have taken Pepper's (1942) idea that the root metaphor for contextualism is the real historic event in all its dynamic activity. To this end we have examined the contributions of a number of different theorists, some of whom are more strongly identified with contextualism than others. The writing of Margaret Mead, for example, has been included here because of the contribution she made to highlighting the significance of culture in understanding and interpreting development. In this, she shares some affinity with the writings of John Dewey. There is no doubt that contextualism has had, and continues to exert, a strong impact on the study of child development today, especially under the influence of Bronfenbrenner's theorizing.

9 Sociocultural influences on development

Introduction

We saw in the previous chapter how certain theorists acknowledged the importance of environmental contexts in children's development. The total context consists of all the conditions surrounding an event, including the physical and social world. In Bronfenbrenner's account, the outermost 'ring' of the environment is the sociocultural context within which the inner environmental systems operate. It is this sociocultural context, according to Georgioudi and Rosnow (1986), that gives meaning to the event. However, the field of child development, as understood by ourselves and (presumably) most of our readers, is a product of western society, and so it can be questioned how far theorizing about development is truly sensitive to sociocultural issues.

Vygotsky's dialectical theory (see Chapter 7) is nowadays given a prominent place in child development textbooks, and provides a framework for understanding how language-based cognitive processes, especially, are determined by culture. Nevertheless, it remains the case that our understanding of child development is based almost entirely on a very narrow sample of the world's children, namely those from North America and western Europe. Criticisms of the underlying assumption of universality – that theories of child development that have arisen within these cultures can be applied to children worldwide – are gradually gaining influence. Indeed, the very scientific status of developmental psychology has been questioned, on the grounds that the discipline neglects the majority of its subject matter and, even when expanding its horizons, applies a particular value system that prizes above all individualism and cognitive competence (Nsamenang, 1999). This emphasis places traditional models and methods of developmental psychology at odds with the interdependence that is central to most cultures of the world, and neglects socioemotional development in favour of rational thought. As Nsamenang and others have noted, western writings often carry the implication that alternative notions of childhood are faulty, thus leaving them open to accusations of racism.

It seems to be the case, therefore, that whenever one tries seriously to address questions about culture and development, one inevitably becomes embroiled in philosophical, epistemological, ethical and political issues, as will be apparent in this chapter.

Culture and development

By and large, developmental psychology is written by western researchers, and conducted on western people – mainly from the United States, with some influence from other parts of the English-speaking world (Burman, 1994). There have also been highly influential western European contributors, such as Freud and Piaget and, increasingly, the West is recognizing the Soviet tradition embodied by Vygotsky.

Despite the overwhelming bias towards US samples and values in developmental research, it is nevertheless the case that some very influential work recognizing the role of culture in development has emerged from the United States, notably from individuals with strong overseas links. We saw in the previous chapter how the anthropologist Margaret Mead, on the basis of many years of fieldwork, identified the characteristics of different kinds of culture that shape children and families. Bronfenbrenner, too, as we observed above, included culture as an overarching environmental influence on development. As Ritchie and Ritchie (1979) noted, Bronfenbrenner's 1970 account of the importance of peer influences on children's development in the USA and Russia was greeted with great interest, while the same point had been made by cross-cultural psychologists, but gone unrecognized, for the previous 30 years.

An important figure in this area is Erik Erikson, whose theory we briefly mentioned in Chapter 5. He was born in 1902 in Germany of Dutch parents and moved to the United States as an adult. He was influenced by Freud (undergoing psychoanalysis with Freud's daughter, Anna) and by Mead. He is probably best remembered for his emphasis on stages of development throughout the lifespan, but he also made an important contribution to understanding development in relation to culture. In his book *Childhood and Society,* first published in 1950, he described his work with the Sioux and Yurok, indigenous peoples of North America. In contrast to typical western approaches to indigenous peoples as primitive or infantile, he recognized that they had their own ways of dealing with the world and bringing up their children. He argued that stages of development are marked by the resolution of normative crises resulting from the interaction between the biological plan for the species and the cultural environment.

Vygotsky also made a great contribution to understanding sociocultural influences on development. Although, like Piaget, his focus was on cognitive development, for Vygotsky this development was inseparable from the influence of more experienced members of the culture. The Vygotskian recognition of the importance of learning from others, and the co-construction of learning within the zone of proximal development, is illustrated by Pere's (1982) description of how New Zealand's Maori children are taught cultural tasks:

> Within the Maori context, the teacher–pupil relationship is an intimate one based on high expectation with both the more learned and the learner working together on a set task. For example, a grandmother teaching her grand-daughter(s) about the mythology and art of finger weaving…. The pupil(s) and the teacher are in a position jointly to evaluate the ongoing process and development of their efforts. When the pupil proves that she has learned the necessary skills, knowledge and understanding to perform the task on her own, both teacher and pupil are then ready to move on to another task.
>
> (Pere, 1982: 67)

As we saw in Chapter 7, Vygotsky's theory of thought was that the interpersonal becomes internalized as the intrapersonal, so that the way a person thinks is inculcated through linguistic interaction with others, the nature of which is culturally determined. That cultural differences can operate even at the perceptual level was brought home to him when he discovered that, in Uzbekistan, the visual illusions that fooled city folk did not work. Vygotsky's work was little recognized by western developmentalists until the 1980s.

While Vygotsky's theory acknowledged that culture plays an integral role in development, developmental researchers have often seen sociocultural variables as something to be *controlled* in studies to enable 'pure process' to be observed. A shift from this type of thinking is becoming apparent, however, in the direction of thinking about the place of social environmental variables as something to be *studied* to enable development to be understood. This shift is acknowledged by the more recent versions of Bronfenbrenner's theory described in Chapter 11. Bronfenbrenner and Morris (1998: 1016) provide a quotation from a 1995 work by Steinberg and colleagues that makes this point well:

> [I]t made no sense at all to control for ethnicity, social class, or household composition in an attempt to produce 'pure' process. No process occurs outside of a context. And if we want to understand context, we need to take it into account, not pretend to control it away.

Like Bronfenbrenner, the dialectical psychologist Riegel developed his theory in the USA in the 1970s (see Chapter 7). Influenced by the earlier Soviet-based work of Rubinstein rather than Vygotsky, he maintained that it was inappropriate to study the isolated individual as the focus of development: rather, the individual can only be understood in relation to historical and societal changes related to issues such as demography, political structures and majority/minority group relations. Thus, the individual does not just exist within the boundaries of the body, but within a 'psychological space' that encompasses interactions with family, friends and the broader culture (Meacham, 1999).

In a similar vein, Joan Miller (1999) draws a distinction between eco-logical perspectives and the approach of cultural psychology. The former sees culture as merely providing a context for development: development happens through universal processes and mechanisms, with culture merely providing specific content. The cultural approach, by contrast, is con-cerned with shared meaning systems, so that psychological notions such as 'mind', 'self' and 'emotion' are themselves culturally created and under-stood. From the perspective of cultural psychology, cultural practices are not based only on adaptive considerations, but may be non-rational, such as when members of a culture refuse to eat certain animals for cultural rea-sons although they are edible. Thus, psychological explanations need to take account of not just the person and the ecological context, but also the culture.

Indeed, culture itself can be seen as subject to evolutionary processes: rather than viewing humans as 'biologically complete hominids' who 'sud-denly invented culture' (Miller, 1999: 87), the cultural view sees culture itself as a factor contributing to evolutionary selection. Thus, apart from some innate propensities in infancy and some involuntary responses, devel-opment must occur within a cultural setting for most psychological processes to develop. This more radical approach owes much to the views of the dialectical psychologists and, as Miller observes, presents a major challenge to the Piagetian theory that development occurs independently of enculturation. Rather, research indicates that the stages and end-points of cognitive development are dependent upon the provision of culturally specific support.

One anecdotal example we are aware of is that Australian Aboriginal children in some remote communities, who 'should' be in the concrete operations stage, have a well-developed understanding of abstract econom-ic principles derived from their involvement in a local economic system based on bartering six-packs of beer. Formal research can provide similar examples. In general terms, Miller points out the need to recognize that all research findings are dependent upon the constructs that underlie them, and that these may be culture-specific. She suggests that cultural psych-ology may best be seen not as a separate area of inquiry within psychology, but as a perspective that can inform whatever field is under consideration.

It is certainly the case that mainstream developmental psychology pays far more attention to cultural influences on development than previously. A cross-cultural study of infant temperament (de Vries, 1984) was (by chance) particularly telling in terms of the differing perceptions about chil-dren that parents in some cultures hold in comparison with western researchers' beliefs. The notion of differences in temperament between infants was being studied, researchers in the USA having established that infants vary in how easy or difficult they are to manage. The researchers applied their temperament criteria to infants of Masai parents (people of Kenya and Tanzania). Then, a tragic drought occurred in which many infants died; it turned out that the survivors were the 'difficult' babies, who had, presumably, demanded more frequent feeding than the 'easy' babies and survived as a result. Furthermore, Masai parents valued more assertive characteristics in children, perhaps the very characteristics that US parents regarded as difficult to handle, but that promoted survival for the Masai. Thus, a characteristic that is valued in one culture may not be highly valued, and may even be detrimental to survival, in another. This illustrates the notion of 'goodness-of-fit' between a child's propensities and the environment in determining development (Thomas and Chess, 1977).

Parental ethnotheories, or parental belief systems, are now being proposed as a way of capturing the link between cultural forces and parenting practices (Harkness *et al.*, 2001). Researchers draw upon both anthropology and developmental psychology (following in the footsteps of Mead and Erikson), and note the need for tolerance of research methods coming from different traditions. This cross-cultural approach aims to elicit the often implicit theories that parents have about the correct way to raise children. As Ritchie and Ritchie (1979: 147) noted,

> ... socialisation is not conducted in terms of the literature on child development but in terms of cultural goals. Adults everywhere want their children to grow up not simply to be good human beings in universal terms but to be good people in their own cultural terms.

In the new millennium, the beliefs of middle-class parents and teachers across seven western countries are being investigated through the Parenting-21 project. Although some have argued that the sample is too homogeneous for this to constitute a true cross-cultural study, differences in parenting beliefs between, and in some instance within, countries, have emerged (Harkness *et al.*, 2001). For example, Dutch parents value rest, expect their babies to sleep through the night at an early age and have babies who sleep long hours; US parents, by contrast, value both rest and stimulation, have more trouble settling their babies to sleep and have infants who in fact sleep less than their Dutch counterparts. Thus cultural influences are apparent even in a behaviour as heavily biologically determined as sleep.

With an increasing recognition of such cultural differences, Nsamenang (1999) has proposed that editors of textbooks and journals, and scientific panels, should have multicultural audiences in mind. As Australian researchers, we are often made acutely aware that there is still a long way to go. Our research samples appear to be perceived by international (generally US) journal editors as oddities, and we are frequently requested to specify in the titles of our journal articles that the study is Australian. By contrast, US authors are rarely required to specify this in their titles, presumably because they are perceived by the journal editors as the norm. One of us also has the experience of having a paper rejected by the editor of a journal solely on the grounds that the topic was no longer relevant to a US readership because of US policy changes – the fact that the journal had an international readership, that the issue was still a major consideration elsewhere in the world, or that US readers might benefit from exposure to overseas experience, was apparently not of interest. In such ways do the guardians of knowledge unwittingly operate to perpetuate a particular hegemony.

One psychology or many?

Considering such matters – the factors that determine which articles find their way into journals, and how cross-cultural issues are portrayed – leads us into some radical territory. Some workers considering cultural influences on development question the very philosophical basis of psychology, an issue we originally raised in Chapter 1. This view represents a change in epistemology from the modern, positivist tradition to which most psychology students are still exposed in their education, to a postmodern perspective. The explicit recognition that cultural, historical and political factors are crucial in developmental psychology is part of a broad, emerging field under the name of 'critical psychology'. This term is being used to cover a variety of areas of endeavour, such as feminist psychology, which have been around for some years, but existed at the margins of the discipline (Ussher and Walkerdine, 2001). We will consider feminism further in the following chapter. From a postmodern perspective, subjectivity, ethical and power issues are central, and qualitative methods provide the major methodological approach.

Burman (1994) has reviewed developmental psychology from a critical perspective. She observed that, in the mid-nineteenth century, non-western peoples, along with infants and animals, were studied as examples of the 'primitive' mind, thus serving the perspective of European (especially British) imperialists that their own race was superior. This perspective continued into the twentieth century. Even Vygotsky, who did so much to foster understanding of cultural influences on individual thought, regarded some cultures as inferior to others (Wertsch and Tulviste, 1992). More subtle and implicit inferences that some cultural achievements are to be valued more highly than others can still be found. For example, in writing about theories of children's language development, Garton and Pratt (1998: 68) observed that

> The empiricist and nativist theories ... cannot adequately account for
> the development of reading and writing. These latter aspects are

definitely not innate, since there are cultures where the written word does not exist. Indeed, the development of reading and writing can be regarded as an indication of a culture 'coming of age'.

We mentioned above our own experience of US culture being taken as the norm, and Burman observes that this is also apparent in the organization of child development textbooks – for example, developmental tasks across the lifespan are culture-bound (Havighurst explicitly acknowledged this). With increasing recognition of cross-cultural issues, textbooks often contain a cross-cultural applications section, but Burman maintains that the underlying message is that the processes and stages described are universal, with only the *content* varying cross-culturally. She notes, for example, that cognitive development is often linked in texts with physical development, giving it pride of place after the biological, with emotional development seen as secondary (we will return to the theme of emotional development theories later).

Dudgeon and Pickett (2000), writing about psychology and reconciliation between Australia's indigenous and non-indigenous communities, have similarly observed that, like anthropology, psychology is based in western culture. While purporting to be objective and apolitical, it is in fact a value-laden discipline, based on individualism and granting only a peripheral role to cultural contexts, largely ignoring historical, cultural and social factors. Psychology promotes individualism to the neglect of the community and family welfare, which are central to many indigenous cultures. Nsamenang (1999) has similarly observed that developmental psychology is a scientific endeavour rooted in a particular culture and worldview, and as such cannot be divorced from it. However, alternative psychological perspectives such as community, narrative and discursive psychology are now appearing, which recognize issues such as as multiple truths and social justice, and are explicitly concerned with social change and valuing the marginalized (Dudgeon and Pickett, 2000). Thus, rather than speaking of a universal 'psychology', the possibility is raised of the development of specific psychologies.

This recognition of the value of alternative perspectives has extended to calls for psychology not to remain isolated from other relevant disciplines (Gridley *et al.*, 2000) and, from the perspective of critical psychology, that psychology as a discipline should entertain critique based within social, political and cultural analyses of today's world (Bendle, 2001). Such a perspective has implications for the work of mental health professionals: culturally competent practice includes acknowledging and accepting cultural differences and biases, recognizing racism and oppression in society, and acknowledging the fact that the mental health professions are unavoidably political (a point also raised by feminists).

These views follow from a consideration of the epistemological issues raised by Teo (1997), as discussed in Chapter 1, and also from an acceptance of Vygotsky's theory: if thought is culturally determined, why would a system of thought such as developmental psychology be exempt? Riegel, too, specifically maintained that developmental theorizing must be understood in relation to its sociohistorical context. Such a perspective throws up serious challenges to traditional developmental psychology, which aims not only to produce universal truths about development, but sees the researcher as a neutral observer. Nsamenang comments that western psychologists 'tend to focus more on measuring research participants, they rarely listen to them in their own terms' (1999: 164). Nsamenang's perspective is in accord with Taft's (1987) advice that developmental psychology would benefit greatly from taking into account alternative sources of information, including historical, demographic and anthropological.

Nsamenang supports the use of 'participatory and interpretive research that values both qualitative and quantitative methodologies' (1999: 164). The developmental psychology literature remains firmly grounded in traditional science and quantitative methods, but postmodern approaches and qualitative methods are slowly gaining ground. For example, in our own work on aggression in children and adolescents, we have come to value both approaches: quantitative data can capture succinctly differences in types of aggression across ages and gender (e.g. Owens, 1996), while in-depth qualitative investigations complement this by providing deeper insights into participants' experiences of aggressive behaviour (e.g. Owens *et al.*, 2000). However, fence-straddling can be decidedly uncomfortable! Most psychologists remain firmly quantitative, and the debate between the two sides continues (see, for example, a series of discussion papers on qualitative psychology in a special issue of *The Psychologist* edited by Henwood and Nicolson, 1995). We will revisit these issues in the following chapter, on feminism, and in Chapter 11 we will examine whether it is possible to reconcile the positivist and postmodern perspectives.

Culture, history and developmental theories

Let us at this point examine further the criticism that developmental psychology has tended to neglect historical influences. As mentioned above, Bronfenbrenner observed that culture is more stable than the inner ecosystems, but nevertheless, it does change, and this change was central to Riegel's theory of development. According to Ho *et al.* (2001), researchers often overlook this, treating culture as if it is 'frozen in time' – a background variable to be controlled. They use changes in the People's Republic of China since the mid-twentieth century to illustrate how traditional parenting practices are being challenged by various historical forces. In the case of China, these include increased openness to western ideas, official ideology and the one-child policy. Their research indicates that

Chinese parents are increasingly turning to western-influenced psychology for guidance on raising their children, resulting in a move towards more child-centred, individualistic ideals, with the pressure on children to achieve academically causing much distress. In contrast with the typical western finding that poverty places children at greater risk for poor developmental outcomes, more behavioural problems in China are found among the children of the rich. Finding such a difference within 'the world's largest geopolitical community' makes it much more difficult for western commentators to dismiss such results as anomalies to be found occasionally in small, exotic communities (Goodnow, 2001).

If we accept the need to consider the role of culture in developmental psychology theorizing and practice, and that culture is not frozen in time, then there is clearly an important place for a historical perspective for creating a deeper understanding of the field itself. As Valentine (1998) has observed, although 'psychology par excellence does not occur in a social or political vacuum', history and philosophy are often marginalized, for reasons such as a positivist inheritance and an emphasis on short-term gain (1998: 167). It is certainly the case that child development textbooks, including this one, generally give a brief description of various views of childhood that have existed in previous historical times. This in itself demonstrates that views of childhood are changeable and relative, and yet the implication generally seems to be that, now that we have reached the era of scientific understanding, we are finally on the right track and nearer to the truth. What we generally fail to stop and consider are issues such as why those particular figures became influential, or why certain theories have gained prominence over others (after all, history is written by the winners). We have already seen, in Chapter 2, that close analysis indicates that Darwin may not be as strongly deserving of acclaim as a founder of developmental psychology as is often claimed. Here, we will consider a further example of how historical and cultural factors conspired to influence theorizing about a specific area of child psychology: emotional development.

Magai and McFadden (1995) have observed how the long-held view in western culture that the emotions are inferior to the intellect, and need to be tamed, is reflected in the history of the study of emotional development. For example, John Watson, who performed the famous experiment on conditioned fear with Little Albert in 1920, gave advice to parents on child-rearing that advocated the avoidance of 'mawkish sentimentality' (see Chapter 6). It has been suggested that Watson's stance was influenced not only by prevailing western approaches to emotion, but by his own upbringing, which combined religious fundamentalism with an alcoholic father prone to violent outbursts. The topic of emotional development became increasingly neglected during much of the twentieth century. This was reflected in its gradually being squeezed out of child development textbooks over the years, and in the difficulty reported by researchers on emotion, such as Carroll Izard, in gaining funding and becoming published in the area (he reported receiving dismissive reviews of papers he submitted to scientific journals, and having to maintain his academic reputation by undertaking research on cognition).

As well as demonstrating how the western belief in the superiority of cognition over emotion influenced the course of child development research, Magai and McFadden have provided an enlightening analysis of how historical factors influenced twentieth-century theorizing about the development of infant emotions. Watson's proposal that infants express three basic emotions (fear, rage and love) was disputed in the 1930s by Kathryn Bridges, who maintained that the emotions of young infants are initially undifferentiated, and only become differentiated gradually through a process of conditioning. Her work was later criticized for its lack of descriptive detail of infant behaviour and her use of institutionalized infants, who are unusually lacking in emotional expression, as we saw in Chapter 5. Nevertheless, her theory of emotional development was accepted for many years and completely overshadowed research undertaken by another woman, Charlotte Bühler, whose work demonstrated the existence of discrete emotions in infants. Her research included painstaking, detailed observational work and experiments, including one that was, in effect, the first demonstration of object permanence in infants. Yet how many psychology students today have heard of Bühler? The first demonstration of object permanence is firmly ascribed to Piaget, whose work, in terms of experimental rigour, was arguably outstripped by Bühler's.

The influence of these three individuals on child development theory appears to have resulted from historical factors, with Bühler working in the German language and remaining untranslated into English, while Piaget's work was translated from French into English from the 1930s onwards. With English-language publications being the most influential in developmental psychology, Piaget became known as a 'giant' of developmental psychology, Bridges' notion of undifferentiated emotions held sway for many years, and Bühler's work has remained little acknowledged, even in modern German-language accounts of the history of emotional development, which have drawn upon English-language accounts.

An exercise such as Magai and McFadden's is a historical and not a scientific one, but can it be denied that it throws valuable light upon theorizing in developmental psychology? It shows us how certain theories and theorists gain credence and others disappear because of cultural factors such as prevailing views about which topics are worthy of publication, what languages are influential and, as we shall see in the next chapter, the gender of the researcher. To use Bronfenbrenner's language, there may be much value in paying closer attention to the chronosystem as it applies to the development of our discipline.

Indigenous psychology

Interest in indigenous psychology – especially in the experience of indigenous people themselves – is very new in the history of psychology. This area of inquiry can only thrive when members of the dominant culture are prepared to recognize the impact of colonialism on indigenous peoples. This is consistent with Riegel's perspective that individual development can only be understood in relation to cultural and historical change, and the relations between majority and minority groups. As recently as 1988 the International Congress of Psychology, held in Australia, was devoid of indigenous content, a fact raised by a New Zealand community psychologist at the closing ceremony (Gridley *et al.*, 2000). This galvanized some Australian psychologists into action, so that by the turn of the millennium articles on indigenous issues were published in journals of the Australian Psychological Society. Furthermore, non-traditional types of journal article and review processes were accepted, guidelines for psychologists working with indigenous peoples had appeared and Aboriginal issues and presenters have regularly been included in conferences. It has also become usual for conferences to include a welcome from local indigenous elders, although we know of one dispossessed Kaurna elder who will only 'greet', not 'welcome', visitors on to her traditional land, on which our university has been built. The editorial of a special issue on indigenous issues of the journal *Australian Psychologist* (Sanson and Dudgeon, 2000) noted that in some of the articles the authors had chosen to be explicit about their own background. This recognition of subjectivity (that disclosure of where a writer is coming from personally is relevant to the understanding and interpretation of their writing on psychological matters – and that journal editors should encourage this) represents a radical and, as yet, rare, shift from the traditions of science.

If indigenous psychology is new, then the specific area of indigenous *developmental* psychology barely exists. However, given the various arguments that culture is a crucial influence on children's development, it is important to consider broader issues, such as history and ethics. For example, Davidson *et al.* (2000) raise the issue of what should be done with a century of psychological research on indigenous peoples which those peoples regard as an aspect of colonial oppression, and question whether social responsibility (a moral precept) is compatible with science. They observe that twentieth-century research on indigenous Australian people was typically based on identifying 'deficits', which were attributed to genetic and cultural inferiority to the majority culture. Similarly, in New Zealand, considering the educational difficulties of Maori children, 'the dominants assume they are dealing with quirks of personality or ethnic traditions created in pre-European history when most often they are dealing with modern class problems which are largely the creation of the dominants themselves' (Burch, 1967, cited in McDonald, 1973).

In the Australian case, Aboriginal children's cognitive and motivational 'shortcomings' with regard to education, and the 'incompetence' of Aboriginal parents, were identified by western researchers, and gave succour to arguments for the removal of Aboriginal children from their parents. Evidence from Aboriginal people and others that many children (predominantly those of mixed ancestry) were indeed removed from their communities and placed in white families, leading to intergenerational social and psychological problems, was presented in a Royal Commission report *Bringing them Home* (HREOC, 1997) and dramatized in the film *Rabbitproof Fence*. Yet, at the turn of the millennium some (white) influential Australian voices were continuing to question the existence of stolen generations of indigenous children. In this regard, the issue of the privileging by the dominant culture of written evidence over oral history has further marginalized the histories of indigenous peoples.

Researchers working with indigenous peoples have been challenged by the constructivist movement away from a universalist approach to indigenous psychology (Davidson *et al.*, 2000). These writers observe a disillusionment with mainstream psychological approaches to indigenous issues, born of concern that traditional approaches were not delivering benefits to indigenous communities together with a growing awareness of ethical obligations to give research participants greater involvement in research aims, processes and outcomes. They take up the issue that psychology's position as a value-neutral science is being challenged by the view that psychology cannot be apolitical and value-free because it is itself a cultural phenomenon.

Despite the assertion referenced in Chapter 2 that developmental psychologists often have melioristic aims, Davidson *et al.* cite examples from the USA, Australia and South Africa to support the argument that it cannot be assumed that psychology will automatically work towards social justice (indeed, South Africa's leading advocate of apartheid, Verwoerd, was a psychologist). Members of the dominant culture tend to see that culture as being the national culture, ignoring the perspectives of other groups within it (Davidson *et al.*, 2000). How well this is illustrated as we write this chapter, on Australia Day weekend: the *Weekend Australian* newspaper incorporates a major feature on the British explorer Matthew Flinders (for whom our university is named) who undertook the first circumnavigation of Australia 200 years ago. The paper headlines this as 'our greatest voyage' (*Weekend Australian*, 26–27 January 2002). How might an indigenous reader, with a history of dispossession by the British of land, language, culture and family, respond to this?

Nsamenang (1999) has suggested that it is necessary to integrate traditional psychology with indigenous psychologies and to take account of the subjectivity of the researcher. An article by Clark (2000) is an example of a study by an Aboriginal person, with Aboriginal participants, using a constructivist framework but also drawing upon mainstream social psychological theory. The politicohistorical context of the participants' experience (e.g. government policies concerning Aboriginal people) is outlined. Participants were asked about their experiences with regard to being taken away from their families as children. The dominant theme to emerge concerned confusion over identity while growing up, with all participants seeking, recovering and/or maintaining their Aboriginal identities, while also experiencing other identities. This can be viewed in terms of self-categorization theory, which 'emphasises the dynamic and contextual nature of self and identity that are always the outcome of a particular social relational context' (2000: 152). See also Box 9.1.

Drummond (personal communication) has described three models of human development derived from different cultures. It is interesting that she takes Bronfenbrenner's ecological theory as an example of a western model, since it is clearly not typical in that it explicitly sets out to encompass a broad range of developmental environments – in other words, to be

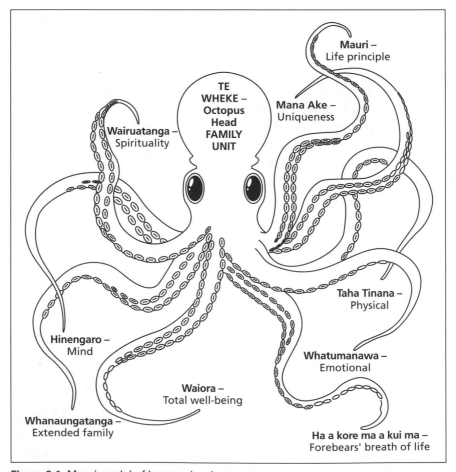

Figure 9.1 Maori model of human development

cross-culturally applicable. The systemic nature of Bronfenbrenner's model, with its dynamically interacting levels of analysis, can be seen to have parallels in another model of development described by Drummond (personal communication), specific to the Maori people of New Zealand and developed by Pere (Figure 9.1). This is based on Te Wheke, or the octopus, with tentacles representing various aspects of Maori life such as spirituality, material and bodily needs, and *Mauri* (life principle), which includes respect for the environment. The intertwining tentacles represent connections between these various aspects, and the interconnectedness and mutual reliance of the parts on one another is very reminiscent of systems theory (see Chapter 11).

A major difference can be identified, however, between the Bronfenbrenner and the Maori model: Bronfenbrenner's scheme of nested levels of the environment places the individual at the centre, whereas the head of the octopus represents not the individual, but the family unit. Factors unique to the individual are placed within a single tentacle; while inseparable from the whole, giving sustenance to the whole and receiving it, the individual is not at the centre. By comparison, we can see how the individual-centred ecological systems model still bears the hallmarks of the western thinking that influenced its development.

Drummond also describes a Philippine model of development, centring around church, family and broader community, and reflecting aspects of both Asian identity and western influence resulting from colonization and, to western eyes, containing many paradoxes, such as the coexistence of strong women and machismo, and Christianity and belief in spirits.

Box 9.1 The five 'worlds' of Aboriginal adolescents: culture and cognition creating each other

... five major worlds ... are significant for Aboriginal adolescents as they seek to form their personal and cultural identity ... the family, the Aboriginal community, the wider society, peers and the school.... Each world has a virtually limitless series of patterns and models for identity and cultural formation, including a range of expectations about values, beliefs, behaviours, and different patterns of control, relationships and communication. Between each world there are real or potential boundaries created by individual and group perceptions of the value and importance of the other worlds and their members. Within each world there are tensions as individuals and groups challenge accepted values and norms, seeking to create their own identities and cultures.

(Groome, 1995: 18–19)

Earlier, Ritchie and Ritchie (1979) also observed apparent contradictions in Polynesian society, such as admiring individual prowess but also valuing cooperation. They cited Redfield's proposal that the very 'work' of culture might be to reconcile such inconsistencies, but also expressed concern about the infiltration into Polynesian society of western-based literature on good parenting. Drummond similarly observes that today's globalized world is exposing people to alternative views of development, with contemporary Maori writing on human development incorporating ideas such as Vygotsky's notion of the zone of proximal development, and Bruner's concept of scaffolding. These notions are clearly consonant with their own cultural experiences, as illustrated by the example early in this chapter of how Maori children learn finger weaving.

Conclusions

Nsamenang considers the notion of culture so central that he defines developmental psychology as 'the science of human development in context' (1999: 163). We have observed in this chapter an increasing recognition by western psychologists of the centrality of cultural influences on development through theorists such as Vygotsky and Bronfenbrenner. This has involved a shift towards attending to cultural influences rather than simply controlling for them. We have also attempted to outline some of the very fundamental challenges to traditional developmental psychology put forward by postmodern, critical and indigenous perspectives. We believe that theories and knowledge gained through the traditional scientific method are very valuable, but provide only a fragmentary picture of development. While there is evidence that western developmental psychology is influencing indigenous psychologies, it is heartening to observe that this is not a one-way street representing yet another aspect of colonialism: western developmentalists are increasingly willing to recognize alternative perspectives that come from listening to, rather than simply experimenting on, peoples from various cultures. It is to be hoped that such cross-fertilization of ideas will be enriching to all.

10 Listening to different voices: feminism and developmental psychology

Introduction

We discussed previously the fact that Darwin is often cited as the father of the field of child development, even though this claim may not stand up strongly to close scrutiny (see Chapter 2). Darwin's pre-eminent position as the writer of the first child study – a diary account of one of his own infants – can also be challenged by the fact that there were many earlier such observational diary studies, including many by women, which have been overlooked by history (Bradley, 1989, cited in Burman, 1994; see also Pollock 1983). Indeed, as we noted in the opening chapter, a gendered approach to child study was soon apparent, whereby fathers, but not mothers, were seen to have the necessary emotional detachment to carry out proper scientific studies of their children (Burman, 1994).

We closed Chapter 5 by acknowledging some of the lasting contributions of Freudian theory to understanding children's development, while also recognizing the lack of support for his Oedipal theory. According to that theory, the young girl believes she has lost her penis, the ultimate compensation for this being to produce a baby (the penis–baby equation). Fisher and Greenberg (1996) suggest that what this is all about is the female being obliged to orientate herself in a male-centric, phallically defined world. She must 'construct an illusory maleness' (1996: 165). They suggest that this is an example of women being required to define themselves in comparison with male body standards, as discussed by the prominent feminist psychologist Sandra Bem (1993).

These two examples serve to illustrate that the field of child development 'is associated with the rise of science and modernity, subscribing to a specific, gendered model of scientific practice' (Burman, 1994: 10). Until very recently, girls' and women's values and experiences were missing from developmental psychology (with the notable exception of the emphasis on mothers, rather than fathers, as parents). The fact that women's and men's worlds differ in many ways was illustrated as I (RS) was drafting this chapter, when my 21-year-old daughter arrived home from playing in a soccer

match. Her team lost 2–0 and she ruefully explained that she was responsible for letting in one of the goals. She had apologized to her team-mates,
and I asked how they had reacted. She said that the team as a whole had
accepted responsibility for letting the ball reach the opponents' goalmouth,
and the person who had let the other winning ball get past also admitted
her part in the team's loss. While not all women's teams might react like
this (and some men's teams might), on the whole we both suspected that a
male soccer player in her position could have expected a rather different
response. It has become something of a truism that males' social relationships are concerned primarily with status, and females' with affiliation
(although truisms should always be viewed with healthy scepticism, as will
become apparent later in this chapter!).

Feminists argue that women's experiences, values and contributions
have been sidelined historically, and are beginning to raise some very fundamental questions about the masculine (androcentric) approach taken to
theory, research and practice in developmental psychology. However, it is
our experience (supported by comments by Rosser and Miller, 2000) that
feminism is given at best a marginal place in the teaching of developmental
psychology, and unless they have taken topics in fields such as women's
studies or sociology, many of our readers will not be familiar with it. We
therefore begin this chapter by outlining the common themes of feminist
theories, and then present an overview of the different kinds of feminist
theories and their relationship to developmental psychology. All question
patriarchal assumptions about what should be studied and how, and what
the underlying mechanisms are, with profound implications for theorizing
and research in child and adolescent development. We go on to discuss
feminist views on research methods, metaphors and the theorizing behind
clinical practice, and also explore whether feminist theorizing might benefit from a consideration of the work of developmental psychologists.

Common themes of feminist theorists

Feminist scholars have come from a wide range of disciplines, and there is
no single feminist theory (Griffin, 1995). Nevertheless, some common
themes can be discerned that have relevance for developmental psychology. We have drawn here upon Worrell and Etaugh's (1994) analysis,
which identified six such themes.

1. Almost all feminist theories challenge the tenets of traditional scientific
   inquiry in the ways we identified in the first chapter. For example, it is
   maintained that science is not objective and value-free, and that a broad
   range of data-gathering methods should be recognized as valuable.
   Qualitative methods are especially valued.
2. There is a focus on the lives and experiences of women. For example,
   women are seen as worthy of study apart from the standard of male

norms; gender differences are examined from the perspective of social-ized power differentials and research questions relevant to women's lives are explored.

3. There is a view of power relations as the basis of patriarchal political social arrangements. For example, it should be recognized that women's social status results from unequal power distribution and not their deficiencies.

4. Gender is seen as something to be analysed, rather than an explanation of difference in itself. For example, the situational contexts of gender as an active process structuring social interactions should be examined.

5. There is concern with the role of language, including explicit 'naming' of otherwise hidden phenomena, such as sexual harassment, restructur-ing language to be inclusive, and reducing the public–private polarity in women's lives.

6. Finally, there is a common concern with social activism, such as recon-ceptualizing theories, methods and goals, in the interests of promoting gender justice.

Specific feminist theories and developmental psychology

Although these common themes are identifiable, there are nevertheless important differences between various feminist standpoints. Rosser and Miller (2000) have discussed these and examined their relationship to developmental psychology, although it should be noted that only one of the theories (psychoanalytic feminism) is specifically developmental.

Liberal feminism is the variation that developmental psychologists have been most open to, presumably because it does not question the tradition-al, positivist approach to developmental inquiry, but rather seeks to make it more inclusive. An example is the extension of Kohlberg's research on moral development by Carol Gilligan to include notions of care and responsibility (Gilligan, 1982). Gilligan's groundbreaking work in this area was triggered by dissatisfaction with Kohlberg's male-based model of moral development, which was derived from a longitudinal study of Chicago boys. Indeed, Kohlberg proposed that women's moral develop-ment was limited by their inability to see beyond personal relationships (Kohlberg, 1971).

Gilligan observed that women were dropping out of Kohlberg's univer-sity classes on moral development because the perspective he presented was not relevant to their own experiences. Gilligan's research indicated that women's view of moral dilemmas lay in a consideration of conflicting responsibilities rather than rights, although more recent research suggests that care and justice perspectives are not the exclusive preserve of either gender. Gilligan's contribution in broadening perspectives on moral development is well accepted in mainstream developmental psychology and her work regularly gains a prominent place in developmental texts. Her broader importance lies in the fact that she has alerted psychologists to the neglect of female experiences in developmental psychology.

Types of feminism other than liberal feminism question positivism and the possibility of scientific objectivity. Developmentalists appear to be either less familiar with, or less receptive to, these more radical ideas (Rosser and Miller, 2000). Feminism's concern with social justice takes on different emphases in different approaches. Marxist and socialist feminism are concerned with the oppression of women on the grounds of both class and gender. This approach draws attention to a covert value system that privileges certain topics and interpretations in developmental psychology over others. For example, the negatively toned finding that sons of single mothers were 'less masculine' than those raised with fathers actually reflected the fact that they were less aggressive, which can be seen as positive (Rosser and Miller, 2000). They also suggest that socialist feminism is consistent with Vygotskian concepts of development – indeed, Vygotsky's very interest in the social, rather than individual, origins of cognitive development reflected his Soviet background.

Other forms of feminism, such as African-American feminism, place more emphasis on race and ethnic issues, while postcolonial feminism maintains that patriarchy continues to influence countries that were previously colonized by western oppressors. Developmental psychology has given little consideration to such cultural changes, however, as we discussed in the previous chapter, with specific reference to the experience of indigenous Australians.

Essential feminism does not appear to have a strong place in developmental psychology. It emphasizes biological differences between men and women, something which most feminists have fought against – for example, viewing sociobiology as providing a rationale for female inferiority/ keeping women in their place. Existentialist feminists, by contrast, argue for the social contruction of gender – that it is not biological differences, but societies' interpretations of them, that lead to women being defined as 'the Other' in contrast to male norms. Many examples of this exist in the developmental literature, such as in the concept of 'mastery' and in androcentric definitions of aggression (Rosser and Miller, 2000). There is also the example of Freud's Oedipal theory. Feminists often fought against Freudian notions of biology as destiny, but there has been some interest in object relations (see Chapter 5) with regard to the construction of gender and sexuality. Rosser and Miller make a link with another issue raised in that chapter: the recent notion of infants' 'working models' of the self, others and relationships developed through interactions with their caregivers.

Radical feminists maintain that women's oppression is the deepest and most widespread kind, with men dominating most institutions, including science. The historical privileging of male baby biographers such as Darwin over mothers' accounts is an example of this; we might also note that, despite the pre-eminent role of mothers in bearing and rearing children, the field of developmental psychology has identified a father, rather than a mother, figure as its originator. Radical feminists reject existing scientific and theoretical frameworks and focus upon women's experiences in women-only groups, and support education in all-female environments. Little developmental research has taken female experiences as a starting point, Gilligan's work being a notable exception (Rosser and Miller, 2000). On the contrary, Piaget paid very limited attention to girls in his research on moral reasoning, as he could not understand the relational nature of their games; he focused instead upon boys' games of marbles and their understanding of rules. Thus, Piaget's theoretical framework privileged masculine, as well as rational and western, forms of reasoning (Burman, 1994). Box 10.1 addresses another suggested link between Piaget's research and masculine values.

Postmodern feminism rejects the universality of the female in favour of diversity of experiences. It also challenges the assumption of 'progress' towards a defined end-point (e.g. adult standards of functioning) and emphasizes instead discontinuities, regressions and diverse pathways and end-points. Coming from a very different perspective, we will see these ideas also reflected in dynamic systems theory, in Chapter 11.

Box 10.1 Did the space race influence developmental psychology?

The socialist-feminist focus on the power of the dominant group raises the question of why, in developmental psychology, certain topics, subject groups and interpretations of data are privileged over others. ... Does this privileging reflect the interests and values of a dominant class of middle-class white males? In the 1960s and 1970s, developmental psychologists' receptivity to Piaget's focus on children's scientific concepts may in part have reflected anxieties about the position of the United States in the cold war, including the space race with the Soviet Union. Concerns about the effects of working mothers (but not working fathers) and 'cocaine mothers' (but not 'cocaine fathers') on development imply blame on only part of the population. Day care and latchkey children are seen as a problem of working mothers but not working fathers. ... These examples suggest that a covert social value system steers developmental psychology.

(Rosser and Miller, 2000: 16–7)

Of these varieties of feminism, Rosser and Miller say that liberal feminism provides the weakest challenge to traditional developmental psychology, and postmodern and radical feminism the strongest. They also suggest that feminist theories could well take a more developmental perspective, an idea we expand on later. For example, radical feminism could take the experiences of girls as well as women as their starting point. An example of such an approach is our own qualitative work with Larry Owens in exploring teenage girls' experiences of social aggression (e.g. Owens *et al.*, 2000). While we have succeeded in publishing this work in mainstream psychology journals, it has not been without receiving along the way occasional referees' comments to the effect that this research would be excellent if only it were quantitative.

Methodology

This brings us to the issue of methodology. As we have seen, most versions of feminism challenge the epistemological underpinnings of traditional scientific inquiry. For example, the dichotomy between the objective observer and the research subject breaks down into a concern with inter-subjectivity between researcher and participant (Griffin, 1995). What has been called feminist-standpoint research is concerned with reducing any power differential that favours the researcher. It acknowledges that no research is value-free and explicitly considers the effect of the researcher on the participant. In ensuring that participants' voices are heard, qualitative methods such as interviews, focus groups and discourse analysis have particularly been favoured, as they provide the opportunity for more open-ended gathering and interpretation of data than do quantitative methods. Griffin suggests that it would be beneficial to focus more on the political aims of research in empowering women, rather than expending too much energy debating the nuances of various qualitative methods.

In any case, feminism in general has focused on women rather than children and, clearly, such methods have their limitations when working with children. Try holding a focus group with one year olds! Obviously, other methods, such as observation, must be used in some circumstances. The concern with intersubjectivity still holds true, however, and the researcher must be conscious of her or his own impact upon the child. As we discussed in Chapter 4, this lesson was learned through Margaret Donaldson and her colleagues' now-classical demonstrations (such as the 'Naughty Teddy' study) that how a young child performs on cognitive (Piagetian) tasks depends upon the child's understanding of the social context surrounding the task (Donaldson, 1978). Ways in which interviewers in various contexts (including research) can take account of children's perspectives and linguistic skills have been discussed in a useful book edited by Garbarino and Stott (1989).

While not arguing with the general feminist push in favour of qualitative methods, Hyde (1994) has pointed out that no research method is, of itself, sexist or feminist, and that quantitative methods can also serve feminism. What matters is the theoretical framework for the research, the questions posed, the interpretations made and the application of the findings. She and others have undertaken meta-analyses of results of studies in a number of areas to debunk some popular myths about gender differences. For example, she examined the textbook 'fact' that boys perform better than girls at maths, meta-analysing results from studies with over three million people in total. The result showed a small difference dropping to a non-existent one in the more recent research, with the magnitude of difference varying by ethnicity. This is consonant with the concern of many feminist psychologists, that issues of race/ethnicity and social class need to be considered along with gender. The 'fact' that females are biologically predisposed to outscore males in verbal ability has also been challenged by meta-analysis; again, the gender differences found have shifted historically from small to non-existent. Hyde raises the question of how such shifts could occur over time if the differences were biologically determined. This kind of analysis is extremely valuable for demonstrating biased synthesis and reporting of research findings but, of course, it cannot address bias in other issues such as selection of research questions, selection of studies for publication or, as we discuss below, the metaphors used in publications.

Psychologists in the quantitative tradition are often highly suspicious of qualitative methods, seeing them as providing an undisciplined approach to research. It is possible, however, to adopt qualitative methods which meet standards of rigour that are analogous to those applied to quantitative research, such as reliability and validity, although such an approach would be rejected by many postmodernists. Readers are referred to a useful paper by Sandelowski (1986), which outlines this approach, and to our papers with Owens on girls' aggression, which exemplifies it.

Metaphors

As we mentioned above, one of the concerns of feminism is the use of language and how it defines our thinking. Scholnick (2000) has discussed the notion of metaphor in developmental theorizing, on the basis that metaphors reflect choices about what aspects of development are to be highlighted. She describes four metaphors used in developmental theory, arguing that these reflect masculine values such as rationality, conflict and hierarchy.

Two of these metaphors concern how change occurs. The first is 'argument' – that development occurs through a series of confrontations between different perspectives, one of which wins following a tussle. Examples include Kohlberg's view that moral development arises from engagement in moral disputes, and the Piagetian notion that new, higher-order schemas are formed through resolving the contradictions between clashing schemas. The second metaphor for developmental change that she discusses is 'survival of the fittest'. An example is the connectionist view of neural pruning in early brain development in terms of competition between nodes and connections.

The other two metaphors concern the direction of change. One is the 'arrow' metaphor of development as launched (like a military attack) from a starting point, passing through consecutive points until it reaches the target of maturity. Scholnick suggests that this metaphor reflects three modern concerns of developmental theory: biology (the launcher); ideal cognitive solutions; and linearity. The fourth metaphor is that of 'building', with lower-order functions providing the platform for building higher-order ones. Again this implies linear progression, with obstacles being overcome to reach a superior position. Scholnick maintains that the traditional, masculine metaphors produce a picture of 'an abstract, timeless, universal child' (2000: 40).

Scholnick proposes some alternative, feminine metaphors for covering the same developmental ground as the masculine ones that are generally employed. One is 'friendship' rather than antagonism, reflecting respectful negotiation between parties who come from different perspectives. She claims that such notions are creeping into developmental writing, with a breakdown of the notion of warring dichotomies such as nature *versus* nurture and an increasing recognition of mutuality and cooperation – a theme we take up in Chapter 11 in our discussion of reciprocity and systems theory.

The second metaphor, related to the first, is 'conversation', as both a means of creating cultural meanings and as a way of conceiving of development. Unlike arguments, which are about conquering through seeking vulnerabilities, conversations promote growth through intersubjectivity. Perhaps this is what the focus group students who discussed this book with us were getting at when they said they were frustrated with only being told what was *wrong* with developmental theories. They are not alone in their concerns about the university culture of critique (Tannen, 2000).

Scholnick's third metaphor is 'apprenticeship', as used by feminist theorists, Vygotsky and later cultural developmental psychologists. Rather than the fittest surviving in a given environment, the picture is of the novice being encouraged by experts in that environment to succeed in it.

Finally, there is the 'narrative', or storytelling metaphor, which acknowledges that narratives take roundabout paths and regressions, and do not just proceed linearly. It also permits metaquestions such as who is the listener or the narrator (whose 'voice' is speaking).

Despite initial appearances, Scholnick is not falling into the trap of setting up yet more false dichotomies (masculine vs feminine metaphors), but suggests that both may have a place and create balance in what has, until now, been a very unbalanced field of inquiry. The value of presenting alternative metaphors is in inviting reflection about how knowledge is acquired, understood and valued, both in terms of the field of inquiry itself (developmental psychology) and in our understanding of the development of children's own knowledge. It enables us to stand back from our traditional positivist position and see things we normally overlook about how the field of developmental psychology came to be as it is, and how it might be different and richer.

Theorizing behind clinical practice

While feminist theory has certainly influenced professional practice with children and adolescents in the education system (e.g. Gilbert and Gilbert, 1998; Mills, 2001), we are not aware that clinical child psychology has been similarly affected. However, feminism has touched adult clinical psychology and family therapy. Whether we prefer to understand children's development through a social learning theory framework, a Vygotskian one or a systemic approach, we can propose that how women are conceptualized and treated clinically will indirectly affect girls (and boys) through its effects on the family and broader social contexts in which they are growing up. We take two examples here of how feminism has impacted upon clinical psychology: the origins and diagnosis of mental disorder, and family therapy.

The American Psychiatric Association's *DSM* project is concerned with classifying individuals as having/not having a mental illness, and determining which diagnosis or diagnoses are applicable to them, on the basis of predetermined criteria (this is an example of Pepper's 'formism' metaphor). In Chapter 2, we commented that the *DSM* project, while purporting to be scientific, has been criticized as being based on clinical judgement influenced by covert social and political agendas. Feminists have been especially active in criticizing aspects of this project as being damaging to women, and have succeeded in influencing the process (Butler, 1999; Franklin, 1987).

For example, in the mid-1980s, there was a move to include 'masochistic personality disorder' in the revised third edition (*DSM-III-R*) of the manual. Feminists, including psychologists working with women and children subjected to domestic violence, were outraged, as the diagnosis could have been used to pathologize those suffering in abusive relationships. For example, women's failure to leave abusive partners could be attributed to their seeking gratification through suffering, rather than because of a realistic fear of severe retribution against themselves or their families (many women who do leave are relentlessly pursued and even murdered by their former partners). Such a perspective would locate blame for the situation with the victim rather than the perpetrator of the abuse. Even changing the name of the 'disorder' to 'self-defeating personality disorder' did not silence the critics, since its 'symptoms' (such as turning down opportunities for pleasure and engaging in excessive self-sacrifice) captured the traits society fosters in women, such as being deferential and putting others' needs before one's own.

Blaming women in regard to mental illness also took another form, in theories that attributed disorders such as schizophrenia and autism to poor mothering. Damaging terms such as 'refrigerator mother' were used. Feminists raised awareness of this 'blame the mother' syndrome. Something of a reversal has been observed of late, with (absentee) fathers being blamed for the psychological ills of their children (Edgar, 1998), although the overwhelming assumption remains that mothers, and not fathers, are responsible for their children's welfare, as evidenced by the debate on out-of-family care discussed in Chapter 5.

Family therapy is not concerned with diagnosing mental disorder, but views the child within the context of reciprocal relationships between members of the nuclear family. Theorizing in family therapy has been profoundly influenced by feminist theory, introducing the important notions of power and gender hierarchy, as well as insisting that women's experiences should be heard (Gladding, 1998). The pioneers of family therapy included only one woman, Virginia Satir, whose theoretical contribution did not receive the recognition it deserved, in comparison with other schools of family therapy (Breunlin et al., 1992). A number of reasons have been proposed for this: she was the only female (and only social worker) in the field; her approach was a relational one, concerned with communication; and there was a general lack of recognition of women's contributions to (western) society at the time family therapy was beginning, in the middle of the twentieth century (Breunlin et al., 1992). These authors point out that it was 1975 before the first feminist critique of the field appeared, and that paper (by Humphrey) was ignored. It was as late as 1978 before a paper by Hare-Mustin appeared that had a major impact, and that was followed by numerous further critiques. The Women's Project in Family Therapy (Walters et al., 1988) was especially influential.

The central issue raised by feminists was that, in emphasizing reciprocal relationships between family members, family therapists had made the assumption that all parties had equal options for changing the relationships, ignoring the gender inequality in society which meant that, in practice, women had less power than men. As a result of clinical experience and research, including work on domestic violence, the behavioural marital therapist Jacobson came to realize that this power differential could not be ignored (e.g. Jacobson, 1989: 32):

> Marital therapists come face to face on a daily basis with the products of an antiquated, patriarchal marital structure which

manifests itself in a power differential almost always favoring men. ... when a therapist knows that they are observing a structure which oppresses women, they can not help but either contribute to the perpetuation of that oppression or ally themselves with its removal.

Prior to such realizations, although family therapy theorists had taken the important step of moving beyond conceptualizing psychological dysfunction as an individual process, they had ignored broader societal issues impacting upon family relationships.

Feminists were critical of a number of central aspects of family therapy theory. It had been accepted previously that the therapist should remain a neutral observer (like the objective scientist), but the feminist challenge was that therapy can never be value-free and, as Jacobson observed, a therapist who fails to challenge sexism implicitly condones it. They also seriously challenged the accepted notions that power is merely an illusion and that there is an accepted hierarchy within family relationships, both of which supported the status quo and female oppression. Breunlin *et al.* described such notions of hierarchy as 'outdated, unethical and unhelpful' (1992: 245), and the idea of enmeshment (overinvolvement between family members) as 'conceptually and politically archaic' (1992: 246) – it, in effect, blamed women for taking on the role in the family historically allotted to them. For all these reasons, some feminists simply regarded family therapy as inappropriate, but others, such as Breunlin *et al.*, took the concerns on board and incorporated feminist notions into their theorizing and practice. It has been suggested that the next step from specifically feminist therapy is 'gender-sensitive' family therapy, which incorporates a broad understanding of gender in society, with such issues central to the training of therapists (Gladding, 1998).

A developmental perspective on feminism

It will have become obvious above that theorizing about links between developmental psychology and feminism is a very recent enterprise, with feminism focusing upon adult women rather than girls. While we have discussed some ways in which feminism might affect developmental psychology, it is clear that the reverse – the potential for developmental psychology to inform feminism – has been paid even scantier attention. Indeed, Gilligan's contribution and that of (outdated) psychoanalytic theory are the only ones regularly mentioned in feminist writings (Scholnick and Miller, 2000). Scholnick and Miller provide examples of some of the potential contributions that developmental psychology could make, including cognitive theorizing about categorization and reasoning, parent–child relationships and perspective-taking. Here, we give a couple of examples to illustrate their ideas.

There is common ground between feminists and cognitive developmental psychologists in dissatisfaction with classical models of categorization (the 'formism' metaphor applies again here). Feminists are dissatisfied with dichotomous (and value-laden) male/female labels and, in support of feminist concerns, cognitive researchers have demonstrated that people's actual categorization of objects is fuzzier than formal logic would predict. Nevertheless, people may readily draw upon stereotypes, such as gender stereotypes, as these are more accessible and easier to process. Gender schema theory can also contribute by explaining why individuals are biased to select information consistent with the stereotypes they have learned (Martin and Halverson, 1981). Vygotsky's theory (see Chapter 7) could also be helpful in explaining how children are socialized by more experienced members of the culture, such as parents, and internalize culturally defined social prescriptions, such as gender roles, in the process. However, children do not passively imbibe these typical cultural lessons: their understanding of gender can be transformed by interactions with those with alternative perspectives, and through their own efforts to make sense of the world, in the ways proposed by organismic and systemic theories.

These examples serve to illustrate Scholnik and Miller's contention that developmental psychology can offer new perspectives to feminism in terms of the understanding and practice of gender – in their terms, developmental theory can 'change the toolbox' available to feminist theorists.

A personal note

Our conversations with young people today suggest that they often do not really appreciate how much, and how recently, feminism has transformed women's positions in many western societies. We saw in Chapter 4 how Eleanor Maccoby was obliged to take a rear entrance to her university's faculty club in the mid-twentieth century. Even though in many respects there is still a long way to go, many young women today seem to take for granted the position they now have. At this point, therefore, one of us (RS), as the female half of our writing team, would like to provide a personal story to illustrate some gendered aspects of academic life in the final part of the twentieth century, and demonstrate the context within which academic women and developmental psychology operated (in the UK and Australia) in the recent past. Readers are also referred to Wilkinson's (1990) account of a British Psychological Society working party report on gender representation in psychology; she noted that the report's suggestion that women may have different experiences of psychology from men was especially contentious.

We mentioned above the importance that feminists place on language. Today, our professional organizations and universities have guidelines on gender-appropriate language, and it is accepted practice that one uses gender-neutral language in academic writings. This has only been the case since the late 1980s. As an undergraduate and postgraduate, and earlier in my academic career, every hypothetical person was referred to as 'he' unless there was a very specific reason to state otherwise and, indeed, this can be observed in some of the quotations used in the present book, which originated prior to 1990. In about 1970, I became aware that the accepted focus of psychological research was on males, noting in an undergraduate assignment that a particular published study only had male subjects, and that this might have affected the results; however, I felt very uncertain about whether it was proper to make such a comment, never having seen this issue raised anywhere during my studies.

Radical feminists would have approved of my education at an all-girls' school, followed by a university college that had formerly been all-female, and therefore still had a good representation of women academics. I had been so socialized to expect teachers to be of either gender that I received a shock on attending a staff meeting in my first university post in 1972, when I suddenly realized that I was the only woman in the room; I later understood that my earlier exposure to women academics was quite atypical for the time. Today, I work in a department that has good gender balance on its staff, including at senior levels of appointment, in contrast to the situation in the 1970s, when the first female staff member received an invitation for 'Dr K. and Mrs K'. to attend an official university function (she replied that, unfortunately, her mother-in-law was unable to attend!). In a previous position during the 1980s I had discovered that the only woman on the staff of mature years lived in rented accommodation, unlike her male colleagues, who owned their homes; the reason was that women were not granted mortgages in those days.

During that decade, I was heavily involved in committees of the British Psychological Society, and once sent my apologies to a departmental staff meeting as I was attending a meeting of the Society's top executive committee, several hours' journey away (where, incidentally, I was the only woman and the only non-professorial member). I later discovered how masculine social constructions could influence the lack of recognition of women's professional contributions when I discovered that the reason for my absence had not been reported to the staff meeting, and one of my male colleagues had assumed I must have been at home because 'one of the kids must have had a cold or something'.

I had previously taken several years out of paid employment in order to raise my young family, but when I later wished to mention this in the biographical 'blurb' for a book, I was prevented from doing so on the grounds that it was irrelevant and would place my biography out of step with those of colleagues, thus forcing my personal story into the same mould as male and childless female academic colleagues, and preventing my attempt to close the public–private gap.

I faced a re-run of some earlier professional experiences in the early 1990s, when I served on a research funding body: I was the only woman (and the only non-medic) on the committee. As a university sexual harassment officer at the turn of the millennium, I was still observing (and intervening in) some worrying gender-related situations, but overall the position of women was improving.

A section such as this one in a book like this would have been out of the question until recently, yet the increasing (though far from universal) acceptance that female voices should be heard enables me to 'risk' such a personal note. I hope it serves to illustrate for our younger readers the male-dominated academic world that existed even quite late in the twentieth century. I hope it will enhance an appreciation of the social landscape in which developmental theorizing, research and practice were occurring at the time, and foster an appreciation of the changes that the feminist movement has brought about.

Conclusions

Feminists have argued that developmental psychology is, historically and currently, an overwhelmingly gendered, androcentric, undertaking, which we have sought to illustrate by examples from the literature and personal experience. In this chapter, we have outlined a variety of feminist theories, which have begun, in recent years, to influence theory, research and practice in developmental and family psychology. Some, such as liberal feminism, are more easily accommodated by traditional developmental psychology than others, such as radical feminism. All, however, have some common aims and issues, such as promoting the use of non-gender-biased language and the taking of a social justice perspective. In the latter respect, links with sociocultural theories of development are especially apparent. The field of developmental psychology has itself the potential to inform feminist theory. To date, however, such mutual exchange has barely begun.

11 Putting it all together: towards theoretical integration

Introduction

When we convened a focus group of psychology students to seek their opinions about what they would like to see in a book such as this, one member said that learning developmental psychology was like going into a dark room with a torch (flashlight, for our US readers) – one only ever sees bits and pieces and cannot put the whole picture together. He hoped that a book of this sort might be able to act like a switch to illuminate the whole room. While it would be overambitious to claim that we have achieved this, we do see the present chapter as a particularly important one since it addresses recent attempts to provide more integrative approaches to understanding child and adolescent development. Theoretical approaches with claims to holism include family therapy theories, biopsychosocial theories (especially bioecological theory), dynamic systems theory and evolutionary developmental psychology. We have also provided a reminder about general systems theory as it has provided the theoretical basis for numbers of these approaches. We also consider whether a *rapprochement* between positivism and postmodernism is possible.

The Tower of Babel

In Chapter 1, Figure 1.1 was developed to facilitate our understanding of various theoretical schools of thought. Students of psychology frequently comment on the apparent 'oil and water', or incompatible, nature of the various theories, especially when considering an overview like that presented in Figure 1.1. Their lament is often for 'just one theory which will explain everything'. Lewis (2000) notes that the traditional theoretical orientations have each in their own right contributed some unique insight into the corpus of our understanding regarding human nature and human behaviour. Mechanistic theories have been 'valuable for modeling the rule-based regularities in development, especially those that are common to human and non-human information-processing' (Lewis, 2000: 37).

Learning theories have helped us better understand the nature of the transfer of knowledge from the world to the child, and the organization of that knowledge. Organismic theories have helped us better understand the concept of stages of development, while contextualist theories have helped our understanding regarding interaction and 'goodness-of-fit' between children and their environments. Nativist theories aid our understanding of species-specific cognitive and emotional development. Notwithstanding these advantages of the various schools of thought, Lewis acknowledges that they produce very diverse accounts of development.

Within the various schools of thought, further diversity can be identified. The ethologist Robert Hinde (1992a) noted that although psychology gained respectability as a science by 'aping physics', the strengths of the standard scientific approach can also be weaknesses. He observed that science proceeds by analysis, to the neglect of synthesis. There has been a gradual breaking up of the discipline of psychology into subdisciplines, which has tended to divorce developmental psychology from other relevant areas such as social and clinical psychology, and has also isolated it from other relevant fields of inquiry, such as biology. This tendency has been called 'regressive fragmentation', although some have seen it as inevitable and a healthy state of affairs (Sternberg and Grigorenko, 2001).

More recently, Sawyer (2000), like Hinde, has bemoaned the isolation of psychology from other fields. This situation reflects the reductionist paradigm of methodological individualism – the study of mental activity in isolation from social or cultural context, which dominates APA journals, as discussed in Chapter 9. Sawyer suggests that this approach will ultimately render psychology redundant, reducing explanations of human behaviour to a biomedical level, an issue we raised in Chapter 2 (but provided an argument against in Chapter 7). Indeed, attempts to reduce explanations of human development and behaviour to the level of genetics have already occurred, in the field of sociobiology – paradoxically, this form of reductionism has been claimed as a unifying force, since all aspects of human activity and development are seen as ultimately being aimed towards the single end of gene reproduction (Lerner and von Eye, 1992). However, this is an example of an explanation of behaviour in terms of ultimate function, whereas most of the theories we have encountered in this book offer explanations of development in terms of *mechanisms*, which rarely span different levels of analysis. Sawyer notes the rarity of anti-reductionist, interdisciplinary approaches to human behaviour that use psychological theory to link culture and biology, and that recognize 'emergent properties' (a concept we will explain later).

Thus, concern has been expressed in recent years that developmental psychology has become isolated both from other relevant disciplines, such as biology and sociology, and from other areas within psychology. Furthermore, as we mentioned earlier in this book, there has been a move within developmental psychology itself away from 'grand theories' and towards many mini-theories. For example, Underwood *et al.* (2001) have expressed their concern that the field of aggression is in danger of going the same way as observed by Watkins in the field of memory – into a stage of 'personalized theorizing', 'in which theories become much like tooth-brushes in that everyone must have one of her own' (2001: 275). Weinert and Weinert (1998: 25) appear resigned to this situation, stating that 'The time of the "large theories" and broad theoretical controversies is past. Micromodels and microtheories have dominated the field for some time'. While they see an advantage in that this diversity accommodates a wide variety of phenomena and empirical data, they also acknowledge that com-prehensive pictures of phenomena are unlikely to emerge. Similarly, in her book on child development theories, Miller (1993) concluded that, 'Although it is tempting to tidy up the assortment of theories presented here by offering an orderly set of conclusions, that aim is unrealistic' (1993: 426). Lewis (2000: 36) has noted the difficulty developmental psychologists themselves have of making sense of the proliferation of theoretical approaches, which he describes as constituting a 'Tower of Babel'. Little wonder, then, that students of psychology are equally perplexed!

Despite the apparent surrender of some to the dominance of micro-theories, as the twentieth century gave way to the twenty-first, there was also a discernible thrust in the direction of integration. Sternberg and Grigorenko (2001) have called for a 'unified psychology', citing the well-known parable of the blind men touching various parts of an elephant and each conceiving of it as a very different creature. They cite work from the 1950s by Berlin, which drew upon another animal analogy in the words of the Greek poet Archilocus: 'The fox knows many things, but the hedgehog knows one big thing'. They call for a more hedgehog-like approach to psy-chology. They endorse the suggestion that this need not be through the old 'grand theory' approach, but through interlevel and interfield theories, in a similar way to that proposed by Hinde. Interlevel theories seek to bridge more fundamental levels of analysis (such as basic learning principles) with more molar levels (such as language learning). Interfield theories adopt a combination of approaches, such as biological and psychological, to prob-lems. Sternberg and Grigorenko call for a 'converging operations approach' in which psychology operates on the basis of phenomena under investiga-tion, rather than separate fields of inquiry, with varieties of perspectives and methodologies applied. They acknowledge the difficulty of achieving this given that the status quo values narrow specialization in psychology, a point also made by one of the present authors in calling for an integrative approach to developmental psychology (Shute and Paton, 1992).

Research and theories based on narrow perspectives can be especially frustrating for practitioners, who are not working with 'children doing strange things in strange situations' (to paraphrase Bronfenbrenner), but who are working with real, whole children, with their physical endowment, cognitions, emotions and behaviours, within their families, peer groups, schools and broader cultures. It is perhaps not surprising, then, that some of the thrust towards more holistic and integrative approaches to child development has come from those concerned with applied issues. In the present chapter and the final one, which addresses applied issues, we will draw upon our own fields of interest (childhood chronic illness and peer relationships), among others, to exemplify the importance of having integrative theories upon which practitioners can draw.

General systems theory

As outlined in Chapter 3, Ludwig von Bertalanffy (1968), a biologist, developed general systems theory in the mid-twentieth century. He observed that, unlike non-living systems, which move towards entropy, or disorder, living organisms tend towards greater order and complexity. He conceptualized an organism as being composed of mutually interdependent parts (see Box 11.1). The theory thus represented a move away from notions of linear ('A causes B') causality, towards a view of cause in terms of circularity and feedback loops. Organisms change and develop over time, and a key aspect of the theory is that constituent parts may come together to produce new, emergent, properties; the whole is thus more than the sum of the parts.

As we shall discuss later, both Bronfenbrenner, and Thelen and Smith, have developed theories based on general systems theory, the latter authors noting that systems notions have often appeared in accounts of development 'because they provide a logically compelling formulation for the complexities of developmental change' (Thelen and Smith, 1994: xx).

Box 11.1 Aesop's fable of mutual interdependence

The members of the Body once rebelled against the Belly. 'You', they said to the Belly, 'live in luxury and sloth, and never do a stroke of work; while we not only have to do all the hard work there is to be done, but are actually your slaves and have to minister to all your wants. Now, we will do so no longer, and you will have to shift for yourself for the future'. They were as good as their word, and left the Belly to starve. The result was just what might have been expected: the whole Body soon began to fail, and the Members all shared in the general collapse. And then they saw too late how foolish they had been.

(From *Aesop's Fables*, 1979, 128)

Reciprocalism and holism in developmental psychology

Central to systems theory is the notion of reciprocal influence. That this is a crucial issue in developmental psychology has become increasingly acknowledged. Particularly influential in this acceptance was the notion of infant temperament, with Thomas and Chess (1977) suggesting that how an infant's temperament influences later development depends on the 'goodness-of-fit' between the child's temperament and the physical and social environment. We can observe a connection here with Vygotskian and neo-Vygotskian concepts: the zone of proximal development, which represents the child's potential level of development when operating in collaboration with a more capable member of the culture, will be greater if the child is interacting with a person who is sensitive to his/her level of development and who therefore provides the appropriate level of scaffolding. These are examples of a growing appreciation within developmental psychology that children's social relationships are *transactional*. This concept of mutual influence has provided a bridge between mechanistic theories of development (which saw the child as being passively acted upon by the environment) and organismic theories (which saw the child as an active creator of his or her environment). It has become clear that, in the social as well as the non-social world, the child and environment are mutually influential.

The notion of reciprocal influence can be applied not just within a single level of analysis but also between levels of analysis. Hinde (1992a), in his expression of concern about the fragmentation and isolation of areas of inquiry within and beyond psychology, commented that the child's physiology and psychology are embedded in a network of immediate social relationships, broader society, the physical environment, sociocultural values and so forth. These levels of analysis have their separate properties but dynamically interact with one another. Thus, each level must be considered in terms of the processes involved in these dialectical interactions.

Although Hinde did not specifically mention in this article either general systems theory or Bronfenbrenner's ecological theory, elements of both are apparent in his description, including a rejection of explanations of developmental phenomena in terms of linear causality and an emphasis on dialectical relationships between different levels of analysis. As an example of the limitations of existing theories, Hinde mentioned the inadequacy of modelling and reinforcement to explain the finding that early experiences of parenting are translated into later long-term behaviour changes such as peer interactions; cognitive intermediaries – such as 'internal working models' of the self, others and the world – can help to bridge the gap. This approach is integrative, in bringing together research from cognitive psychology, developmental psychology and psychopathology, and is couched in terms of mutually influential systems.

At the same time as Hinde was writing this, one of the present authors was also drawing attention to trends in psychology towards greater integration between subfields, in relation to childhood chronic illness (Shute and Paton, 1992). For example, evidence was accumulating that cognitive development could be promoted through social interaction and also that cognitive performance was influenced by social context (neither of which findings would have been a surprise to Vygotsky). Also, not only were biological factors seen to affect the child psychologically (e.g. illness might have emotional effects) but psychological factors were becoming seen as capable of influencing biology (as when the course of a chronic illness is affected by stress). In addition, links between physical health and social relationships were being found, such as children's diabetic control being related to the parental marital relationship. Thus, evidence was accumulating for important causal and reciprocal linkages between various facets of development (e.g. Johnson, 1985; Kazak, 1992).

In considering evidence for reciprocity within and between different levels of analysis, we can also revisit the theme of gene–environment interactions discussed in Chapter 2. While there are arguments that genes can influence the environment in which the child develops (for example, through niche-picking) current biological knowledge indicates that the environment cannot normally change genetic make-up (exceptions are genetic manipulation by scientists and genetic damage by, for example, toxins). This suggests that we are at the limits of reciprocal influences, with the environment normally unable to change genes. However, although the environment cannot usually change genetic *structure*, it may change the ways in which that genetic structure is *expressed*: there is biological evidence (Campbell, 1996) that environmental changes (through a series of intermediate processes) can turn genes on or off (and, in some cases, feedback loops can reverse this process). Hence, we have direct evidence that the notion of reciprocal influence also applies when considering gene–environment interactions.

Both Vreeke (2000), and Bronfenbrenner and Morris (1998) take issue with those such as Scarr and Plomin who maintain that genes are the major determinants of developmental outcome, maintaining instead that an interactive, or dynamic, developmental view best accords with the evidence. Citing work by Molenaar *et al.*, Vreeke proposes that the distance between a genotype and the ultimate phenotype is great, because the phenotype is reached via a network of epigenetic, non-linear processes. The fact that correlations are found between genotype and phenotype should not be interpreted as providing information about development – rather, they are an artefact of the statistical methods used, which assume separateness of the variables. Vreeke proposes that alternative statistical methods need to be applied – non-linear statistics that do not make this assumption.

In this section, we have provided some examples to illustrate the rising acceptance of notions of interaction and transaction in theorizing about development. Similar trends have also become apparent in other fields of psychological inquiry; for example, the social psychologists Doise (1986) and Hogg (1992) have called for integration of different levels of explanation in order to fully understand social phenomena. Ideas about interaction and transaction certainly represent considerable progress in comparison with earlier ideas of one-way causality, and these terms have been described by Thelen and Smith as 'everyone's comfortable buzzwords, and the preferred 'solution' to the nature/nurture dichotomy' (1994: xv). However, as we shall explain further later, these writers maintain that these ideas in fact provide no such solution.

Family therapy and beyond

The above examples demonstrate that the notion of reciprocal, non-linear influences on development, within and between levels of analysis, was slowly taking hold in developmental psychology research towards the end of the twentieth century. The applied field of family therapy must also be credited with taking up, at an even earlier stage (from the 1940s), notions of mutual influence, within the specific area of the family, as we mentioned in Chapter 4 in our outline of Bateson's work. Various schools of family therapy have been developed by a range of professionals, including psychologists, psychiatrists and social workers (Gladding, 1998). These include the psychoanalytic and Bowen schools, experiential family therapy, behavioural and cognitive-behavioural family therapies, structural, strategic and systemic family therapies. They vary in many ways, such as whether emphasis is placed on historical family factors or present symptoms, the length of therapy, the nature and strength of their theoretical basis and the specific therapeutic emphases and techniques; however, they are all, to a greater or lesser degree, based on addressing psychological problems by considering reciprocal influence between family members, rather than focusing on factors within the individual. The notion that repetitive patterns of interaction develop over time is crucial, and therapy is aimed at identifying and changing such patterns when they are dysfunctional. The term 'circularity' is often used to refer to these patterns, but the term 'recursion' may be preferable as this better captures the notion that repeated patterns within systems are never actually identical (Breunlin *et al.*, 1992).

While those who devised family therapy took pride in their breadth of vision and their move away from the narrow individual focus of other therapies, more recent clinical developments have seen even family therapy as too narrowly focused. Breunlin *et al.* (1992) have developed a 'metaframework' approach. They point out that most family therapy models ignore the intrapsychic aspects of family members, yet at times these may be important to address. Furthermore, systems beyond the family (such as the peer group) may sometimes need to be considered to understand their role in the presenting problem. They observe that it is especially ironic that, although claiming to be anti-reductionist, family therapy gave a reductionist account of the environmental context – as consisting of just the family – ignoring broader sociocultural contexts, as we mentioned in the previous chapter in connection with societal gender relations. Similarly, under the influence of Bronfenbrenner's theory, 'multisystemic therapy' has been devised, based on a consideration of the broader ecological systems in which children and adolescents develop (Henggler *et al.*, 1998). Multisystemic therapy has been shown to be effective in especially difficult clinical situations, such as working with youths involved with the juvenile justice system.

Biopsychosocial models

While Bronfenbrenner's ecological systems theory was becoming influential in persuading some therapists to consider ecosystems beyond those of the family, Bronfenbrenner was, ironically, coming to accept that his original theory was too narrow: while it emphasized the nested environmental contexts in which children develop, it neglected to provide structures to encompass the characteristics of the developing person, including biological and psychological aspects (Bronfenbrenner and Ceci, 1994; Bronfenbrenner and Morris, 1998). In the field of medicine, Engel (1977) had earlier proposed that a comprehensive 'biopsychosocial' approach should be taken, and during the 1980s health psychologists increasingly advocated this approach, which recognizes reciprocal interactions between the person's biology, psychology and social contexts. Consistent with this were the trends we noted above towards comprehensive and dynamic systems approaches coming from those with applied interests in child development, especially child health, where a major concern was to promote good adjustment in children faced with challenges over and above the usual ones.

While there was general recognition of the need to acknowledge such linkages between different levels of analysis, a general and holistic model of child development was still absent when one of the present authors (RS), in the late 1980s, was addressing the role of peers in the development of children with chronic illnesses. We were unaware of any broad theoretical framework for understanding development and adjustment that explicitly linked peer relationships and cognitive development (Shute and Paton, 1990). Taking up an earlier suggestion by Butterworth (1982) that systems theory might offer a way of integrating social and cognitive aspects of development, blended with Vygotskian notions of social/cognitive links, we outlined a theoretical framework by which a process of 'social cognitive monitoring' provides a reciprocal link between the child's cognitive/emotional systems and social world, which consists of environmental systems including home, school and hospital (similar to Bronfenbrenner's microsystems, although we were unfamiliar with his work at the time). Within each, the child experiences relationships with both adults and peers. These are differentially involved in cognitive development, given that age–peer relationships are based on equality (which Piaget said was necessary for certain aspects of development such as moral understanding) while relationships with adults (and older peers) are asymmetrical, influencing cognitive development in the way proposed by Vygotsky (Foot *et al.*, 1990; Hartup, 1980).

However, we also acknowledged that cognition could interact with non-social features of the world, in the way proposed by Piaget (and in accordance with Vygotsky's notion of early infant development). The importance of development over time was also acknowledged, with 'adjustment' being characterized by different criteria at different developmental stages, but in general terms defined as 'the degree to which he or she functions at age-appropriate levels in the social, cognitive and academic spheres, while maintaining good disease management and high self-esteem' (Shute and Paton, 1990: 332). The concern with adjustment, rather than just development, reflected the clinical thrust of the work.

We developed this integrative approach 'on the run', as it were, to provide a framework for a specific purpose: to encompass the multiplicity of factors and processes under consideration in addressing some practical issues concerning child health management. Today we would not have had to undertake this exercise, as we would have found a well-developed framework already in existence encompassing many of the ideas (and many more) that we were attempting to pull together: the latest version of Bronfenbrenner's theory. This has evolved over time from the ecological model (described in Chapter 8) into his 'bioecological model' (Bronfenbrenner and Morris, 1998), one of the most comprehensive models of child development to date. A complete exposition of this theory is beyond the scope of the present book, but a few key points will be made.

The original theory corrected previous neglect of contexts of development, but what it prompted were many studies of 'context without development' (Bronfenbrenner and Morris, 1998: 994). Bronfenbrenner now places much more emphasis on developmental *processes*, giving pride of place to proximal processes – interactions between the organism and environment, which are the primary mechanisms for development (our notion of social-cognitive monitoring similarly was aimed at capturing child–social interactions as the primary driving force for development). However, as in our framework, Bronfenbrenner also allows for development through interaction with the non-social world. Proximal processes vary as a function of aspects of the developing *person*, their *environmental contexts* and *time*, factors we had also incorporated into our framework. Bronfenbrenner and Morris further categorize person characteristics into *dispositions, resources* and *demand characteristics*, concepts that are also applied to the nested environmental systems such as the microsystem.

The notion is also introduced that features of the environment may not just foster, but interfere with, the development of proximal processes. While we were specifically concerned with adjustment of the child with chronic illness, Bronfenbrenner and Morris incorporate the notion that developmental outcomes for all individuals represent competence or dysfunction, something that reflects a growing interest in the idea that factors both internal and external to the child contribute to risk for, or resilience against, poor developmental outcomes, as mentioned in Chapter 5. There is also an increased concern with time (the chronosystem), and this is reflected in their definition of development as 'stability and change in the biopsychological characteristics of human beings over the life course and across generations' (1998: 995). A link with evolutionary theory is made in that it is assumed that biological and evolutionary factors both set limits to and provide imperatives for development.

Bronfenbrenner regards his theory as being suitable for research in what he calls 'discovery mode' rather than 'verification mode', with propositions for testing being drawn (at least initially) more from theory than from research findings. An implication of this is that one should be less concerned about making Type I error (falsely claiming to have found an effect) and be more accepting of the possibility of making Type II errors (overlooking a 'real' effect) since even a marginal finding may in fact be a useful pointer towards new discoveries. This is especially important given that, in development, small initial influences may become magnified over time and, ultimately, powerful predictors of outcome. Thus, as with systems approaches in general, Bronfenbrenner's theory challenges traditional hypothesis-testing and the use of linear statistics in developmental psychology.

Dynamic systems theory

The term dynamic systems theory has recently been introduced to describe a new and well-articulated theory of development (Thelen and Smith, 1994). It is strongly based upon the principles of general systems theory, which means, of course, that, despite its name, it is not unique in its dynamic emphasis. As with Bronfenbrenner's most recent (bioecological) theory, central notions are holism, mutual influence within and between traditionally separate levels of analysis, and a focus on process rather than structure. However, the two theories differ strongly in the emphasis placed upon biology. Although Bronfenbrenner now acknowledges the biological (specifically, the genetic) contribution to development, he does not detail biological processes at all. On the contrary, Thelen and

Smith set out deliberately to create a theory that was biologically valid, to the extent that they explicitly reject models of development that use machine or computer analogies, and use biologically appropriate terminology instead. They question the common usage of the term 'biological' to refer exclusively to genes, neurology, hormones, etc. – the things that psychologists call 'biological bases' of behaviour. They argue that aspects of the environment, such as social environments that enable language to develop, are no less biological.

In addition to biological plausibility, Thelen and Smith spell out five other requirements for a developmental theory: to understand the origins of novelty; to reconcile global regularities with local variability, complexity and context-specificity; to integrate developmental data at many levels of explanation; to understand how local processes lead to global outcomes; and to establish a theoretical basis for generating and interpreting empirical research.

They argue that the appearance of development as being orderly, progressive, incremental and directional, which gives the impression of a pre-determined plan, is illusory. For example, the development of infants' ability to walk has long been regarded as a series of invariant stages determined by maturation, as described by Gesell (see Chapter 3); Thelen and Smith present evidence that, on closer inspection, development is much 'messier' than this, with component processes moving along in fits and starts, and sometimes regressing rather than progressing. On closer investigation, then, the grand plan seems to disappear, as it does also if one examines cognitive development. Effectively, group averages are masking individual differences that are important for understanding the true nature of development, a point also made by Hinde (1992a). They observe that descriptions of typical developmental stages have become mistaken for explanations.

Thelen and Smith also argue that the notion that there is a 'plan for the adult' encapsulated in the genes is illogical, as is any 'plan' encoded in the environment. Both these extreme views, they maintain, lead to an impossible infinite regress of coded instructions for development, which is not solved by interactionism: a theory of development must explain how novelty and complexity in structure and function arise, and simply claiming that the answer is 'through gene–environment interactions' does not explain *how* new forms and behaviours come about. Their answer is that one has to explain development from the bottom up, not from a top-down plan. Various factors interact to create novelty in the way described above for general systems theory – so that new properties emerge, rather than being predetermined. An important feature of this is that some abilities may be present but hidden, only coming into play when other aspects of development catch up and enable them to operate. For example, it has been discovered that infants can step with alternate legs on a treadmill from early infancy, if their weight is supported; normally, this ability is not apparent until they can also support their own weight, and balance, in order to walk (Thelen and Smith, 1994). This conception helps to address one of developmental psychology's perennial questions – 'Does development happen in discrete stages or is it a continuous process?' The answer may be that it is both, with continuity in subabilities or attributes leading to relatively sudden change as the subabilities operate together to form an emergent property.

Piaget's theory fits well with this perspective, being organismic and systemic, but Thelen and Smith note that much research inspired by his theory has been more concerned with structure than process. Apart from general systems theory, other important theories that have influenced their work include Edelman's (1992) theory of neuronal group selection and Eleanor Gibson's work in ecological psychology and the notion of affordance (see Chapter 3).

From the perspective of their theory, Thelen and Smith say that one of the questions that has so vexed psychologists over the years – 'What is innate and what is learned?' – is uninteresting. This echoes earlier comments by Jeffrey Gray (1985) that the fondness psychologists have for (false) dichotomies often stands in the way of understanding the phenomena at hand. Psychologists are as fond of linear causality and traditional research and analytic methods as they are of dichotomies; such approaches do not lend themselves well to investigations in the mould of dynamic systems, and this presents some real challenges for developmental psychology.

Evolutionary developmental psychology

As mentioned in Chapter 2, it has been proposed that evolutionary developmental psychology is another approach that has the potential to act as an integrating force. Geary and Bjorklund (2000) describe it as an emerging interdisciplinary field, a sister discipline to evolutionary developmental biology, with the goals of identifying 'the social, psychological, cognitive, and neural phenotypes that are common to human beings, and to other species, and to identify the genetic and ecological mechanisms that shape the development of these phenotypes and ensure their adaptation to local conditions' (2000: 57).

The above definition makes it clear that this field is inclusive of all aspects of development traditionally studied as separate subdisciplines. Geary has proposed a hierarchically organized system of modules and submodules of the mind that enable the individual to manage the social environment (e.g. theory of mind) and the natural environment (e.g. spatial representation). These modules have evolved to subserve survival and reproduction, and one issue for evolutionary developmental psychology is to relate to modern environments mechanisms that evolved under past evolutionary pressures. This level of explanation is, of course, like genetic determinism, concerned with ultimate functions of behaviour and development, rather than with mechanisms, understanding of which must draw upon other theoretical frameworks. In making this point, Dunbar has applauded the potential of evolutionary psychology to 'weld together the innumerable cracks that threaten to tear psychology apart' (2001: 421).

We discussed in Chapter 2 the criticism that evolutionary psychology creates *post hoc* explanations. As noted by Ketelaar and Ellis (2000), critics observe that it accounts for an endless range of phenomena, and when the phenomena change the explanations change: essentially, evolutionary-derived hypotheses are unfalsifiable. While Ketelaar and Ellis accept that the field was indeed open to such charges in the past, they argue that it has now matured, and is able to produce surprising and testable new hypotheses. The essence of their argument rests upon adopting the philosophy of science articulated by Lakatos, which we outlined in Chapter 1. They suggest that evolutionary theory constitutes a 'metatheoretical research program', based on certain core assumptions. This core is surrounded by a 'protective belt' of middle-level theories such as attachment theory, parental investment/sexual selection theory and reciprocal altruism theory. Rather than experimental results leading to all-or-none acceptance or rejection of the basic metatheory, they should contribute to making a decision about whether the metatheory in general is progressive or degenerative. Thus, even if the weight of evidence were, say, to destroy attachment theory, provided the weight of evidence still favoured other middle-level theories, the basic evolutionary metatheory would still stand. Ketelaar and Ellis argue that evolutionary theory has the status of a progressive metatheory, in being able both to accommodate major anomalous findings and to generate novel predictions and explanations. An example of the former is altruism, which was initially considered a major threat to evolutionary theory, but was later accommodated within it. An example of the latter was a challenge to the accepted 'fact' that males are superior to females in spatial ability: it was predicted, and supported by various studies (e.g. McBurney *et al.*, 1997), that males would tend to be superior on mental rotation tasks, based on the assumption that ancestral males needed such skills to hunt and kill animals, while females would be superior in remembering static locations of objects, based on an ancestral role in gathering food from static sources.

In adopting an evolutionary approach, it will be important for psychologists to ensure that their theories about the operation of ancient societies do not become outdated. Also, postmodern approaches to scientific inquiry should lead us to maintain a healthy scepticism about taken-for-granted archaeological assumptions; for example, a feminist approach might lead us to inquire closely into the truth of tales of brave, strong (male) hunters. As explained by Dincauze (2001), research has shown that archaeological sites with large animal bones are more highly valued and researched than those without them; there has thus been a privileging, in research, of carnivory and hunting over other nutritional strategies such as gathering plant materials or trapping small animals. One might therefore question just how much evolutionary pressure really came from hunting. It has also been proposed that where hunting of large animals did occur, it served the purpose of achieving and validating male status. If so, a hunting-based explanation of male spatial rotation superiority would have to posit a cultural rather than a nutritional selection pressure.

If the overall position that evolutionary theory acts as a metatheory is accepted, this adds philosophical weight to the argument that it has the potential to act as a unifying force across many diverse areas of psychology. We began this book with the suggestion (not entirely unchallenged) that Darwinian theory can be taken as the starting point for the various schools of developmental theory that have arisen. It is fascinating, therefore, that the wheel has turned full circle and the evolutionary approach is now being proposed as a novel means of reunifying the field.

Critical state theory

We referred above to to the notion that psychology can be seen as having 'aped physics', the implication being that this has had some disadvantages as well as advantages. We would like to be very speculative here and suggest the possibility that some recent advances in theoretical physics may in the future impinge upon our understanding of human development and behaviour as we begin to take a more systemic approach.

Science is traditionally concerned with the predictability of events, yet theoretical physicists carried out a wide range of studies during the 1980s and 1990s, which showed that many natural events within complex systems are unpredictable (Buchanan, 2000). It appears that catastrophic events such as earthquakes, major forest fires and species extinctions are not events that can be predicted and controlled, although the likelihood of occurrence of a particular-sized event can be calculated mathematically. The larger an event, the less likely it is to happen, but at any time the interacting factors underlying the event may reach a critical state of hidden instability such that an additional, minor change to the system can trigger a catastrophic event (this is like the notion of emergent properties). For example, an extensive and intricate pattern of fault lines in the earth's crust may be balanced on the edge of instability, but this only becomes apparent when one small movement of the earth triggers a shift in the entire system; like a house of cards tumbling down as one card is placed slightly carelessly, the result is a massive earthquake.

Evidence is accumulating that that these laws of non-equilibrium physics apply not just to events in the physical world, but to human activities such as stock market crashes and world wars. There seems no reason to suppose

---

Box 11.2 Twenty-first-century challenges for developmental psychology

The following extract comes from a section of a textbook headed 'The emerging challenge to causal thinking'.

> All the sciences of Western industrialized society are based on a traditional mode of thought that can be traced back to Aristotle, at least, but was codified and established within the scientific enterprises of the seventeenth, eighteenth and nineteenth centuries. ... This mode of thinking, amounting to a world-view, an article of faith in the way the world works, assumes direct linearity in causation. ... Whether from the perspective of 'normal' science or the new sciences of complexity, the advantages of multidisciplinary studies of complex systems are impressive. The compartmentalized disciplines of modern science have each special strengths for investigating a circumscribed range of phenomena. None can exhaust the complexities of any aspect of the world, but each can specify the likely states of some variables, and the relationships between variables within parts of a given system.
>
> (Dincauze, 2000: 35)

After reading the present chapter, these ideas should sound familiar. However, this passsage comes not from a developmental psychology text, but from a book on environmental archaeology. Issues concerning systems, complexity and the value of multidisciplinary collaboration have come to the forefront in many sciences concerned with change, such as meteorology, geology and epidemiology. In these respects, developmental psychology may find that it has more in common with these sciences than with other fields of psychology.

---

that these laws might not also apply to aspects of the developing individual, their family or community. Indeed, if we take a broad systemic view of development, which includes cultural, historical and even evolutionary change, we can say that there is already strong evidence that development is subject to these influences. The challenge that this new approach presents is addressed in Box 11.2.

Can postmodern and scientific approaches be reconciled?

At first sight, the answer to this question might seem to be an obvious no. Throughout this book we have contrasted positivist and postmodern notions of inquiry, and observed that they have arisen from different philosophical approaches. A postmodern perspective such as that articulated by Gergen (2001) holds that all knowledge is relative, and there is no such thing as reality, but only individuals' constructions of reality. Thus, any perspective on child development, including ones derived from scientific inquiry, would be no better than any other. The result would appear to be an unhelpful anarchy and nihilism. Indeed, as Martin and Sugarman (2000) have observed, if one takes such views of postmodernism literally, 'psychology and education are not only problematized, they are liquidated!' Yet it is hard to ignore the fact that, without the critique offered by postmodernism, developmental psychology would be even more ethnocentric, androcentric, ignorant of its history and disempowering to research participants than it already is.

In an earlier chapter we described ourselves as 'fence-sitters' on the science/postmodernism issue, for example, acknowledging the value of both quantitative and qualitative research methods, and suggesting that a reconciliation between the two might be possible. It seems that we are not alone in seeking such a solution. Martin and Sugarman (2000: 398) have observed that some psychologists

> ... resonate to postmodern themes of difference, plurality, peculiarity and irregularity as refreshing changes from past adherence to sameness, regularity and strict rationalism ... in effect, having labored within the straitjacket of modernity, they enjoy the full ludic romp of postmodernism's radical problematizing without really believing its full social constructionist and deconstructive implications for themselves and their everyday and professional practices.

They suggest that attempting to have the best of both these worlds is a rather sensible approach. It is helpful to note that the term 'postmodernism' does not cover a single approach, and that there are philosophical debates within the field. Gergen's version, which seems so irreconcilable with a scientific approach to child development, is an extreme one. Martin and Sugarman resist a forced choice between 'the unsustainable myths of modernity on the one hand and some of the more excessively radical medicine of postmodernism on the other'. They propose a middle-ground philosophical perspective that draws upon the work of Vygotsky and Mead as well as other scholars.

In this view, the non-human world of physical and biological objects ('natural kinds') really exists, independently of the humans who study it. 'Human kinds' also exist, but they are themselves heavily implicated in this reality: as humans are aware and reflective, their actions and ways of being are affected by the classification of societies and cultures, and by their own reactions to these classifications. Thus their actions are influenced not only by the culture of which they are a part, but by their own unique experiences within it. Their reflections and actions may in turn change the available societal classifications. An example of this provided by Martin and Sugarman is changes to *DSM* classifications resulting from the activities of advocacy groups, as we discussed in Chapters 2 and 10. Another example of the mutual co-creation of the cultural and the psychological was provided by the example in Chapter 9 of the five worlds of Aboriginal adolescents. The implications of Martin and Sugarman's position for a *rapprochement* between reality-based science and postmodern constructionism is captured in the following extract (2000: 403):

> In the dynamic, developmental scenario we have painted, the possibility of reflexive subjectivity is developmentally emergent within human embeddedness in real and preexisiting physical, biological and sociocultural contexts. Although precise forms of emergent subjectivity are necessarily historically and contextually contingent and thus variable, some such emergence (given the physical, biological, and sociocultural conditions of human existence) is existentially inevitable.

In deciding how to respond to postmodern critiques, readers may find Box 11.3 helpful.

Box 11.3 How should we respond to non-traditional theoretical approaches?

Teo has performed a valuable service in bringing to our attention the diversity of theoretical traditions that address the contexts, phenomena and issues that are central to developmental psychology. In particular, Teo has identified the three extended theoretical families that include the critical-theoretical approaches, the postmodern, post-structuralist, deconstructionist approaches, and the feminist and multicultural approaches ... there are several alternative visions of the relationships among families of theoretical traditions that might guide us in our reading, understanding, and evaluation of Teo's article. From the exclusivist perspective, we would finish reading the article and ask, 'What can I do to demonstrate how these alternative theoretical perspectives are wrong?' From the inclusivist perspective, we would ask, 'What can I borrow from these alternative theoretical traditions to strengthen my own?' From a detached perspective, we would merely dismiss the article and not return to it again. And from a caring perspective, we would now be asking, 'What can traditional developmental psychology offer to strengthen these alternative theoretical traditions?'

(Meacham, 1997: 211–15)

Conclusions

In previous chapters, we outlined some historical and current trends within a range of different theoretical approaches to child and adolescent development, each of which tells a partial story. In the current chapter, we have observed some dissatisfaction with fragmentary approaches, with some strong moves apparent in the direction of more integrative and holistic approaches. The implication is that developmental theories at a purely psychological (or any other) level of analysis will necessarily be incomplete. As Lerner (1998: 1) has observed,

> ... in contemporary developmental theories, the person is not biologized, psychologized or sociologized. Rather the individual is 'systemized' – that is his or her development is embedded within an integrated matrix of variables derived from multiple levels of organization, and development is conceptualized as deriving from the dynamic relations among the variables in this multi-tiered matrix.

We wonder whether a future path might lie in even further integration of the approaches outlined here. Evolutionary theory provides a basis for understanding some of the biological imperatives for and limits to human development, while the bioecological approach encompasses the interactions between the person and environment over both micro and macro levels and timescales (thus, potentially covering even the evolutionary timescale). Dialectical theory helps to provide crucial links between individual cognition and the social/cultural world, while general (and dynamic) systems theory provides an overall framework for understanding interactions between systems at different levels of analysis, and provides for the existence of emergent properties and a reconciliation between stage theories and continuity theories of development. Finally, and most speculatively, we wonder whether approaching developmental psychology from the perspective of critical state theory might indicate that aspects of development also follow ubiquitous principles that defy prediction.

However, we regularly hear psychologist colleagues claiming to be unimpressed when holistic models are presented, and to be much more impressed by small models that are directly testable by standard experimental methods – in line with the mini-theory approach. While we believe that this approach has an important place, as practitioners we are actually much more excited by the current thrust towards holism and integration, and are appreciative of the enormous intellectual effort that goes into developing such approaches, which can provide the big picture into which the smaller models fit. As with postmodernism, these newer approaches certainly present significant challenges for traditional scientific methods.

Nevertheless, we recognize that many colleagues will remain as unmoved by integrative approaches as by postmodernism; and surely many of us will feel some alarm about the prospect of a theory that will not permit us to predict significant (including catastrophic) events! We leave it to our readers to determine which of the possible paths they believe are most worthy of pursuit. Finally, we would do well to recall George Kelly's view that each theory not only has its own limited 'range of convenience', but that all theories are ultimately expendable.

12 From theory into practice

Introduction

Throughout this book, we have made reference to real-life applications of child development theory. For example, children's behavioural, emotional and social problems have been approached from perspectives such as medical diagnosis, family systems and social information processing; theories such as those of Dewey, Piaget and Vygotsky have been applied educationally; and attachment and learning theories have been implicated in debates about the best way to raise children. Practice informed by theory is sometimes referred to as 'praxis'. Equally, we have seen that policy decisions concerning children can fly in the face of what theory and research suggest will promote positive development, as in the case of Australian Aboriginal children removed from their attachment figures. Alternatively, practice that promotes positive development can occur in the absence of a theoretical basis, as in the case of the nineteenth-century South Australian infants who were fostered rather than institutionalized.

In this final chapter we turn to a more in-depth discussion of the links between child development theory and real-world practice. A broad consideration of the contribution of the philosophy of science to psychology will provide a backdrop for a discussion of the manner in which theories of child development impact on practice. To facilitate this discussion we briefly address a number of terms that have been emerging in the psychology and educational literature in recent years including 'scientist-practitioner', 'applied developmental psychology' and 'developmentally appropriate practice'. These ideas issue some interesting challenges to researchers and writers enmeshed in the world of theory. As stated in various chapters throughout this book, and as witnessed by a considerable body of literature, developmental psychology is almost embarrassed by an excess of riches in relation to theoretical development. The application of this body of knowledge to practice and as a means of informing policy development is, to some extent, uncharted territory. In a reciprocal fashion, there is a challenge to better understand how practice in the field can inform theory development.

Psychology and the nature of knowledge

Throughout this book we have sought to place developmental theory in a historical and cultural context and to present ideas regarding the conduct of science. As we noted in Chapter 1, philosophers have long debated the means by which we attain knowledge or truth. Empiricists such as Locke, Berkeley and Hume posited that knowledge exists outside the individual and that humans acquire knowledge through the senses. Locke (1690/1947: 22) argued that 'The senses at first let in particular ideas, and furnish the yet empty cabinet, and the mind by degrees growing familiar with some of them, they are lodged in the memory ...'. In contrast, the rationalists, such as Descartes, Spinoza and Kant, argued that reason is more important than experience. For example, Kant, while not denying the existence of experience, identified two elements of knowledge: (i) what is given, principally through the senses; and (ii) what is posited by the thinking subject. Rationalists argue that we can be deceived by our senses, as in the case of perceptual illusions, and so the senses cannot be trusted to provide reliable knowledge. Postmodern views of knowledge propose a very different outlook concerning the nature and development of knowledge and in turn, there are obvious links with practice. For example, in family therapy the postmodern trend to use narrative therapy (White and Epston, 1989) emphasizes practice that attempts to understand how the client construes the world in order to best facilitate client change.

Writers such as Teo (1997) and Valentine (1998) believe that, while developmental psychology draws upon disciplines such as biology, anthropology and sociology, it has been rather reluctant to consider recent developments in the philosophy of knowledge. Teo suggests that the primary reason for this has to do with the rise and dominance of empiricism, particularly as reflected in mainstream North American psychology (see Chapter 6). Perhaps associated with this point we would also note that, politically, the focus on the *individual's* development that has taken place in the majority of the theories is essentially consistent with mainstream western political democratic development. Developmental psychology, with few exceptions, is not a socially or politically critical enterprise and so much mainstream theorizing reflects dominant hegemonic thought. In the postmodern context we have elaborated on some contemporary influences on child development theory including feminist theory (see Chapter 10) and indigenous theory (see Chapter 9). The thinking and theorizing in these fields has considerably enriched our understanding of human development. The implications for practice are significant. For example, the Australian Mental Health Strategy (2000) document stepped outside mainstream empirical theorizing that focuses on linear causal explanations and took into account more systemic, multifactorial explanations for the development of protective factors influencing young people's mental health, in a manner consistent with the more recent, integrative approaches to development outlined in the previous chapter.

A related and important issue in considering theory–practice links is the role of universities in creating knowledge, and particularly the type of knowledge created. Western universities have generally engaged in the conduct of science to develop and test theories and hypotheses. Best and Tiernay (2001) have summarized the modernist paradigm as encapsulating linear, causal reasoning with an overarching search for theories and universal truths. Consistent with a positivist view of science, the university has generally been represented as a community of scholars dispassionately engaged in the conduct of science and in the pursuit of knowledge unfettered by political or social constraints. As Tierney (2001: 355) notes, 'A modernist stance on knowledge production proceeds from the belief that objective scientists from particular disciplines undertake neutral investigations' (see Chapter 1). The right of the scholar to speak independently has been, and still is, a jealously guarded one. As we discuss further below, some would argue that in the face of current funding trends, where the issue of intellectual property has risen to prominence, the need to protect the independence of scholarship is seen by some academics as a high priority.

The role of the university as the sole repository of knowledge is also being challenged in a postmodern context in which the term 'knowledge society' (Stehr, 1994) implies that knowledge is produced by and across society. Moreover, the type of knowledge so prized by universities, namely 'contemplative knowledge', which seeks to 'describe the world, to represent the world' (Barnett, 2000: 410) is increasingly being understood as only one of many types of knowledge. Tierney (2001: 353) has noted that 'proponents of modernism have assumed that rational, objective knowledge discovered by scientific inquiry ultimately will set humanity free, or at least improve the lives of men and women'. This view is under challenge from new emergent forms of knowledge, identified as 'performative knowledges' (Gibbons *et al.* 1994) or 'forms of action and engagement with and in the world' (Barnett, 2000: 410). The implications are that, while theory can inform practice, greater consideration is needed of the possibility that practice (representing a form of knowledge in its own right) can also inform theory.

It has further been argued that knowledge generated by universities has less status now and simply takes its place alongside a range of other 'knowledges' (Gokulsing and DaCosta, 1999). The privileging of knowledge generated by universities, perceived as representing the sectional interests of a small group of academics, is now being questioned in some quarters, although the issue of the existence of other forms of knowledge that might exist outside of the university research setting is still a debate largely waiting to be had. The outcome is that universities are being challenged to take their knowledge to the market-place to compete with other forms of knowledge (Barnett, 2000).

This brief description of the philosophical background to developmental psychology, the nature of knowledge, and links with practice, helps set the scene for the following discussion regarding the manner in which theory has informed (or not!) the link between theory and practice. In order to facilitate this discussion we describe three rather disparate models of theory–practice links relevant to developmental psychology.

Models of theory–practice links

In 1950 the formulation of the scientist-practitioner model (Raimy, 1950) was facilitated by funding from the United States government to provide rehabilitation and other services for servicemen and women returning from duty in the Second World War. The Boulder Conference in 1949 had preceded Raimy's publication and essentially produced a model of education and training rather than a model of professional practice. As a result, there was a call for clinical psychologists to be trained both as scientists and practitioners (Shapiro, 2002). At the time, the body of psychological knowledge resided principally with academics working in university settings. The dominant influence of behaviourism in American psychology

> ... meant that many of the academic psychologists who would be involved in the training of practitioners would be more likely to be familiar with laboratory procedures for the experimental investigation of animal learning and the intricacies of Hullian learning theory than the psychological problems confronting veterans in their everyday lives.
>
> (John, 1998: 25)

In the field of developmental psychology, we can hear these sentiments echoed in Bronfenbrenner's concern that research efforts have mainly concentrated on the decontextualized child.

John has further argued that the prevailing positivist influence of the time 'enabled academic psychologists, the exponents and self-declared custodians of these procedures, to position themselves as the arbiters of psychological knowledge claims of any kind' (1998: 25). The implications for scientific practice were almost self-evident and were reflected in 'a form of instrumental or technical rationality that proceeds by rigorous deduction of prescriptions for practice from these generalizations' (John, 1998: 26). Furthermore, as we discussed in the previous chapter, the current diversity of incompatible theories provides a daunting challenge not only to developmentalists, but to educators and other practitioners working with children (Lewis, 2000).

Those such as John (1994; 1998) who criticize the grounding of the scientist-practitioner model in 'a naive empiricist conception of science' (Cotton, 1998: 31) have drawn attention to the issue of the range of 'knowledges' jostling for a voice in the postmodern dawn. Debate is now turning to a consideration of how sociocultural forces influence psychological research and practice. It has been proposed that science should not be understood in terms of a method, but through its fostering of free inquiry. Given that the latter is the very business of universities, John (1998) regards it as ironic that it is through a dominant positivist outlook that universities train psychologists.

Despite such postmodern critiques, the scientist-practitioner model remains a strong force in clinical psychology. In Australia, for example, university clinical psychology course accreditation depends upon the espousement of the model. There is also a strong push towards the further development of the scientist-practitioner model, with calls for the further integration of science with practice and greater recognition of the need for contextually relevant practice (Lerner, 2000; Shapiro, 2002).

In considering the scientist-practitioner model, it is noteworthy that the practice of clinical child psychology did not arise from developmental psychology theory, but from applied work in child mental health and education (child psychiatry and child guidance). An important aspect of the application of the scientist-practitioner model has been the forging of stronger links between developmental theory/knowledge and clinical applications. For example, learning theory, social learning theory and research on parenting styles have all been very influential in the development of parenting programmes. Nevertheless, the influence of psychiatry remains strong, especially in terms of the application of diagnostic systems, the scientific basis for which is questionable, as discussed in Chapter 2. Alternative methods to diagnosis in formulating an understanding of children's behavioural and emotional problems include functional behavioural analysis (derived from learning theory – e.g. Sonuga-Barke, 1994) and the use of empirically devised classificatory systems such as those developed by Achenbach and colleagues (e.g. 1991; 2001).

The second model of theory–practice links is embraced by the term 'developmentally appropriate practice' (DAP). This is generally used to refer to early childhood education centres in which children are meaningfully engaged in learning activities, using 'hands-on' support material and are seen as actively constructing their own knowledge. Teachers or childcare workers in developmentally appropriate classrooms utilize research on child development and learning, and knowledge of individual children's strengths, needs and cultural and social background to inform their practice. In particular, writers have noted that DAP is underpinned by Piagetian theory (see Chapter 4).

Developmentally appropriate practice has been subject to some critical evaluation. In particular, the underlying assumption that knowledge and theory generated through research directly informs 'best practice' in working with children has been criticized. In defending their position advocates of DAP have noted that, in order to develop a DAP curriculum, it is necessary to address three areas: (a) age appropriateness; (b) individual appropriateness and (c) social and cultural appropriateness (Aldwinckle, 2001). That is, DAP practice is better understood as being informed by a broad range of theoretical and research insights into child development. At this point it appears that the direction of influence is largely one way and it is difficult to see how knowledge gained from DAP informs theory and research.

The third model to be described here is that of 'applied developmental science'. Public anxiety about many social problems affecting children and families became apparent as the twentieth century progressed (Lerner *et al.*, 2000), and international concern regarding the health and well-being of young people is a global concern (Smith, 2002). Such concern shares some interesting parallels to the scientist-practitioner debate, with worldwide concerns regarding issues such as the impact of violence, poverty, health and crime on young people confronting the traditional 'keepers of knowledge' – the universities – with the challenge of better understanding the nature and type of knowledge they are pursuing. They are also being asked to address the ability of such knowledge to successfully address the various and immediate problems facing the world. This call has created a burgeoning interest in linking scholarship and outreach (i.e. in fostering 'outreach scholarship') (Lerner *et al.*, 2001).

An important focus identified by Lerner *et al.* (2000) is that of contextualized knowledge. The idea that all knowledge is related to its context has promoted a change in the typical ontology within current scholarship (i.e. a focus on 'relationism') and has helped to advance the view that all existence is contingent on the specifics of the physical and social conditions that exist at a particular moment of history, as acknowledged by theorists such as Riegel (Overton, 1998; Pepper, 1942; see also Chapter 7). Contrast this view with the idea of the pursuit of knowledge in a context-free, value-free situation. Toffler (1984: xii–xiii) has critiqued the mechanistic worldview that has for so long dominated our understanding of science and scientific inquiry, instead conceiving of science as 'an open system embedded in society and linked to it by very dense feedback loops. It is powerfully influenced by its external environment, and, in a general way, its development is shaped by cultural receptivity to its dominant ideas'. It follows, then, that knowledge separated from its context is not basic knowledge.

As described by Fisher and Lerner (1994), the establishment of applied developmental science began with a meeting of delegates at Fordham University in New York in 1991. In keeping with the 'melioristic' values of developmental psychology we noted in Chapter 2, the purpose of applied developmental science is to utilize descriptive and explanatory knowledge about human development in the interests of pursuing interventions of a preventative or enhancing nature. Lerner *et al.* (2000) have identified three characteristics of applied developmental science. First, it is applied, in the sense that it has direct implications for the behaviour and actions of individuals, families and policy-makers. Second, it has a focus on change across the lifespan. Finally, it stresses the utilization of a diversity of research methods to capture information regarding the phenomena under study.

We have briefly described here some aspects of the scientist-practitioner debate, developmentally appropriate practice and applied developmental science, which all share the idea of linking theory and practice. They differ inasmuch as the scientist-practitioner model represents a more bi-directional relationship between theory and practice, with each informing the other. Developmentally appropriate practice and applied developmental science are more uni-directional in nature, with theory and research informing fieldwork practice and application.

Box 12.1 provides an example of the application of child development theory to interventions with children.

Box 12.1 Theory into practice: children's peer relationships

There has been a great deal of research into children's peer relationships, and this has been closely related to practice (Schneider, 2000), with efforts being made to help children whose peer relationships are problematic. In particular, various methods of social skills training have been devised (McGrath, 1998). These have drawn upon a number of theoretical approaches as described in Chapter 6, including information processing, behaviourism and social learning theory. For example, following an information-processing approach, children are coached or instructed in steps such as interpreting social cues appropriately and selecting suitable responses. Behaviourism may be used, as when children are reinforced for demonstrating appropriate social skills, and social learning theory may be drawn upon, as when adults or other children model appropriate social behaviours for children to imitate. Children might also be taught to give themselves instructions aloud, then to whisper them, and finally just to think them, in the manner of Vygotskian theory about private speech (see Chapter 7). Schneider (2000) has reported that an important aspect of effective social skills training is that the children should feel fully engaged with the process and should have a sense of ownership concerning the programme; this is in accord with the theoretical move promoted by Bandura, from the more mechanistic versions of learning theory to a consideration of notions of personal agency (see Chapter 6).

Current challenges in applying developmental psychology

Up to this point we have been concerned with describing a number of significant changes relating to the nature of knowledge, the role of universities in generating knowledge and the press in applying this understanding to solving significant problems of human development. As we observed earlier, in this postmodern era there has been a significant challenge to the idea that science, driven by its own laws, is somehow conducted in isolation from the world around it. Rather, as we discussed in Chapter 9 and elsewhere, scientists conceive of and conduct research within a broader social context that determines the nature and fate of their work (Fabes *et al.*, 1994; 2000). Fabes *et al.* (2000) have described a model of developmental research in terms of Bronfenbrenner's ecological model. The researcher is at the centre of the organizational system, driven to research by interests and motivation. The microsystem considers those who impact directly on the researcher, including family, colleagues and professionals. The exosystem encompasses community interests and funding agencies, while the macrosystem taps into cultural practices and beliefs, including the politics of the particular time and place that impact on the research process. Understood in this way, the research endeavour is understood to reflect the forces to which it is subject, as it is integrally linked to the context in which it is conducted. Seen in this light, and in line with a postmodern view, it clearly behoves developmental psychologists in industrialized countries to consider very carefully the wholesale export of their knowledge to address concerns elsewhere in the world (see Box 12.2).

Box 12.2 Applying psychology for the Third World

... most cross-cultural psychology ... seems to be more interested in variables than in human problems ... the lack of concern for the Third World among behavioral scientists ... is primarily the product of ideological processes that shape the self-understanding of the 20th century psychologist. ... My personal conclusion about all this is that the first move toward Third World involvement by Western-trained behavioural scientists must be a self-purging of individualistic and scientistic thinking (Habermas, 1971). This would entail a shift from 'pure' research focusing on individual behavior to applied research/intervention of the sort normally associated with primary prevention programs, public health education, family systems approaches, community mobilization strategies, program evaluation, and even world systems analysis.

(Sloan, 1990: 3, 16)

Various writers have observed that researchers are being challenged to apply their knowledge to address some of the supposedly unprecedented ills faced by children and adolescents in the world today (Fabes *et al.*, 2000; Lerner *et al.*, 2000; McCall and Groark, 2000; Shonkoff, 2000). There is an imperative to use knowledge to inform practice and policy in order to better inform the development and delivery of services to address social, economic, environmental and health problems. On the basis of both the scientist-practitioner model and a postmodern perspective, it can be argued that there should be a broader exchange of knowledge, with the opportunity for fieldwork practice to inform research and theory. Indeed, this can be seen to be happening in the case of indigenous psychology, following from disillusionment with the ability of traditional services to deliver benefits to indigenous peoples.

There is no doubt that the discipline of developmental psychology faces significant challenges if it is to achieve this end more broadly:

> Put simply, a scholar's knowledge must be integrated with the knowledge that exists in communities in order to understand fully the nature of human development and, based on this constructed knowledge, to develop and sustain ethical actions that advance civil society.
>
> (Lerner *et al.*, 2000: 27)

The starkness of this challenge is highlighted in the writing of Shonkoff (2000), who has drawn our attention to the three related and separate cultures that have been working to address issues facing today's children and adolescents. In the culture associated with science, practitioners are engaged in theory building, hypothesis testing and research. The culture of policy is a separate world whose practitioners are driven by political, economic and social imperatives, and where science is just one point of view, which is often not the most influential. Finally, the culture of practice refers to domains where clinical judgement or professional experience is valued, which may or may not be based on scientific evidence or bear any relationship to policy imperatives. There are significant 'tensions' among these three separate but related cultures, elegantly summarized as follows:

> Science is focused on what we do not know. Social policy and the delivery of health and human services are focused on what we should do. Scientists are interested in questions. Scholars embrace complexity. Policy makers demand simplicity. Scientists suggest that we stop and reflect. Service providers are expected to act.
>
> (Shonkoff, 2000: 528)

Increasingly, universities and researchers are being challenged to bridge the gap between the world of research and the world of practice and application. This imperative is reflected in practical ways through collaborative research and funding involving industry and universities, a move that is also being urged by reductions in public funding for universities in many countries. A number of writers have issued significant warnings against an uncritical acceptance of this link, maintaining that the universities and academic community have been 'largely silenced as a source of dissent and independent critical thought' (Miller and Philo, 2002: 44). These authors call our attention to the fact that as the linkage between universities and government and corporate bodies strengthens, such external forces exert increased control over research findings and the research agenda itself.

In relation to this danger, one of us (PS) has been directly involved in a number of university–industry collaborative grants. In the finalization of the contracts in every situation quite keen attention has been given to the issue of 'intellectual property' in the contract. In particular, the ability of the university researchers to publish their findings (in some cases adverse ones) has been an issue. Happily enough, the issue has been resolved in every instance, but the article by Shonkoff (2000) has resonated with this personal experience. We are similarly aware that researchers with young people in the USA are constrained by some funding bodies not to focus upon findings that would offend the gun lobby. Miller and Philo (2002: 45) have commented that 'If academics are to give any lead or guidance on such pressing social issues, the universities and research councils must assert their independence from the state'. Corporate sponsorship must not allow the corporations to suppress publications or findings, especially where the findings are not supportive of their product or service. Albee, in an editorial note, wrote, 'The integrity of psychological science is based on the academic freedom to explore fundamental questions about the nature of human behavior, thoughts, feelings, and social process' (2002: 161). In the same article, the ability of psychological research to impact on policy development and inform programme development was alluded to. In this age of globalization and the demise of nation-states, there are some significant issues still to be addressed.

Conclusions

In this final chapter we have argued that, at conception, developmental psychology reflected strong philosophical overtones. In a short time the attachment to philosophy was quickly outgrown, along with a strong identification with the development of science and the scientific method. A significant growth occurred in the body of the subject matter of developmental theory and research during the twentieth century. As developmental psychology struggled to develop its own identity a rather stormy period followed, characterized by significant challenges concerning the content and nature of the subject matter and the knowledge generated by virtue of research and theorizing. Universities vigorously protected their hegemonic claim to the right to generate and disseminate research and theory and, ultimately, arbitrate over what is claimed to represent knowledge. In turn, this had significant ramifications for links between theory and practice. There is currently increasing pressure for the application of research and theory to solve 'real-world' problems. Alongside this view has emerged a strident challenge to the idea that there is only one type of knowledge and that universities are its authors and arbiters. Considerable introspection has followed relating to the manner in which knowledge is understood and sought. Presently, the discipline of developmental psychology is being challenged in terms of its outreach to the world in order to apply the knowledge obtained in the best interests of the children and adolescents whose development it seeks to understand.

We opened this book with a reference to the sheer complexity of child development yet, as we have seen in this final chapter, those concerned with real-world applications often seek simplicity. We end our book with Horowitz's entreaty to developmental theorists (Box 12.3) not to fall into the trap of supplying the person in the street with simplistic answers.

Box 12.3 No simple answers for the person in the street?

A fact is a fact is a fact is not analagous to Gertrude Stein's rose. Moreover, the image of Stein's unyielding rose does not carry with it serious social implications for the fabric of a society. ... The social impact of *our* facts and their interpretation is something we *must* care about. For good or ill, our knowledge base is of enormous interest to the Person in the Street ... if we accept as a challenge the need to act with social responsibility then we must make sure that we do not use single-variable words like genes or the notion of innate in such a determinative manner as to give the impression that they constitute the simple answers to the simple questions asked by the Person in the Street lest we contribute to belief systems that will inform social policies that seek to limit experience and opportunity, and ultimately, development, especially when compounded by racism and poorly advantaged circumstances. Or, as Elman and Bates and their colleagues said in the concluding section of their book *Rethinking innateness* (Elman *et al.*, 1998), 'If our careless, underspecified choice of words inadvertently does damage to future generations of children, we cannot turn with innocent outrage to the judge and say, 'But your Honor, I didn't realize the word was loaded'.

(Horowitz, 2000: 8)

APPENDIX 1

Some historical milestones relevant for developmental psychology

Charles Darwin publishes *The Origin of Species* (1872)

William James's *Principles of Psychology* published; establishes the 'functionalist' approach (1890)

Wundt develops the method of 'introspection'

Titchener establishes the theory of 'structuralism' in the USA

Pearson develops statistical theory of correlation (1896)

Cattell is influential in the development and use of mental tests (1896)

Thorndike performs experiments regarding learning in animals (1898)

Freud presents many of his ideas on psychoanlaysis in *Die Traumdeutung* (1900)

Intelligence is described in terms of general and specific factors by Spearman (1904)

G. Stanley Hall published his findings in educational psychology and adolescent psychology in *Adolescence* (1905)

Binet and Simon devise the first intelligence test for children in France (1905)

Pavlov publishes his findings regarding classical conditioning (1906)

Catherine Helen Spence writes a history of child care in South Australia (1907)

Dewey publishes his ideas regarding problem-solving (1910)

Stern presents the concept of IQ (1911)

Gestalt psychology is presented in Wertheimer's paper on Phi phenomenon (1912)

Watson publishes his ideas on behaviourism (1913)

Binet intelligence test revised as Stanford-Binet by Terman (1916)

Kohler publishes the results of his studies on problem-solving in apes (1917)

Watson and Raynor publish their study on 'Little Albert' (1920)

Mary Cover Jones lays the foundations for behaviour therapy

Piaget publishes his theory of language and thought in children (1926)

Klein influential in object relations school

Pavlov's work on the 'conditioned reflex' published in English (1927)

Margaret Mead's *Coming of Age in Samoa* is published (1928)

Tolman presents his ideas on purposive behaviourism (1929)

Vygotsky presents his 'sociocultural' theory (1930)

Thurstone develops factor analysis (1935)

Bridges and Bühler (independently) work on infant emotion

Skinner publishes *The Behaviour of Organisms,* summarizing research on operant conditioning (1938)

Rubinstein writes on the mind–body question (1940)

Pepper writes on metaphors for developmental psychology (1942)

Hull presents his mathematico-deductive learning theory (1943)

Family therapy is developed

Werner elaborates the 'orthogenetic principle' (1948)

Erikson publishes his psychosocial theory (1950)

Bowlby and Ainsworth carry out work on attachment

Lorenz publishes his ideas on ethology (1952)

Havighurst writes about 'developmental tasks' (1953)

Kelly publishes personal construct theory (1955)

Gibson and Gibson work on infant perception and the notion of 'affordance'

Aries writes about views of childhood (1962)

Vygotsky's *Thought and Language* is translated into English (1962)

von Bertalanffy applies general systems theory to biology (1968)

Kohlberg applies Piaget's theory to moral development

Blurton Jones promotes ethological study of children (1972)

Rutter critiques notion of maternal deprivation (1972)

Riegel develops his transactional theory

Cognitive psychology overshadows other approaches

Humphrey provides first feminist critique of family therapy (1975)

Dawkins publishes *The Selfish Gene* (1976)

Bandura publishes his ideas on social learning theory (1977)

Notion of child–environment 'goodness-of-fit' introduced (1977)

Biopsychosocial perspective on health introduced (1977)

Donaldson publishes *Children's Minds,* critiquing Piaget's theory (1978)

Theory of mind introduced (1978)

Bell proposes that socialization is a two-way process (1978)

Bateson publishes his ideas on systems theory (1979)

Bronfenbrenner publishes his ideas on the ecology of human development (1979)

Baltes establishes lifespan psychology (1979)

Notion of the 'competent infant' is promoted

Connectionism emerges (1980s)

Gilligan's *In a Different Voice* published (1982)

Maturana and colleagues publish ideas on constructivism (1988)

Increasing fragmentation of developmental psychology

Postmodern perspectives on psychology are offered

Behaviour genetics gains currency

Thelen and Smith publish their 'dynamic systems' perspective (1994)

Critical state and complex systems theories gain momentum

Teo provides postmodern critique on the philosophy of knowledge (1997)

Evolutionary developmental psychology gains increasing prominence

Indigenous psychology begins to gain recognition

Draft human genome sequence announced (2000)

Scholnick discusses gendered metaphors in developmental psychology (2000)

APPENDIX 2

Discussion questions, activities and selected websites

Chapter 1

1. Consider the various 'views' of children in Figure 1.1, and identify and discuss their key distinguishing features.
2. Identify the key characteristics and distinguish among the terms 'development', 'maturation' and 'growth'.

Activity

Form small discussion groups. Each group draws an outline of a child on a large sheet of paper approximately 90 cm x 30 cm. Members of the group write on the outline words that they associate with the word 'child'. Allow 10–15 minutes to fill in the outline. Each person then explains the words they have contributed and upon what basis they hold such views. The group then considers how far their views reflect 'the postmodern child'.

Websites

Australian Institute Family Studies http://www.aifs.org.au/
Child Adolescent Psychological Educational Resources
http://www.caper.com.au
Nippon Hoso Kyokai http://www.nhk.or.jp/kosodate/english/index.html

Chapter 2

1. Is evolutionary psychology just a politically correct version of sociobiology?
2. How far did Darwin influence theorizing about children's development?

Activity

Find some newspaper articles about ADHD. How far do they reflect a biological perspective?

Website

The evolutionary psychology FAQ
http://www.anth.ucsb.edu/projects/human/evpsychfaq.html

Chapter 3

1. Identify the key features of the root metaphor of 'organicism' and discuss.
2. Debate the usefulness, or otherwise, of 'stages' in describing development.

Activity

Take a document such as 'Promotion, prevention and early intervention for mental health' (2000), identifying how the document has used the concept of 'stages', and discuss the advantages and disadvantages of this concept for understanding human growth and development.

Websites

Child Adolescent Psychological Educational Resources
http://www.caper.com.au
Nippon Hoso Kyokai http://www.nhk.or.jp/kosodate/english/index.html

Chapter 4

1. After reading Chapters 4 and 7, identify and distinguish between the key features of Piaget's and Vygotsky's view of the child and the factors shaping development.
2. Research and present the identifying features of Jerome Bruner's constructivist understanding of development.

Activity

Search the library shelves or Internet for various journal reviews regarding the nature of the child as an 'active participant' in development. What evidence can you find that contemporary theories of development consider the child from this perspective?

Websites

Flinders Education Website
http://www.ed.sturt.flinders.edu.au/edweb/onpub/WEBLMS/INDEX.HTM
Child Adolescent Psychological Educational Resources
http://www.caper.com.au

Chapter 5

1. Can attachment theory be supported by empirical evidence?
2. What are the advantages and disadvantages of the 'Strange Situation' as a measure of attachment?

Activity

Explore and discuss the status afforded to Freudian theory in some standard textbooks on child development.

Websites

Ethological attachment theory: A great idea in personality?
http://www.personalityresearch.org/papers/pendry.html
The object relations home page
http://www.object-relations.com/index.html

Chapter 6

1. To understand better the contemporary relevance of the research and theory of Watson take and critically examine an article utilizing a behavioural framework in terms of the challenge that it is not really a theory of development.
2. Identify the key elements of Albert Bandura's social learning theory as reflected in his review article 'Social cognitive theory: an agentic perspective' (2001), *Annual Review of Psychology*, **52**, 1–26

Activity

Debate in class the advantages and disadvantages of the theories of Pavlov, Watson, Skinner and Bandura for explaining human development.

Website

Information on self-efficacy (Albert Bandura and social cognitive theory)
http://www.emory.edu/EDUCATION/mfp/effpage.html

Chapter 7

1. Discuss the notion of constitutive relationalism.
2. How do Vygotsky's and Rubinstein's theories differ?

Activity

Observe parents and children engaged in activities together. Look for examples of scaffolding.

Websites

Karl Jasper's forum (a very philosophical article about the subject–object dichotomy)
http://www.douglashospital.qc.ca/fdg/kjf/22-R1MUL.htm
Vygotsky and Special Education
http://www.igs.net/~cmorris/zpd.html

Chapter 8

1. Kalbaugh (1989) has argued that 'contextualism is based on assumptions fundamentally distinct from those of the dialectical (organismic) paradigm'(1989: 4). Debate this argument.
2. Identify the key features of Bronfenbrenner's ideas regarding human development, comparing and contrasting them to the ideas encompassed in lifespan developmental theory.

Activity

Examine the 'milestones' in Appendix 1, identifying the key philosophical, cultural and historical influences shaping new understandings in developmental theory.

Website

Child Adolescent Psychological Educational Resources
http://www.caper.com.au

Chapter 9

1. Discuss the notion of 'cultural evolution' (see *The Meme Machine* website, details below).
2. How might 'folk wisdom' differentially influence the development of a Chinese child and one from the United States?

Activity

Examine a standard textbook on child development. How far does it reflect a western perspective on children's development?

Websites

To imitate is human: a review of *The Meme Machine* by Susan Blackmore
http://www.goertzel.org/dynapsyc/1999/meme.html
American and Chinese have different ways of discovering truth ...
http://www.berkeley.edu/news/media/releases/98legacy/06_09_1998.html

Chapter 10

1. Are women and girls morally underdeveloped compared with men and boys?
2. Discuss Freud's views of femininity.

Activity

Watch a children's cartoon programme on television and the commercials associated with it. Observe any differences between the portrayal of boys and girls (e.g. activities, dress, values, music, toys, voice-overs).

Websites

Gilligan's *In a Different Voice*
http://www.stolaf.edu/people/huff/classes/handbook/Gilligan.html

Chapter 11

1. What contributions to our understanding of development have been made by the various theoretical schools?
2. What holds the most promise as an integrative theory of development?

Activity

Consider the possible reactions to postmodern theories discussed by Meacham (see Box 11.3). In groups, draw up checklists of the advantages and disadvantages of each kind of response.

Websites

Complex Systems
http://www.brint.com/Systems.htm
Dynamic Systems in child development
http://cogprints.ecs.soton.ac.uk/archive/0001425

Chapter 12

1. Identify the key features of the 'scientist-practitioner' model, 'developmentally appropriate practice' and 'applied developmental science', indicating how they each link with scientific practice.
2. What are the implications for developmental theory of the notion that there is more than one 'type of knowledge'?

Activity

Take Shonkoff's (2000) three cultures of 'science', 'policy' and 'practice', and interview a practitioner regarding how these impact on psychological practice.

Websites

Australian Institute of Family Studies http://www.aifs.org.au/
Child Adolescent Psychological Educational Resources
http://www.caper.com.au

While we (the authors) have endeavoured to ensure that the URLs are correct at the time of going to press, we have no responsibility for the websites and cannot guarantee their future accessibility or appropriateness.

Glossary

accommodation in Piaget's theory, the modification of mental structures to incorporate new knowledge.

adolescence a term for teenagers derived from the Latin *adolescere*, meaning 'to grow to maturity'.

affective processes processes regulating emotional states and elicitation of emotional reactions.

agency the idea that people are active in making decisions about their lives.

cognitive processes thinking processes involved in the acquisition, organization and use of information.

associationism the view that all knowledge derives from associating one small item of information with another.

assimilation in Piaget's theory, the incorporation of new information into the child's existing patterns of thought and behaviour.

attachment the primary social bond between one individual and another.

attachment behaviour behaviour that promotes contact and/or proximity of an infant to the caregiver.

behaviourism a reductionist approach that focuses entirely on the overt and visible.

biological determinism the idea that all human behaviour is determined by biology.

Cartesian dualism Descartes' idea that the mind and body are entirely distinct and separate.

classical conditioning learning in which a neutral stimulus elicits a certain response by repeated association with another stimulus that already elicits the response.

cofigurative Margaret Mead's description of a culture in which children learn from their peers.

cognitive processes thinking processes involved in the acquisition, organization and use of information.

cognition the way we know about the world through the use of thinking, reasoning, learning and remembering.

conditioned reflex occurs when a previously neutral stimulus acquires the ability to produce a response through association with an unconditioned stimulus (a stimulus that evokes a response that has not been learned).

conservation in Piagetian theory, the retention by an object or substance of certain properties, regardless of changes in shape and arrangement.

constructive development occurs when a child actively participates by finding personal meaning in a situation, making decisions and sharing viewpoints with peers.

constructivism a school of thought in psychology that emphasizes the subjectivity of experience and the role of individuals in actively construing their world.

constructivist emphasizing the subjectivity of our experience and the role of individuals in actively construing meaning in their world.

development increase in the functional complexity of an organism; changes that take into account the effect of experience on an individual (compare with maturation).

developmental psychology the study of the individual from conception to adolescence.

developmental tasks in Havighurst's theory, tasks that must be completed during certain periods of a person's life.

dialectical proceeding by debate between conflicting viewpoints.

empiricism the approach to understanding the world which assumes that only information that can be detected physically and measured should count as valid knowledge.

epistemological development development of the child's knowledge base.

epistemology the study of the theory of how we acquire knowledge.

existentialism a philosophy emphasizing the importance and value of the individual and the role of freedom, responsibility and choice in determining behaviour.

experiential child refers to the concept that children develop solely as a product of their experience.

feminism the advocacy of women's experiences, values and contributions.

formal operations period Piaget's name for the fourth stage of cognitive development, from about 11 years of age onwards, during which individuals acquire the ability to think in abstract terms.

genes biological units of heredity involving self-reproducing DNA.

genetics the scientific study of heredity.

genotype the actual genetic composition of the organism.

Gestalt a school of thought in psychology suggesting that the perceived organized whole is more than the sum of its parts.

information processing the taking in, storing and using of information by humans and animals.

Lamarck (1744–1829) French naturalist who theorized that acquired characteristics could be inherited.

maturation the changes that occur in an organism as it fulfils its genetic potential (compare with development).

méthode clinique the method of interviewing adopted by Piaget to help him understand the child's thought processes.

organismic emphasizing the contribution individuals make to their own development.

phenotype the physical or behavioural traits in an individual that reflect both genetic and environmental factors.

perceived self-efficacy people's beliefs about their capabilities to produce effects.

positivism a branch of philosophy advocating the use of the methods and principles of the natural sciences in the study of human behaviour.

postfigurative Margaret Mead's description of a culture in which children learn from their forebears.

pre-operational period Piaget's name for the stage between two and seven years of age, during which children acquire the ability to represent the world using symbols, such as language.

preformist refers to the view that a miniature adult exists in the egg or sperm.

reaction range the broadest possible expression of a genotype.

reinforcement any stimulus that increases the likelihood of a behaviour recurring.

self-regulation exercise of influence over one's own motivation, thought processes, emotional states and patterns of behaviour.

scaffolding Vygotsky's term for the way in which a mature person skilfully encourages a learner to acquire a new skill or understand a concept.

schema in Piagetian terms, a pattern of action or a mental structure (plural: schemes or schemata).

scientism the idea that all true knowledge arises from the use of empirical scientific method.

sensori-motor period Piaget's first cognitive development stage, in which infants use their senses and motor skills to explore their environment.

transactional view of development the view that development is a two-way interaction between child and environment; strictly, that the entities concerned do not exist independently.

virtuous child refers to Rousseau's notion that the child is inherently good.

zone of proximal development (ZPD) the 'gap' between what individuals can achieve alone and what they can achieve with the help of a more knowledgeable person.

References

ACHENBACH, T.M. 1991: *Manual for the Child Behavior Checklist* 4-18. Vermont: Dept. of Psychiatry, University of Vermont.

ACHENBACH, T.M. 2001: Challenges and benefits of assessment, diagnosis, and taxonomy for clinical practice and research. *Australian and New Zealand Journal of Psychiatry* 35, 263-271.

AESOP, trans. 1979: *Aesop's fables.* Trans. Vernon, V.S. Heinemann.

AINSWORTH, M.D.S., BLEHAR, M.C., WATERS, E. & WALL, S. 1978: *Patterns of attachment: A psychological study of the strange situation.* Hillsdale NJ: Erlbaum.

AINSWORTH, M.D.S. & WITTIG, B.A. 1969: Attachment and exploratory behaviour of one-year-olds in a strange situation. In Foss, B.M. (ed), *Determinants of infant behaviour.* London: Methuen, Vol.4.

ALBEE, G.W. 2000: Exploring a controversy. *American Psychologist* 57, 161-164.

ALBINO, R.C. & LONG, M. 1951: The effect of infant food-deprivation upon adult hoarding in the white rat. *British Journal of Psychology* 42, 146-154.

ALBRECHTSEN, J. 2002: Your child minds if you're absent. *The Australian* May 29, 2002, 15.

ALDWINCKLE, M. 2001: The DAP debate: Are we throwing the baby out with the bath water? *Australian Journal of Early Childhood* 26, 36-39.

ALLANSON, S. & ASTBURY, J. 2001: Attachment style and broken attachments: Violence, pregnancy, and abortion. *Australian Journal of Psychology* 53 (3), 146-151.

AMERICAN PSYCHIATRIC ASSOCIATION 1994: *Diagnostic and statistical manual of mental disorders* (4th edn). Washington DC: APA.

AMES, A. 1951: Visual perception and the rotating trapezoidal window. *Psychological Monographs* 65 (7), 234.

ANDREWS, B. & BREWIN, C.R. 2000: What did Freud get right? *The Psychologist* 13 (12), 605-607.

ANGLIN, J. M. 1993: Vocabulary development: A morphological analysis. *Monograph of the Society for Research in Child Development* 58, 10.

ARCHER, J. 1999: *The nature of grief: The evolution and psychology of reactions to loss.* London: Routledge.

ARCHER, J. 2001: Evolving theories of behaviour. *The Psychologist* 14 (8), 414-419.

ARIES, P. 1962: *Centuries of Childhood.* New York: Vintage Books.

ASPIN, L. J. 1979: *The Family: an Australian Focus.* Melbourne: Longman Cheshire.

ASTINGTON, J. W. 1993: *The child's discovery of the mind.* Cambridge MA: Harvard University Press.

ATHANASSIOS, P. 1999: Connectionist modeling of speech perception. *Psychological Bulletin* 125, 410-436.

ATKINSON, I. & SHUTE, R. 1999: Managing ADHD: Issues in developing multidisciplinary guidelines. *Australian Journal of Guidance and Counselling* 9 (1), 119-127.

AUSTRALIAN PSYCHOLOGICAL SOCIETY 1998: Society argues the case for

PTSD assessment. In *Psych: The Bulletin of the Australian Psychological Society Ltd* 20, 5.

AVIEZER, O., Van Ijzendoorn, M.H., Sagi, A. & Schuengel, C 1994: 'Children of the Dream' revisited: 70 years of collective early child care in Israeli Kibbutzim. *Psychological Bulletin* 116, 99-116.

BACON, F. 1626: (cited in J. Marias 1967) *History of philosophy.* NY: Dover Publications.

BALTES, P.B. 1979: On the potential and limits of child development: Life-span developmental perspectives. *Newsletter of the Society for Research in Child Development* Summer, 1-4.

BALTES, P.B. 1997: On the incomplete architecture of human ontogeny: Selection, optimization, and compensation as foundations of developmental theory. *American Psychologist* 52, 366-380.

BALTES, P.B., LINDENBERGER, U. & STAUDINGER, U. 1998: Life-span theory in developmental psychology. In Damon, W (series ed) and Lerner, R.M. (vol ed), *Handbook of child psychology. Theoretical models of human development.* New York NY: Wiley, Vol 1, 5th ed, 807-863.

BANDURA, A. 1963: The role of imitation in personality development. *Journal of Nursery Education* 18, 207-215.

BANDURA, A.1971: *Psychological modeling: Conflicting theories.* Chicago: Aldine-Atherton.

BANDURA, A.1986: *Social foundations of thought and action: A social-cognitive theory.* Engelwood Cliffs, NJ: Prentice–Hall.

BANDURA, A. 2000: Exercise of human agency through collective efficacy. *Current Directions in Psychological Science* 9, 75-78.

BANDURA, A. 2001: Social cognitive theory: an agentic perspective. *Annual Review of Psychology* 52, 1-26.

BANDURA, A. & WALTERS, R. H. 1963: *Social learning and personality development.* New York: Holt, Rinehart & Winston.

BASSECHES, M. 1989: Toward a constructive-developmental understanding of the dialectics of individuality and irrationality. In Kramer, D.A. and Bopp, M.J. (eds), *Transformaion in clinical and developmental psychology.* New York: Springer-Verlag, 188-210.

BATESON, G. 1972: *Steps to an ecology of mind.* London: Ronald Press Ballantine.

BATESON, G. 1979: *Mind and nature.* UK: Flamingo.

BATTYE, P. & SLEE, P. T. 1985: The demise of the person in social work. *Australian Social Work* 38, 23-31.

BAUMRIND, D. 1993: The average expectable environment is not good enough: A response to Scarr. *Child Development* 64, 1299-1317.

BEILEN, H. 1992: Piaget's enduring contribution to developmental psychology. *Developmental Psychology* 28, 191-204.

BELL, R. Q. 1978: A reinterpretation of the direction of effects in studies of social-ization. *Psychological Review* 75, 81-95.

BEM, S. 1993: *The lenses of gender: Transforming the debate on sexual inequality.* New Haven, CT: Yale University Press.

BENDLE, M. F. 2001: Being critical in a globalised world. *Australian Psychologist* 36 (1), 81-83.

BERK, L. 2000: *Child Development.* Boston: Allyn & Bacon.

BERTALANFFY, L. von 1968: *General systems theory.* New York: Braziller.

BIGGE, M.L. 1982: *Learning theories for teachers.* 4th edn. New York: Harper & Row.

BJORKLUND, D.E. & PELLEGRINI, A.D. 2002: *The origins of human nature:*

Evolutionary developmental psychology. Washington DC: APA.

BLOOM, B. S. 1964: *Stability and change in human characteristics.* New York: Wiley.

BLURTON JONES, N. 1972: *Ethological studies of child behaviour.* Cambridge: Cambridge University Press.

BOLLES, R.C. 1980: Species-specific defence reactions and avoidance learning. *Psychological Review* 77, 32-48.

BOWLBY, J. 1953: *Child care and the growth of love.* Harmondsworth, Middlesex: Penguin.

BOWLBY, J. 1969: *Attachment.* Harmondsworth, Middlesex: Penguin.

BOWLBY, J. 1975: *Separation.* Harmondsworth, Middlesex: Penguin.

BRANDSTADTER, J. 1998: Action perspectives on human development. In Damon, W (series ed) and Lerner. R.M. (vol ed), *Handbook of child psychology. Theoretical models of human development.* New York NY:Wiley, Vol 1, 5th. ed, 807-863.

BREGMAN, E.O. 1934: An attempt to modify the emotional attitudes of infants by the conditioning response technique. *Journal of Genetic Psychology* 45, 169-178.

BREUNLIN, D.C., SCHWARTZ, R.C. & KUNE-KARRER, B.M. 1992: *Metaframeworks: Transcending the models of family therapy.* San Francisco: Jossey-Bass.

BRETHERTON, I. 1992: The origins of attachment theory: John Bowlby and Mary Ainsworth. *Developmental Psychology* 28 (5), 759-775.

BRITISH BROADCASTING CORPORATION 1990: *The Butterflies of Zagorsk.* London: BBC Education and Training.

BRONFENBRENNER, U. 1974: Developmental research, public policy and the ecology of childhood. *Child Development* 45, 1-5.

BRONFENBRENNER, U. 1979: *The ecology of human development: Experiments by nature and design.* Cambridge, MA: Harvard University Press.

BRONFENBRENNER, U. 1986: Recent advances in research on the ecology of human development. In Silbereisen, R.K., Eyferth, K. and Rudinger, (eds), *Development as action in context: Problem behavior and normal youth development.* New York: Springer-Verlag, 286-309.

BRONFENBRENNER, U. & CECI, S.J. 1994: Nature-nurture reconceptualized in developmental perspective: A bioecological model. *Psychological Review* 101, 568-586.

BRONFENBRENNER, U. & MORRIS, P.A. 1998: The ecology of developmental processes. Ch. 17. In Lerner, R.M. (vol. ed.), *Handbook of child psychology: Theoretical models of human development, 5th edn. Vol. 1* New York: Wiley, 993-1028.

BROUGHTON, J.M. 1987: An introduction to critical developmental psychology. In Broughton, J.M. (ed), *Critical theories of psychological development.* New York: Plenum, 1-30.

BRUNER, J. 1966: *Studies in cognitive growth.* New York: Wiley.

BRUNER, J. 1986: *Actual minds, possible worlds.* Cambridge, Massachusetts: Harvard University Press.

BRUNER, J. 1987: *Child's talk.* New York: Norton.

BRUNER, J. & HASTE, H. 1987: *Making sense. The child's construction of the world.* London: Methuen.

BRYANT, P. E. & TRABASSO, T. 1971: Transitive inferences and memory in young children. *Nature* 232, 456-8.

BUCHANAN, M. 2000: *Ubiquity: The science of history or Why the world is simpler than we think.* London: Weidenfeld & Nicolson.

BURMAN, E. 1994: *Deconstructing developmental psychology.* London: Routledge.

BUS, A. G., VAN IJSDOORN, M. H. & PELLEGRINI, A. D. 1995: Joint book reading makes for success in learning to read: a meta-analysis on intergenerational transmission of literacy. *Review of Educational Research* 65, 1-21.

BUSS, D.M. 1999: *Evolutionary psychology: The new science of the mind.* New York: Oxford University Press.

BUTLER, P. 1999: Diagnostic line-drawing, professional boundaries, and the rhetoric of scientific justification: A critical appraisal of the American Psychiatric Association's *DSM* project. *Australian Psychologist* 34 (1), 20-29.

BUTTERWORTH, G. 1982: A brief account of the conflict between the individual and the social in models of cognitive growth. In G. Butterworth & P. Light (eds), *Social cognition: Studies of the development of understanding.* Brighton: Harvester. pp. 3-16.

CAHAN, E.D. 1992: John Dewey and human development. *Developmental Psychology* 28, 205-214.

CAIRNS, R.B. 1998: The making of developmental psychology. In Lerner, R.M. (vol. ed.), *Handbook of child psychology: Theoretical models of human development, 5th edn., Vol. 1.* NY: Wiley, 25-105.

CAMPBELL, N. (1996). *Biology.* 4th ed. Menlo Park, CA: Benjamin/Cummings.

CARROLL, L. 1982: *Alice's adventures in Wonderland: through the looking glass.* New York: Penguin.

CASE, R. 1998: The development of central conceptual structures. In Kuhn, D. and Siegler, R. (eds), *Handbook of child psychology, Cognition, perception and language.* New York: Wiley. *Vol 2,* 5th ed, 745-800.

CHARLESWORTH, W.R. 1992: Darwin and developmental psychology: Past and present. *Developmental Psychology* 28 (1), 5-16.

CLARK, A. 1993: *Associative engines: Connectionism, concepts, and representational change.* Cambridge MA: MIT Press.

CLARK, Y. 2000: The construction of Aboriginal identity in people separated from their families, community and culture: Pieces of a jigsaw. *Australian Psychologist* 35 (2), 150-157.

CLARKE-STEWART, A. K. 1998: Historical shifts and underlying themes in ideas about rearing young children in the United States: Where have we been? Where are we going ? *Early Development and Parenting* 7, 101-117.

CLEVERLEY, J. & PHILLIPS, D. C. 1976: *From Locke to Spock.* Melbourne: Melbourne University Press.

COLEMAN, J. C. 1988: Social capital and the creation of human capital. *American Journal of Sociology* 94, 95-120.

COLLINS, J. 1975: Adolescent delinquency-orientation. In Collins, J.Y. (ed), *Studies of the Australian Adolescent.* Sydney: Cassell.

COMMITTEE ON TRAINING IN CLINICAL PSYCHOLOGY 1947: Recommended graduate training program in clinical psychology. *American Psychologist* 2, 539-558.

COMMONWEALTH OF AUSTRALIA, *Promotion, prevention and early intervention for mental health 2000.* A monograph. Canberra: Commonwealth of Australia.

COMPAYRE, G. 1896: The Intellectual and Moral Development of the Child, trans. New York: Appleton.

CONNELL, W. F., STROOBANT, R. E., SINCLAIR, K. E., CONNELL, R. W. & ROGERS, K. W. 1975: *12 to 20: Studies of city youth.* Sydney: Hicks Smith and Sons.

COTTON, P. 1998: The framing of knowledge and practice in psychology: A response to John. *Australian Psychologist* 33, 31-38.

CRICK, N.R. & BIGBEE, M.A. 1998: Relational and overt forms of peer victimization: A multiinformant approach. *Journal of Consulting and Clinical Psychology* 66, 337-47.

CRICK, N. R. & DODGE, K. 1999: Superiority is in the eye of the beholder: A comment on Sutton, Smith and Swettenham. *Social Development* 8, 128-134.

CRITTENDEN, P. M. 1988: Distorted patterns of relationship in maltreating families: the role of internal representational models. *Journal of Reproductive and Infant Psychology* 6, 183-99.

DARWIN, C. 1959: *The life and letters of Charles Darwin.* (vol. 2, F Darwin, wd). New York: Basic Books (original work published 1888).

DARWIN, C. 1965: *The expression of the emotions in man and animals.* Chicago: University of Chicago Press (first published 1872).

DAVIDSON, G., SANSON, A. & GRIDLEY, H. 2000: Australian psychology and Australia's indigenous people: Existing and emerging narratives. *Australian Psychologist* 35 (2), 92-99.

DAWKINS, R. 1976: *The selfish gene.* Oxford: Oxford University Press

DEGRANDPRE, R.J. 2000: A science of meaning: Can behaviourism bring meaning to psychological science? *American Psychologist* 55, 721-739.

DEMOS, J. & DEMOS, V. 1969 Adolescence in historical perspective. *Journal of Marriage and Family* 31, 632-638

DEVRIES, M.W. 1984: Temperament and infant mortality among the Masai of East Africa. *American Journal of Psychiatry* 141, 1189-1194.

DEWEY, J. & BENTLEY, A.F. 1949: *Knowing and the known.* Boston: Beacon.

DICKSON, D. 2000: The story so far ... *Nature* 405, 983-985.

DINCAUZE, D. 2000: *Environmental archaeology.* Cambridge: Cambridge University Press.

DIXON, R.A. & LERNER, R.M. 1992: A history of systems in developmental psychology. In Bornstein, M.H. and Lamb, M.E. (eds), *Developmental psychology: An advanced textbook.* 3rd ed. Hillsdale, NJ: Erlbaum, 3-58.

DOBSON, J. C. 1970: *Dare to Discipline.* Wheaton, Illinois: Tyndale.

DODGE, K.A. 1986: A social information processing model of social competence in children. In Perlmutter, M. (ed,) *Minnesota symposium on child psychology.* Hillsdale NJ: Erlbaum, 18, 77-125.

DODGE, K. A., BATES, J .E. and PETTIT, G. 1990: Mechanisms in the cycle of violence. *Science* 250, 1678-1683.

DOISE, W. 1986: *Levels of explanation in social psychology.* Cambridge: Cambridge University Press.

DOISE, W. 1990: The development of individual competencies through social interaction. In Foot, H.C., Shute, R.H. and Morgan, M.J. (eds), *Children helping children.* Chichester: Wiley, 43-64.

DONALDSON, M. 1978: *Children's minds.* Glasgow: Fontana

DUDGEON, P. & PICKETT, H. 2000: Psychology and reconciliation: Australian perspectives. *Australian Psychologist* 35 (2), 82-87.

DUNBAR, R. 2001: Darwinising ourselves. *The Psychologist* 14 (8), 420-421.

EDELMAN, G. 1992: *Bright air, brilliant fire.* New York: Basic Books.

EDGAR, D. 1998: What does Daddy do? The nature of fathers' work affects their children's social competence. *Weekend Australian* May 2-3, 29.

EIBL-EIBESFELDT, I. 1989: *Human ethology.* New York: Aldine de Gruyter.

ELKIND, D. 1974: (2nd edt.) *Children and adolescents.* London: Oxford University Press.

ELKIND, D. 1987: The child yesterday, today and tomorrow, *Young Children* May, 6-11.

EMDE, R.N. 1992: Individual meaning and increasing complexity: Contributions of Sigmund Freud and Rene Spitz to developmental psychology. *Developmental Psychology* 28 (3), 347-359.

ENGEL, G.L. 1977: The need for a new medical model. *Science* 196 (4286), 129-136.

ENRIGHT, R. D., LEVY, V. M., HARRIS, D. & LAPSLEY, D. K. 1987: Do economic conditions influence how theorists view adolescents? *Journal of Youth and Adolescence* 16, 541-59.

ERIKSON, E. H. 1963: *Childhood and Society.* Harmondsworth: Penguin.

ERIKSON, E. 1968: *Identity, youth and crisis.* New York: Norton.

EVANS, C. S. 1979: *Preserving the person: a look at the human sciences.* Illinois: IVP.

FABES, R.A., MARTIN, C.L. & SMITH, M.C. 1994: Further perspectives on child development research: A reconsideration and recall. *Journal of Family and Consumer Sciences* 23, 42-54.

FABES, R.A., MARTIN, C.L., HANISH, L.D. & UPDEGRAFF, K.A. 2000: Criteria for evaluating the significance of developmental research in the twenty-first century: Force and counterforce. *Child Development* 71, 212-221.

FARRELL, B.A. 1951: The scientific testing of psychoanalytic findings and theory. *British Journal of Medical Psychology* 24, 35-41.

FEIBLEMAN, J.K. 1973: *Understanding philosophy: A popular history of ideas.* Condor. New York

FISCHER, K. W. 1987: Relations between brain and cognitive development. *Child Development* 58, 623-32.

FISHER, S. & GREENBERG, R.P. 1996: *Freud scientifically reapraised: Testing the theories and therapy.* New York: Wiley.

FLANAGAN, O. 1991: *The science of the mind.* (2nd. edn.) Cambridge MA: MIT Press.

FLAVELL, J. H. 1992a: Cognitive development: Past, present, and future. *Developmental Psychology* 28, 998-1005.

FLAVELL, J .H. 1992b: Development of children's knowledge about the mental world. *International Journal of Behavioural Development* 24,15-23.

FLAVELL, J. H. 1999: Cognitive development; Children's knowledge about the mind. *Annual Review of Psychology* 50, 21-45.

FLAVELL, J. H. & MILLER, P .H. 1998: Social cognition. In Kuhn, D. and Siegler, R. S. (eds,) *Handbook of child psychology.* Vol 2. Cognition, perception, and language. New York: Wiley.

FOERSTER, H. von 1973: Cybernetics of cybernetics (physiology of revolution). *The Cybernetician* 3.

FOOT, H.C., SHUTE, R.H., MORGAN, M.J. & BARRON, A-M. 1990: Theoretical issues in peer tutoring. In Foot, H.C., Shute, R.H. and Morgan, M.J. (eds), *Children helping children.* Chichester: Wiley.

FOOT, H.C., SHUTE, R.H. & MORGAN, M.J. 1997: Children's sensitivity to lack of understanding.
Educational Studies 23 (2), 185-194.

FRANKLIN, D. 1987: The politics of masochism. *Psychology Today* January, 52-57.

FRANKLIN, D. 1987: *Psychology Today* Jan., 52-57.

FRASER, B. G. 1976: The child and his parents: a delicate balance of rights. In Helfer, R. and Kempe, C.H. (eds), *Child Abuse and Neglect.* Cambridge, Massachusetts: Ballinger.

FRAUENGLASS, M.H. & DIAZ, R.M. 1985: Self-regulatory functions of children's private speech: A critical analysis of recent challenges to Vygotsky's theory. *Developmental Psychology,* 21, 357-364.

FREEDMAN, D.G. 1979: *Human sociobiology: A holistic approach.* New York: Free Press.

FREEMAN, D. 1996: *Franz Boas and the Flower of Heaven: Coming of Age in Samoa and the fateful hoaxing of Margaret Mead.* Harmondsworth: Penguin.

FREUD, S. 1973: *An outline of psychoanalysis.* London: Hogarth.

FREUD, S. 1974: *Two short accounts of psychoanalysis.* Harmondsworth: Penguin.

FREUD, S(ophie), 1998: Freud as a postmodernist. *Families in Society: The Journal of Contemporary Human Services* Sept-Oct.

GALAMBOS, N. L. & LEADBETTER, B. J. 2000: Trends in adolescent research for the new millenium. *International Journal of Behavioural Development* 24, 289-294.

GARBARINO, J., STOTT, F. & THE FACULTY OF THE ERIKSON INSTITUTE 1989: *What children can tell us.* San Francisco: Jossey Bass.

GARMEZY, N. 1985: Stress-resistant children: The search for protective factors. In Stevenson, J.E. (ed), *Aspects of current child psychology research. Journal of Child Psychology and Psychiatry Book Supplement no. 4.* Oxford: Pergamon.

GARTON, A. & PRATT, C. 1998: *Learning to be literate: The development of spoken and written language.* 2nd edn. Oxford: Blackwell

GAULD, A. & SHOTTER, J. 1977: *Human action and its psychological investigation.* London: Routledge and Kegan Paul.

GEARY, D.C & BJORKLUND, D.F. 2000: Evolutionary developmental psychology. *Child Development* 71 (1), 57-65.

GELCER, E. & SCHWARTZBEIN, D. 1989: A Piagetian view of family therapy: Selvini-Palazzoli and the invariant approach. *Family Process* 28, 439-56.

GERGEN, K. 2001: Psychological science in a postmodern perspective. *American Psychologist* 56 (10), 803-813.

GEWIRTZ, J.L. & PELAEZ-NOGUERAS, M. 1992: B.F. Skinner's legacy to human infant behaviour and development. *American Psychologist* 47, 1411-1422.

GIBBONS, M. 1994: *The new production of knowledge: The dynamics of science and research in contemporary societies.* Thousand Oaks, CA: Sage.

GIBSON, E. J. & WALK, R. D. 1960: The 'visual cliff'. *Scientific American* 202, 64-71.

GIBSON J. J. 1979: *The ecological approach to visual perception.* Boston: Houghton-Mifflin.

GIBSON, J .J. & GIBSON, E. J. 1955: Perceptual learning: Differentiation or enrichment? *Psychological Review* 62, 32-41.

GILBERT, R. & GILBERT, P. 1998: *Masculinity goes to school.* St. Leonards, New South Wales: Allen and Unwin.

GILLIGAN, C. 1982: *In a different voice: Psychological theory and women's development.* Cambridge: Harvard University Press.

**GIORGIOUDI & ROSNOW – : Phillip told me this is actually Rosnow & Giorgioudi, but hasn't given me the ref. Will ask him to forward directly. Ros

GLADDING, S.T. 1998: Family therapy: History, theory and practice. 2nd edn. Upper Saddle River, NJ: Prentice Hall.

GLICK, J. 1975: Cognitive development in cross-cultural perspective. In Horowitz, F. (ed), *Review of child development research.* Chicago: University of Chicago Press, Vol. 4, 595-654.

GLICK, J.A. 1992: Werner's relevance for contemporary developmental psychology. *Developmental Psychology* 28, 558-565.

GOKULSING, K. & DACOSTA, C 1997: *University knowledges as the goal of university education.* Lampeter: Edwin Mullen.

GOLDBERG, S. 2000: Attachment and development. London: Arnold.

GOODNOW, J. 2001: Commentary: Culture and parenting: Cross-cultural issues. *International Society for the Study of Behavioural Development Newsletter* 1 (38), 13-14.

GOTTESMAN, I.I. 1974: Developmental genetics and ontogenetic psychology: Overdue entente and propositions from a matchmaker. In Pick, A. (ed), *Minnesota symposium on child psychology*. Minneapolis: University of Minnesota Press.

GOULD, S.J. & LEWONTIN, R.C. 1979: The spandrels of San Marco and the Panglossian paradigm: a critique of the adaptationist programme. *Proceedings of the Biological Society of London* 205, 581-598.

GRAETZ, B., SHUTE, R.H. & SAWYER, M. 2000: An Australian study of adolescents with cystic fibrosis: Perceived supportive and nonsupportive behaviors from families and friends and psychological adjustment. *Journal of Adolescent Health* 26, 64-69.

GRAY, J.A. 1985: A whole and its parts: Behaviour, the brain, cognition and emotion. *Bulletin of the British Psychological Society* 38, 99-112.

GREEN, M. 1989: *Theories of human development. A comparative approach.* Engelwood Cliffs NJ: Prentice-Hall.

GRIDLEY, H., DAVIDSON, G., DUDGEON, P., PICKETT, H. & SANSON, A. 2000: The Australian Psychological Society and Australia's Indigenous people: A decade of action. *Australian Psychologist* 35 (2), 88-91.

GRIFFIN, C. 1995: Feminism, social psychology and qualitative research. *The Psychologist* 8 (3), 119-121.

GROOME, H. 1995: Towards improved understandings of Aboriginal young people. *Youth Studies Australia* Summer, 17-21.

HALFORD, G. S.1982: *The development of thought.* Hillsdale, New Jersey: Lawrence Erlbaum.

HALFORD, G. S. 1989: Reflections on 25 years of Piagetian cognitive developmental psychology 1963-1988. *Human Development* 32, 325-57.

HALL, G. S. 1904: *Adolescence: Its psychology and its relations to physiology, anthropology, sociology, sex, crime, religion and education.* vols 1 and 2. New York: Appleton-Century-Crofts.

HALL, J. A. 1985: *Nonverbal sex differences.* Baltimore: Johns Hopkins Open University Press.

HARKNESS, S., SUPER, C.M., AXIA, V., ELIASZ, A., PALACIOS, J. & WELLES-NYSTROM, B. 2001: Cultural pathways to successful parenting. *International Society for the Study of Behavioural Development Newsletter* 1 (38), 9-13.

HARLOW, H.F & HARLOW, M.K. 1966: Learning to love. *American Scientist* 54, 244-272.

HARRÉ, R. & SECORD, P. F. 1972: *The explanation of social behaviour.* Oxford: Basil Blackwell.

HARRÉ, R. 2000: Varieties of theorizing and the project of psychology. *Theory and Psychology* 10, 57-62.

HARRIS, J.R. 1995: Where is the child's environment? A group socialization theory of development. *Psychological Review* 102, 3, 458-489.

HART, C.H., YANG, C., NELSON, D.A., JIN, S., BUZARSKAYA, N., NELSON, L., WU. X. & WU, P. 1998: Peer contact patterns, parenting practices, and preschoolers' social competence in China, Russia, and the United States. In P.T. Slee & K. Rigby (Eds), *Children's peer relations.* London: Routledge, 3-30.

HARTUP, W. 1980: Peer relations and family relations: Two social worlds. In M.

Rutter (ed), *Scientific foundations of developmental psychiatry.* London: Heinemann.

HAVIGHURST, R. J. 1953: *Human development and education.* New York: Longman.

HAY, D. 1984: Social conflict in early childhood. In Whitehurst, G. (ed.), *Annals of Child Development.* Greenwich: CT JAI, vol.1, 1-44.

HAYES, N. 1995: *Psychology in perspective.* London: Macmillan.

HEBB, D.O. 1949: *The organisation of behaviour.* New York: Wiley.

HENGGELER, S.W., SCHOENWALD, S.K., BORDUIN, C.M., ROWLAND, M. & CUNNINGHAM, P.B. 1998: *Multisystemic treatment of antisocial behavior in children and adolescents.* New York: Guilford.

HENWOOD, K. & NICOLSON, P. 1995: Qualitative research. *The Psychologist* 8 (3), 109-110.

HERLIHY, J. & GANDY, J. 2002: Causation and explanation. *The Psychologist* 15 (5), 248-251.

HETHERINGTON, E.M., REISS, D. & PLOMIN, R. (eds) 1994: *Separate social worlds of siblings: The impact of nonshared environment on development.* Hillsdale, NJ: Erlbaum.

HILGARD, E.R. 1962: The scientific status of psychoanalysis. In Nagel, E., Suppes, P. and Tarski, A. (eds), *Logic, methodology and philosophy of science: Proceedings of the 1960 International Congress.* Stanford University Press, 375-390. Reproduced in Lee, S.G.M. and Herbert, M (1970), *Freud and psychology:* Harmondsworth, England: Penguin, 29-49.

HILL, W.F. 1963: *Learning: A survey of psychological interpretations.* London: Methuen.

HINDE, R. 1982: *Ethology: Its nature and relations with other sciences.* Oxford: Oxford University Press.

HINDE, R.A. 1992a: Developmental psychology in the context of other behavioral sciences, *Developmental Psychology* 28 (6), 1018-29.

HINDE, R.A. 1992b: Commentary. *Human Development* 35, 34-39.

HO, D.Y.F., PENG, S. & LAI, A.C. 2001: Parenting in mainland China: Culture, ideology and and policy. *International Society for the Study of Behavioural Development Newsletter* 1 (38), 7-9.

HOBBES, T. 1931: *Leviathan.* Oxford: Basil Blackwell.

HOGG, M. 1992: *The social psychology of group cohesiveness: From attraction to social identity.* New York: New York University Press.

HOLADAY, B., LAMONTAGNE, L. & MARCIEL , J. 1994: Vygotsky's zone of proximal development. Implications for nurse assistance of children's learning. *Issues in Comprehensive Pediatric Nursing* 17, 15-27

HONSTEAD, C. 1968: The developmental theory of Jean Piaget. In Frost, J.L. (ed.), *Early Childhood Education Rediscovered.* New York: Holt, Rinehart and Winston.

HOROWITZ, F.D. 1987: *Exploring developmental theories: Toward a structural/behavioral model of development.* New Jersey: Lawrence Erlbaum Assoc.

HOROWITZ, F. D. 1992: John B. Watson's legacy: Learning and environment. *Developmental Psychology* 28, 360-367.

HOROWITZ, F.D. 2000: Child development and the PITS: Simple questions, complex answers, and developmental theory. *Child Development* 71 (1), 1-10.

HUMAN RIGHTS AND EQUAL OPPORTUNITY COMMISSION 1997: *Bringing them home: The report of the National Inquiry into the Separation of Aboriginal and Torres Strait Islander Children from their Families.* Sydney: Commonwealth of Australia.

HUNT, J. McV. 1961: *Intelligence and experience.* New York: Ronald Press.

HYDE, J.S. 1994: Can meta-analysis make feminist transformations in psychology? *Psychology of Women Quarterly* (18), 451-462.

INHELDER, B. 1975: Some aspects of Piaget's genetic approach to cognition. In Gants, J. & Butcher, H.J. (eds), *Developmental Psychology.* Harmondsworth, UK: Penguin.

IRVING, K. 1998: The location and arrangement of peer contacts: links with friendship initiation knowledge in 4-7 year olds. In Slee, P.T. & Rigby, K. (eds.) *Children's peer relations.* London: Routledge, 164-183.

JACOBSON, N.S. 1989: The politics of intimacy. *The Behavior Therapist* 12 (2), 29-32.

JAMES, W. 1950: The Principles of psychology: Vol 1 Dover Publications. 1-80, 214-235, 462. (First published in 1890), New York: Holt, Rinehart and Winston.

JAMES, A. L. & JAMES, A. 2001: Tightening the net: Children, community and control. *British Journal of Sociology* 52, 211-228.

JENKINS, H. 1988: Annotations: family therapy – developments in thinking and practice. *Journal of Child Psychology and Psychiatry* 31 (7), 1015, 196-206.

JOHN, I. D. 1994: Constructing knowledge of psychological knowledge: Towards an epistemology for psychological practice. *Australian Psychologist* 2.

JOHN, I. 1998: The scientist-practitioner model: A critical examination. *Australian Psychologist* 33, 24-30.

JOHANSSON, G., VON HOFSTEN, C. & JANSSON, G. 1980: Event perception. *Annual Review of Psychology* 31, 27-63.

JOHNSON, S. B. 1985: Psychosocial factors in juvenile diabetes: A review. *Journal of Behavioral Medicine* 3 (1), 95-116.

JONES, A. 1991: *"At school I've got a chance": Culture/privilege: Pacific Islands and Pakeha girls at school.* Palmerston North, NZ: Dunmore Press.

KAGAN, J., KEARSLEY, R. B. & ZELAZO, P. R. 1978: *Infancy: Its place in human development.* Cambridge, Massachusetts: Harvard University Press.

KAHLBAUGH, P.E. 1989: William James' pragmatism: A clarification of the contextual world view. In Kramer, D.A. and Bopp, M.J. (eds), *Transformation in clinical and developmental psychology.* New York: Springer-Verlag, 73-88.

KAYE, K. 1977: Toward the origin of dialogue. In Schaffer, H.R. (ed.), *Studies in mother-infant interaction.* London: Academic Press.

KAYE, K. 1985: Toward a developmental psychology of the family. In L'Abate, L. (ed.), *Handbook of family psychology and therapy.* Homewood, Illinois: Dow Jones-Irwin.

KEATING, D. P. & BOBBITT, B. L. 1978: Individual and developmental differences in cognitive processing components of ability. *Child Development* 49, 155-67.

KEATING, P. 1980: Thinking processes in adolescence. In Adelson, J. (ed.), *Handbook of adolescent psychology.* New York: Wiley.

KELLY, G. A. 1955: *A theory of personality. The psychology of personal constructs.* New York: W.W. Norton & Company Inc.

KENNEDY, D. 2000: The roots of child study: Philosophy, History, and religion. *Teachers College record* 102, 514-538.

KETELAAR, T. & ELLIS, B.J. 2000: Are evolutionary explanations unfalsifiable? Evolutionary psychology and the Lakatosian philosophy of science. *Psychological Inquiry* 11 (1), 1-21.

KIPLING, R. 1902/1975: *Just so stories.* London: Piccolo.

KNOBLOCH, H. & PASAMANICK, B. 1974: *Gesell and Amatruda's*

Developmental Diagnosis: the Evaluation and Management of Normal and Abnormal Neuropsychologic Development in Infancy and Early Childhood. New York: Harper and Row.

KOFFKA, K. 1925: *The growth of mind.* New York: Harcourt Brace and World.

KOHLBERG, L. 1971: From is to ought: How to commit the naturalistic fallacy and get away with it in the study of moral development. In Mischell, T. (ed), *Cognitive development and epistemology.* New York: Academic Press.

KOHLER, W. 1927: *The mentality of apes.* London: Routledge & Kegan Paul.

KOVACEV, L. & SHUTE, R. 1999: Peer social support in relation to acculturation and psychosocial adaptation in adolescent refugees from the former Yugoslavia. *Poster presented at the 11th Australasian Human Development Association Conference, Sydney, July 1999.*

KRAMER, D.A. 1989: Change and stability in marital interaction patterns: A developmental model. In Kramer, D.A. and Bopp, M.J. (eds), *Transformation in clinical and developmental psychology.* New York: Springer-Verlag, 210-233.

KREITLER, H. KREITLER, S. 1976: *Cognitive orientation and behaviour.* New York: Springer-Verlag.

LAMB, M. 1977: A re-examination of the infant social world. *Human Development* 20, 65-85.

LEAKEY, R. & LEWIN, R. 1996: *The sixth extinction: Biodiversity and its survival.* London: Phoenix.

LERNER, R.M. 1983: *Concepts and theories of human development.* New York: Random House.

LERNER, R. M.1986: (2nd. edt.) *Concepts and theories of human development.* New York: Random House.

LERNER, R.M. 1998: Theories of human development: Contemporary perspectives In W. Damon (Series Ed) & R.M. Lerner (vol. Ed). Handbook of child psychology. Vol 1. Theoretical models of human development. (5th. Edt.) pp 1-24. New York. Wiley.

LERNER, R.M. & STEFANIS, I.D. (2000): The importance of infancy for individual, family and societal development: Commentary on the special section: Does infancy matter? Infant behaviour and Development. 22, 475-482.

LERNER, R.M. DE STEFANIS, I. 2000: The import of infancy for individual, family, and societal development: Commentary on the special section: Does infancy matter? *Infant Behaviour and Development* 22, 475-482.

LERNER, R.M., FISHER, C.B. & WEINBERG, R.A. 2000: Applying developmental science in the 21st century: International scholarship for our times. *International Journal of Behavioural Development* 24, 24-29.

LERNER, R.M. & VON EYE, A. 1992: Sociobiology and human development: Arguments and evidence. *Human Development* 35, 12-33.

LEUNG, C. 2001: The sociocultural and psychological adaptation of Chinese Migrant adolescents in Australia and Canada. *International Journal of Psychology* 36, 8-19.

LEWIS, M.D. 2000: The promise of dynamic systems approaches for an integrated account of human development. *Child Development* 71 (1), 36-43.

LEWIS, M. & ROSENBLUM, L. A. (eds), 1974: *The effect of the infant on its caregiver.* New York: John Wiley & Sons.

LIPPMAN, L. 1970: *To achieve our country: Australia and the Aborigines.* Sydney: Cheshire.

LOOFT, W.R. 1973: Socialisation and personality through-out the life-span: An examination of contemporary psychological approaches. In Baltes, P.B. and Schaie, K.W. (eds), *Life-span developmental psychology: Personality and socialisation.*

New York: Academic Press.

LORENZ, K.Z. 1981: T*he Foundations of Ethology.* New York: Springer-Verlag.

MACCOBY, E. E. & JACKLIN, C. N. 1974: *The psychology of sex differences.* California: *Stanford University Press.*

MAGAI, C. & MCFADDEN, S.H. 1995: *The role of emotions in social and personality development: History, theory and research.* New York: Plenum.

MAHONEY, M.J. 1993: Introduction to special section: Theoretical developments in the cognitive psychotherapies. *Journal of Consulting and Clinical Psychology* 61, 187-193.

MAIN, M., KAPLAN, N. & CASSIDY, J. 1985: Security in infancy, childhood, and adulthood: a move to the level of representation. In Bretherton, I. and Waters. E. (eds), Growing points of attachment theory and research. *Monographs of the Society for Research in Child Development,* 50, nos. 1-2.

MAIN, M. & SOLOMON, J. 1990: Procedures for identifying infants as disorganized/disoriented during the Ainsworth Strange Situation. In Greenberg, M., Cicchetti, D. and Cummings, M., *Attachment in the preschool years: Theory, research and intervention.* Chicago: University of Chicago Press, 121-160.

MAINE, S. 2001: Parents supporting youth: Risk and resilience in youth suicide prevention. *Paper presented at Helping Families Change Conference, Melbourne, February 2001.*

MALONE, J. C. 1990: *Theories of learning. A historical approach.* California: Wadsworth Publishing Company.

MARTIN, C.L. & HALVERSON, C.F. 1981: A schematic-processing model of sex typing and stereotyping in children. *Child Development* 52, 1119-1134.

MARTIN, J. & SUGARMAN, J. 2000: Between the modern and the postmodern: The possibility of self and progressive understanding in psychology. *American Psychologist* 55 (4), 397-406.

MASSON, J.M. 1984: *The assault on truth: Freud's suppression of the seduction theory.* New York: Farrar, Straus & Giroux.

MATURANA, H. R. and VARELA, F. J. 1988: *The tree of knowledge. The biological roots of human understanding.* Boston: New Science Library.

MCBURNEY, D.H., GAULIN, S.J.C., DEVINENI, T. & ADAMS, C. 1997: Superior spatial memory of women: Stronger evidence for the gathering hypothesis. *Evolution and Human Behavior* 18 ,165-174.

MCCALL, R.B. & GROARK, C. 2000: The future of applied child development research and public policy. *Child Development* 71, 197-204.

MCDONALD, G. 1973: *Maori mothers and pre-school education.* Wellington New Zealand: Council for Educational Research.

MCGARRIGLE, J. & DONALDSON, M. 1974: Conservation accidents. *Cognition* 3, 341-50.

MCGRATH, H. 1998: An overview of prevention and treatment programmes for developing positive peer relations. In Slee, P.T. and Rigby, K. (eds), *Children's peer relations.* London: Routledge, 229-241.

MCGURK, H. 1975: *Growing and changing: A primer of developmental psychology.* London: Methuen.

MEACHAM, J. 1997: Relationships among theoretical traditions. *Human Development* 40, 211-215.

MEACHAM, J. 1999: Riegel, dialectics, and multiculturalism. *Human Development* 42 (3), 134-144.

MEAD, M. 1970: *Culture and commitment.* New York: Doubleday, Garden City.

MEADOWS, S. 1986: *Understanding child development.* London: Hutchinson.

MEDINNUS, G. R. 1976: *Child Study and Observation Guide* New York: Wiley.

MILLER, D. & PHILO, G. 2002: Silencing dissent in academia. The commercialisation of science. *The Psychologist* 15, 44-46.

MILLER, J. 1993: *Theories of developmental psychology.* New York: Freeman.

MILLER, J. G. 1999: Cultural psychology: Implications for basic psychological theory. *Psychological Science* 10 (2), 85-91.

MILLS, M. 2001: *Challenging violence in schools.* Buckingham: Open University Press.

MINUCHIN, P. 1985: Families and individual development: Provocations from the field of family therapy. *Child Development* 56, 289-302.

MIYAKE, K., CHEN, S.J. & CAMPOS, J.J. 1985: Infant temperament, mother's mode of interaction, and attachment in Japan: An intermin report. In Bretherton, I. and Warers, E. (eds), Growing points of attachment theory and research. *Monographs of the Society for Research in Infant Development* 50 (1-2, Serial no. 209).

MORAWSKI, J. 2001: Gifts bestowed, gifts withheld: Assessing psychological theory with a Kochian attitude. *American Psychologist* 56, 433-440.

MORELLI, G., ROGOFF, B., OPPENHEIM, D. & GOLDSMITH, D. 1992: Cultural variation in infants' sleeping arrangements: Questions of independence. *Developmental Psychology* 28, 604-613.

NEIL, A. S. 1968: *Summerhill.* Harmondsworth, UK: Penguin.

NEWELL, A. & SIMON, H. 1972: *Human problem solving.* Engelwood Cliffs, NJ: Prentice Hall.

NSAMENANG, B. 1999: Eurocentric image of childhood in the context of the world's cultures. *Human Development* 42, 159-168.

OAKLEY, A. 1972: *Sex, gender and society.* Melbourne: Sun Books.

OCHILTREE, G. 1994: *Effects of child care on young children: Forty years of research.* Melbourne: Australian Institute of Family Studies.

O'CONNOR, P. 1985: *Understanding Jung: Understanding yourself.* Sydney: Methuen.

OVERTON, W.F. 1998: Developmental psychology: Philosophy, concepts, and methodology. . In Damon, W. (ed in chief) and Lerner, R.M. (series editor), *Handbook of child psychology. Theoretical models of human development.* New York NY: Wiley, Vol 1, 5th ed, 107-189.

OWENS, L 1996: Sticks and stones and sugar and spice: Girls' and boys' aggression in schools. *Australian Journal of Guidance and Counselling* 6, 45-55.

OWENS, L., SHUTE, R., & SLEE, P. 2000: "Guess what I just heard..." Indirect aggression among teenage girls in Australia. *Aggressive Behavior* 26, 67-83.

PAINTAL, S. 1999: Banning corporal punishment of children. *Childhood Education* 2, 36-39.

PAVLOV, I. P. 1927: *Conditioned reflexes* (trans. G. V. Anrep) London: Oxford University Press.

PAVLOV, I. P. 1970: The discovery of the conditioned reflex . In Gantl, W. H., Pickenhain, L. and Zwingman, C. H. (eds.), *Pavlovian approaches to psychopathology.* Oxford: Pergamon Press. (First published in 1928).

PELLEGRIN, A.D. & BLATCHFORD, P. 2000: The child at school. Interactions with peers and teachers. In Smith, P.K. (series ed), *Tests in Developmental Psychology.* London: Arnold Hodder.

PEPLER, D., CRAIG, W. M. & O'CONNELL, P. 1999: Understanding bullying from a dynamic systems perspective. In Slater, A. & Muir, D. (eds), *Developmental psychology.* London: Blackwell Publishers.

PEPPER, S. 1942: *World hypotheses: A study of evidence.* Berkeley: University of

California Press.

PERE, R.M. 1982: Concepts and learning in the Maori tradition. *Working paper No. 17,* Dept. of Sociology, University of Waikato, Hamilton, New Zealand.

PERRY, B.D. 1997: Incubated in terror: Neurodevelopmental factors in the "Cycle of violence." In Osofky, J.D. (ed), *Children in a violent society.* New York: Guilford.

PETERSON, D 2000: Scientist-practitioner or scientific practitioner. *American Psychologist* 55, 252-253.

PERVIN, L.A. 1968: Performance and satisfaction as a function of individual-environment fit. *Psychological Bulletin* 69, 56-68.

PHILLIPS, J. L. 1969: *The origins of intellect: Piaget's Theory.* San Francisco: W. H. Freeman.

PIAGET, J. 1954: *The construction of reality in the child.* London: Routledge and Kegan Paul.

PIAGET, J. & INHELDER, B. 1969: *The psychology of the child.* New York: Basic Books.

PIAGET, J. 1985: *The equilibration pf cognitive structures: The central problem of intellectual development.* Chicago: University of Chicago Press.

PICK, H. L. 1992: Eleanor J. Gibson: Learning to perceive and perceiving to learn. *Developmental Psychology.* 28, 787-794.

PILGRIM, D. 2000a: Psychiatric diagnosis: More questions than answers. *The Psychologist* 13 (6), 302-305.

PILGRIM, D. 2000b: Declining credibility of medical approaches. Letter, *The Psychologist* 13 (11), 547.

POLLOCK, L. 1983: *Forgotten children.* Cambridge: Cambridge University Press.

POPPER, K. 1972: *Objective knowledge. An evolutionary approach.* Oxford: Clarendon Press.

PREMACK, D. and WOODRUFF, G. 1978: Does the chimpanzee have a theory of mind? *Behavioural and Brain Sciences* 1, 515-526.

PROSSER, B., REID, R., SHUTE, R. & ATKINSON, I. 2002: Attention Deficit Hyperactivity Disorder (ADHD): Special education policy and practice in Australian. *Australian Journal of Education* 46 (1), 65-78.

RAIMY. V. 1950: *Training in clinical psychology.* Engelwood Cliffs, NJ: Prentice-Hall.

RAMSAY, W., STICH, S.P. & GARON, J. 1991: Connectionism, eliminativism, and the future of folk psychology. In Ramsey, W. Stich, S.P. and Rumelhart, D.E. (eds), *Philosophy and connectionist theory.* Hillsdale NJ: Erlbaum, 199-228.

REEVES, J.W. 1965: *Thinking about thinking.* London: Methuen.

REID, R. & MAAG, J.W. 1997: Attention deficit hyperactivity disorder: Over here and over there. *Educational and Child Psychology* 14 (1), 10-20.

RILLING, M. 2000: John Watson's paradoxical struggle to explain Freud. *American Psychologist* 55, 301-312.

RITCHIE, J. & RITCHIE, J. 1979: *Growing up in Polynesia.* Sydney: Allen and Unwin.

ROBERTSON, J. 1953: A two-year-old goes to hospital [Film]. Tavistock Child Development Research Unit, London (available through Penn State Audiovisual Services, University Park, PA).

ROBINSON, J.A. 1999: Update on attachment theory and research. *Paper presented to Child and Adolescent Mental Health Service,* Norwich House: Adelaide, April 1999.

ROGOFF, B. 1990: *Apprenticeship in thinking: Cognitive development in social context.* Oxford: Oxford University Press.

ROGOFF, B. & GARDNER, ? 1984: Adult guidance of cognitive development. In B. Rogoff & J. Lane (eds.) Everyday cognitive development in a social context. pp 96-116. Cambridge MA: Harvard University Press.

ROGOFF, B. & MORELLI, G. 1989: Perspectives on children's development from cultural psychology. *American Psychologist* 44, 343-348.

ROSE, H. & ROSE, S. 2001: Much ado about very little. *The Psychologist* 14 (3), 428-429.

ROSE, S. P. & FISCHER, K.W. 1998: Models and rulers in dynamical development. *British Journal of Developmental Psychology* 16, 123-131.

ROSENBLITH, J.F. 1992: A singular career: Nancy Bayley. *Developmental Psychology* 28 (5), 747-758.

ROSENZWEIG, M.R. 1996: Aspects of the search for neural mechanisms of memory. *Annual Review of Psychology* 47, 1-32.

ROSSER, S.V. & MILLER, P.M. 2000: Feminist theories: Implications for developmental psychology. In Miller, P.K. and Scholnik, E.K. (eds), *Toward a feminist developmental psychology*. New York: Routledge, 11-28.

ROUSSEAU, J. J. 1914: *Emile on Education, trans. B.ÿFoxle*. New York: Basic Books (first published 1762).

RUSSELL, B. 1974: *History of Western Philosophy*. London: George Allen and Unwin.

RUTTER, M. 1972: *Maternal deprivation reassessed*. Harmondsworth: Penguin.

SAGI, A. & AVIEZER, O. 2001: The rise and fall of children's communal sleeping in Israeli Kibbutzim: An experiment in nature and implications for parenting. *Newsletter of the International Society for the Study of Behavioral Development* 1 (38), 4-6.

SAMEROFF, A. 1975: Transactional models in early social relations. *Human Development* 18, 65-79.

SAMEROFF, A. J. 1983: Developmental systems: Contexts and evolution. In Kessen, W. (ed.), *Handbook of child psychology*. Vol. 1, History, theory and methods. New York:Wiley, 237-294.

SANDELOWSKI, M. 1986: The problem of rigor in qualitative research. *Advances in Nursing Science* 8 (3), 27-37.

SANSON, A. & DUDGEON, P. 2000: Guest editorial: Psychology, indigenous issues, and reconciliation. *Australian Psychologist* 35 (2), 79-81.

SAWYER, R.K. 2000: Connecting culture, psychology and biology: Essay review on Inghilleri's *From subjective experience to cultural change*. *Human Development* 43, 56-59.

SAWYER, R.K. 2002: Emergence in psychology: Lessons from the history of non-reductionist science. *Human development* 45, 2-28.

SCARR, S. 1985: Constructing psychology: making facts and fables for our times. *American Psychologist* 40, 499-512.

SCARR, S. 1992: Developmental theories for the 1990s: Development and individual differences. *Child Development* 63, 1-19.

SCARR, S. & DUNN, J. 1987: Mother Care/Other Care. Harmondsworth: Penguin.

SCHACHTER, S. & SINGER, J. E. 1962: Cognitive, social and physiological determinants of emotional state. *Psychological Review* 69, 379-99.

SCHAFFER, R. 1989: Early social development. In Slater, A. and G. Bremner, G. (eds), *Infant development*. Hove: Lawrence Erlbaum, 189-210.

SCHAFFER, R. 1996: *Social development*. Oxford: Blackwell.

SCHAFFER, R, & EMERSON, P.E. 1964: The development of social attachments in infancy. *Monographs of the Society for Research in Infant Development* 29, (3 Serial No. 94).

SCHLINGER, H.D. 1992: Theory in behavior analysis. *American Psychologist* 47, 1396-1410.

SCHNEIDER, B.H. 2000: *Friends and enemies: Peer relations in childhood.* London: Arnold.

SCHOLNIK, E.K. 2000: Engendering development: Metaphors of change. In Miller, P.H. and Scholnik, E.K. (eds), *Toward a feminist developmental psychology.* New York: Routledge. 29-42.

SCHOLNIK, E.K. & MILLER, P.H. 2000: Engendering development: Developing feminism. In Miller, P.H. and Scholnik, E.K. (eds), *Toward a feminist developmental psychology.* New York: Routledge, 241-254.

SCHORSCH, A. 1979: *Images of Childhood.* New York: Mayflower Books.

SCHUTZ, A. 2001: John Dewey's conundrum. Can democratic schools empower? *Teachers College Record* 103, 267-302.

SCRATON, P. (ed.) 1997: *Childhood in crisis.* London: UCL Press.

SEARIGHT, H.R. & MCLAREN, A. L. 1998: Attention-Deficit Hyperactivity Disorder: The medicalisation of misbehavior. *Journal of Clinical Psychology in Medical Settings* 5 (4), 467-495.

SEGAL, L. 2001: Main agendas and hidden agendas. *The Psychologist* 14 (8), 422-423.

SEIFERT, K.L. 2000: Uniformity and diversity in everyday views of the child. *New Directions for child and adolescent development* 87, 75-91.

SELIGMAN, M. E.P. 1972: Phobias and preparedness. In Seligman, M.E.P. and Hager, J.L. (eds), *Biological boundaries of learning.* New York: Appelton-Century-Crofts.

SELVERSTONE, R. 1989: Adolescent sexuality: developing self-esteem and mastering developmental tasks. *SIECUS Report* 18, 1-4.

SENECHAL, M. 1997: The differential effect of storybook reading on pre-schoolers: Acquisition of expressive and receptive vocabulary. *Journal of Child Language* 24, 123-138.

SHANAHAN, M.J. SULLOWAY, F. HOFER, S.M. 2000: Change and constancy in developmental contexts. *International Journal of Behavioral Development* 24, 421-427.

SHAPIRO D. 2002: Renewing the scientist-practitioner model. *The Psychologist* 15, 232-234.

SHONKOFF, J.P. 2000: Science, policy, and practice: Three cultures in search of a shared mission. *Child Development* 71, 181-187.

SHUTE, R., DE BLASIO, T. & WILLIAMSON, P. 2002: Social support perceptions of Australian children. *International Journal of Behavioral Development* 26 (4), 318-326.

SHUTE, R., FOOT, H. & MORGAN, M. 1992: The sensitivity of children and adults as tutors. *Educational Studies* 1 (1), 21-36.

SHUTE. R. & MIKSAD, J. 1997: Scaffolding effects of computer-assisted instruction on the cognitive development of preschool children. *Child Study Journal* 27 (2), 237-253.

SHUTE, R. & PATON, D. 1990: Chronic childhood illness: The child as helper. In Foot, Morgan and Schute (eds), *Children helping children.* Chichester: Wiley.

SHUTE, R. & PATON, D. 1992: Understanding chronic childhood illness: Towards an integrative approach. *The Psychologist: Bulletin of the British Psychological Society* 5, 390-394.

SKINNER, B. F. 1979: My experience with the baby-tender. *Psychology Today* March, 29-40.

SLEE, P. T. 1987: *Child observation skills.* Beckenham, Kent: Croom Helm.

SLEE, P. T. 2001: *The P.E.A.C.E. Pack: A program for reducing bullying in our schools.* Adelaide: Flinders University.

SLEE, P.T. (2002) (2nd Edn). *Child, adolescent and family development.* Melbourne: Cambridge University Press.

SLOAN, T.S. 1990: Psychology for the Third World? *Journal of Social Issues* 46 (3), 1-20.

SLUCKIN, W. 1970: *Early learning in man and animal.* London: Allen and Unwin.

SMITH, E. R. 1996: What do connectionism and social psychology offer each other? *Journal of Personality and Social Psychology* 70, 893-912.

SMITH, E. R. 1999: What do connectionism and social psychology offer each other? *Journal of Personality and Social Psychology* 70, 893-912.

SMITH, M.S. 1987: Evolution and developmental psychology: Toward a sociobiology of human development. In Crawford, C., Smith, M. and D. Krebs, D. *Sociobiology and psychology: Ideas, issues and applications.* Hillsdale, New Jersey: Lawrence Erlbaum. 225-252.

SMITH, P.K., COWIE, H. & BLADES, M. 1998: *Understanding children's development.* 3rd edn. Oxford: Blackwell.

SMITH, P. K. 2002: *Violence in schools: The response in Europe.* (in press)

SNOWLING, M. 2000: *Dyslexia.* (2nd edn). Oxford: Blackwell.

SONUGA-BARKE, E.J.S. 1994: Annotation: On dysfunction and function in psychological theories of childhood disorder. *Journal of Child Psychology and Psychiatry* 35, 801-815.

SOUTHEY, R. 1925: *The Life of Wesley,* London, Vol 2. 304-305.

SPENCE, C.H. 1907: *State children in Australia: A history of boarding out and its developments.* Adelaide: Printed by Varolen and Sons Ltd.

STERNBERG, R.J. & GRIGORENKO, E.L. 2001: Unified psychology. *American Psychologist* 56 (12), 1069-1079.

STEVENS, G. & GARDNER, S 1982: *The women of psychology.* vol. 2: Expansion and refinement. Cambridge, Massachusetts: Schenkman.

STORER, D. 1985: *Ethnic family values in Australia.* Sydney: Prentice-Hall.

SUTTON, J. and SMITH, P. K. 1999: Bullying as a group process: An adaption of the participant role approach. *Aggressive behaviour* 25, 97-111.

SUTTON, J., SMITH, P. K. and SWETTENHAM, J. 1999: Bullying and 'theory of mind': A critique of the 'social skills deficit' view of anti-social behaviour. *Social Development* 8,117-127.

TAFT, R. 1987: Presidential address: Cross-cultural psychology as psychological sience. In Kagitcibasi, C. (ed.), *Growth and progress in cross-cultural psychology.* Berwyn, PA: Swets North America. 3-9.

TANNEN, D. 2000: Rites of demolition. *The Australian, April* 12, 41.

TEO, T. 1997: Developmental psychology and the relevance of a critical metatheoretical reflection. *Human Development* 40, 195-210.

TEO, T. 1999: Functions of knowledge in psychology. *New Ideas in Psychology* 17, 1-5.

TEES, R.C. 1986: Experience and visual development: Behavioral evidence. In Greenough, W.T. and Juraska, J.M. (eds), *Developmental neurobiology.* New York: Academic Press. 317-361

THELEN, E. and ADOLPH, K. E. 1992: Arnold L. Gesell: The paradox of nature and nurture. *Developmental Psychology* 28, 368-380.

THELEN, E. & SMITH, L.B. 1994: *A dynamic systems approach to the development of cognition and action.* Cambridge, MA: MIT Press.

THELEN, E. & SMITH L. B. 1998: Dynamic systems theories. In Damon, W. & Lerner, R. M. (1998) *Handbook of child psychology* (5th edt). New York: John Wiley and Sons Inc., 563-630.

THOMAS, A. & CHESS, S. 1977: *Temperament and development.* New York: Bruner/Mazel.

TIERNEY, W.G. 1996: The academic profession and the culture of the faculty: A perspective on Latin American universities. In Kempner, K. & Tierney, W. G. (eds), *The social role of higher education: Comparative perspectives.* New York, NY:Garland Publishing, 11-26.

TIERNEY, W.G. 2001: The autonomy of knowledge and the decline of the subject: Postmodernism and the reformulation of the university. *Higher Education* 41, 353-372.

TINBERGEN, N 1973: *The animal in its world: Explorations of an ethologist, 1932-1972,* Vols. 1 & 2. Cambridge: Harvard University Press.

TOLAN, P. H. (ed.), 1990: *Multi-systemic structural-strategic interventions for child and adolescent behavioural problems.* New York: Hawarth Press.

TONNESSEN, F.E. 1999: Options and limitations of the cognitive psychological approach to the treatment of dyslexia. *Journal of Learning Disabilities* 5, 386-395.

TOWNSEND, S. 1982: *The secret diary of Adrian Mole age 133/4.* London: Methuen.

UNDERWOOD, M.K., GALEN, B.R. & PAQUETTE, J.A. 2001: Hopes rather than fears, admirations rather than hostilities: A response to Archer and Bjorqvist. *Social Development* 10 (2), 275-280.

USSHER, J.M. & WALKERDINE, V. 2001: Guest editorial: Critical psychology. *Australian Psychologist* 36, 1, 1-3.

VALENTINE, E. 1998: Out of the margins. *The Psychologist* 11 (4), 167-168.

VALENTINE, G. 1996: Children should be seen and not heard? The roles of children in public space. *Urban Geography* 17, 205-220.

VAN DER MOLEN, M. W. & RIDDERINKHOF, K. R. 1998: The growing and aging brain: Life-span changes in brain and cognitive functioning. In Demetriou, A., Doise, W. and van Lieshout, C. *Life-span developmental psychology.* Chichester: Wiley.

VAN DER VEER, R. 1986: Vygotsky's developmental psychology. *Psychological Reports* 59, 527-536.

VAN GEERT, P. 1998: A dynamic systems model of basic developmental mechanisms: Piaget, Vygotsky, and beyond. *Psychological Review* 105, 634-677.

VIADERO, D. 1988: Corporal punishment. *Education Week* 1, 38-39

VIOLATO, C. & WILEY, A.J. 1990: Images of adolescence in English literature: The middle ages to the modern period. *Adolescence* 25, 253-64.

VON BERTALANFFY, L. 1968: *General system theory.* New York: George Brazillier.

VREEKE, G.J. 2000: Nature, nurture and the future of the analysis of variance. *Human Development* 43, 32-45.

VYGOTSKY, L.S. 1962: *Thought and language.* Cambridge, MA: MIT Press.

VYGOTSKY, L.S. 1978: *Mind in society: The development of higher mental processes.* Cambridge, MA: Harvard University Press. (Originally published in 1930, 1933 & 1935.)

WACHTEL, E. F. 1990: The child as an individual: a resource for systemic change. *Journal of Strategic and Family Therapies* 9, 50-8.

WAHLSTEN, D. 2000: Analysis of variance in the service of interactionism. *Human Development* 43, 46-50.

WALTERS, M., CARTER, B., PAPP, P. & SILVERSTEIN, O. 1988: *The invisible web: Gender patterns in family relationships.* New York: Guilford Press.

WANGANEEN, R. undated: *Discussion paper: Spiritual healing using loss and grief.* Adelaide: Sacred Site Within Healing Centre.

WATSON, J.B. 1913: Psychology as the behaviorist views it. *Psychological Review* 20, 158-177.

WATSON, J. B. 1914: *Behaviour: An introduction to comparative psychology.* New York: Norton.

WATSON, J.B. 1928: *Psychological care of the infant and child.* New York: Norton. 81-82

WATSON, J. B. 1930: *Behaviourism.* New York: Henry Holt.

WATSON, J.B. 1936: Autobiography. In C. Murchison, C. (ed), *A history of psychology in autobiography* 3, 271-278. Worchester, MA: Clarke University Press.

WATZLAWICK, P., WEAKLAND, J. H. and FISCH, R. 1974: *Change: Principles of problem formation and problem resolution.* New York: Norton.

WEINERT, F.E. & WEINERT, S. 1998: History and systems of developmental psychology. In Demetriou, A., Doise, W. and van Lieshout, C. *Life-span developmental psychology.* Chichester: Wiley. 1-33

WELLS, A. 2000: Subtle interplay (book review). *The Psychologist* 13 (12), 624-625.

WERNER, H. 1948: *Comparative psychology of mental development.* New York: International Universities Press.

WERNER, H. & KAPLAN, B. 1963: *Symbol formation.* New York: Wiley.

WERTSCH, J.V., & TULVISTE, P. 1992: L.S. Vygotsky and contemporary developmental psychology. *Developmental Psychology* 28 (4), 548-557.

WESTALL, C. & SHUTE, R. 1992: OKN asymmetries in orthoptic patients: Contributing factors and effects of treatment. *Behavioural Brain Research* 49, 77-84.

WHITE, M. & EPSTON, D. 1989: *Literate means to therapeutic ends.* Adelaide: Dulwich Centre Publications.

WHITE, S. 1992: *G. Stanley Hall: From philosophy to developmental psychology. Developmental Psychology* 28. 25-34.

WILKINSON, S. 1990: Gender issues: Broadening the context. *The Psychologist 3* (9), 412-414.

WILLIAMS, R. 1976: *Keywords: A vocabulary of culture and society.* New York: Oxford University Press.

WILSON, E.O. 1975: *Sociobiology: The new synthesis.* Cambridge MA: Harvard University Press.

WINNICOTT, D.W. 1953: Transitional objects and transitional phenomena. *International Journal of Psychoanalysis* 34, 1-9.

WOHLWILL, J. F. 1973: *The study of behavioural development.* New York: Academic Press.

WOOD, D. 1998: *How children think and learn.* 2nd edn. Oxford: Blackwell.

WOOD, D.J., BRUNER, J.S. & ROSS,G. 1976: The role of tutoring in problem solving. *Journal of Child Psychology and Psychiatry* 17 (2), 89-100.

WOOD, D.J., WOOD, H.A & MIDDLETON, D.J. 1978: An experimental evaluation of four face-to-face teaching strategies. *International Journal of Behavioral Development* 1, 131-47.

WORRELL, J. & ETAUGH, C. 1994: Transforming theory and research with women. *Psychology of Women Quarterly* 18, 443-450.

WYN, J. & WHITE R. 1997: *Rethinking youth*. London: Sage Publications.

WYNESS, M. 2000: *Contesting childhood*. London: Palmer Press.

YOUNG, K. T. 1990: American conceptions of infant development from 1955 to 1984: What the experts are telling parents. *Child Development* 61, 17-28.

Index